THE BEGINNER'S WORKSHOP
Part I

THE BEGINNER'S WORKSHOP

by

IAN BRADLEY

MODEL & ALLIED PUBLICATIONS
ARGUS BOOKS LTD
Station Road, Kings Langley, Hertfordshire
England

Completely Revised 1975

© Model & Allied Publications 1967

ISBN 0 85242 428 0

Printed in Great Britain by
REDWOOD BURN LIMITED
Trowbridge & Esher

INTRODUCTION

ALTHOUGH this book is intended primarily for the ever increasing number of those fitting up small workshops in the home, when adopting light engineering work and model engineering as a hobby, the more experienced worker may find in its pages much of practical interest.

Within the space available it is hardly possible to do more than start the novice on the right road, but as his skill and experience grow he will, we hope, be able to profit from the more advanced publications available on this subject.

In order that progress, both in equipping the workshop and in the use of tools, may be made step by step, Part I of this book has been devoted to hand tools, whilst in Part II the selection and practical use of the electrically-driven drilling machine, the grindiug machine, and the lathe are described.

Moreover, to help the novice to gain proficiency and to maintain his interest, some examples of work have been included which will not only enable him to put his reading into practice but will, at the same time, serve to add to his workshop equipment.

Hungerford 1975

CONTENTS PART I

PAGE

CHAPTER ONE   **PLANNING A WORKSHOP**   I
General Considerations—Benches—Storing Tools—Tool Racks—Shelving—Cupboards—Chests of Drawers—Heating and Lighting—The Floor—Methodical Working

CHAPTER TWO   **WORKSHOP EQUIPMENT**   12
The Vice — Hand Tools — Files — Hacksaws — Hand Drills—Drills—Screwthreading Equipment — Shears — Chisels — Scrapers — Tools used for Assembling Work — Spanners — Screwdrivers— Pliers — Hammers — Punches — Soldering Equipment—Oil Stones

CHAPTER THREE   **EQUIPMENT FOR MEASURING AND MARKING-OUT**   41
Callipers—Rulers—Micrometers—Depth Gauge—The Protractor—Drill Gauge—Marking Out—Equipment Required—Marking-out Sheet Metal Work—Witness Lines—Marking-out Solid Objects—Marking-out a Bearing Bracket—Marking-out the Centre of a Shaft—Reading Machine Drawings

CHAPTER FOUR   **USING HAND TOOLS**   66
Filing — Pinning — Draw Filing — Filing Aluminium — Scraping — Sawing Metal — Marking-out the Work — Using the Hacksaw — Sawing Curves — Cutting Metal — Cold Chisels — Hand-Drills — The Drilling Operation — Polishing — Reaming—Screw Threading—Cutting Threads—Soldering—Hardening and Tempering

CHAPTER FIVE   **TOOLS TO MAKE**   100
A Simple Depth Gauge—A Rule Stand

CONTENTS PART II

PAGE

CHAPTER ONE THE DRILLING MACHINE 109
Lever-feed and Rack-feed Types—Electric Drilling Machine — Driving the Machine — Drilling Speeds—Machine Vice—Table V Blocks—Work Clamp—Drill Chuck—Table Stop—Depth-drilling Stop and Gauge—Drilling Operations—Drilling into a Cross-hole—Drilling on an Inclined Surface—Cross-drilling Shafts—Drilling for Tapping—Tapping in the Drilling Machine—Countersinks—Counterbores and Pin Drills

CHAPTER TWO THE GRINDING MACHINE 135
The Grinding Head—Driving the Machine—Electric Grinding Machine—Angular Grinding Rest — Grinding Operations — Grinding Twist Drills

CHAPTER THREE THE LATHE 147
General Description—Types of Small Lathes—Methods of Driving—Lathe Accessories—Lathe Maintenance

CHAPTER FOUR DRIVING MACHINE TOOLS IN THE WORKSHOP 163
Setting out the Machine Tool Bench—Lineshafts and Countershafts—Direct Drive from Electric Motors—Installation of Motors

CHAPTER FIVE OPERATING THE LATHE 173
*Lathe Tools—Measuring Instruments—Chuck Work—Sliding—Surfacing—Boring—Use of the Faceplate—Turning Work between Centres—
—Mounting the Work—Use of Steadies—
—Boring Work on the Saddle—Drilling from the Tailstock—Depth-drilling—The D Bit—Tapping and Dieing—Screwcutting—Turning with Hand Tools*

CHAPTER SIX TOOLS AND EQUIPMENT TO MAKE 211
Colleted Die Holders—Drilling Machine Tapping Handle—A Countersink—Pin Drills—Drilling Machine Table Stop—Centre Finder—Angular Rest

INDEX 239

DRAWINGS BY IAN BRADLEY

CHAPTER ONE

> General Considerations — Benches — Storing Tools—Tool Racks—Shelving—Cupboards—Chests of Drawers—Heating and Lighting—The Floor—Methodical Working.

IF my own first workshops are any guide, you must not expect to start with a fully-equipped shop. For one thing, this would be expensive, and, on the other hand, you

PLANNING A WORKSHOP

could hardly expect to be able, straight away, to make proper use of a large number of special tools. Far better to start with a few good quality simple tools and to add to these later on as they are required.

The question of the quality of the tools must be stressed ; always buy the best tools you can afford or are otherwise able to procure. Do not be put off with any poor quality equipment that may be offered to you, and, when buying tools, you will find it a good plan to persuade a friend with knowledge of the subject to accompany you, for if he is a practical man his timely help may save you much disappointment later on.

A good tool will last a lifetime, and the money spent on it will be amply repaid by years of good service.

As the choice of tools calls for some experience, I shall give later some hints on what to look for and what to avoid when buying tools.

First of all, however, the question of the workshop itself must be considered.

If you have a parent or a relation who is himself a model engineer or is interested in the use of tools, in all probability this question will already have been solved. If not, it will be a matter of persuading the household authorities to let you have a place, be it a room, an outbuilding, or even the corner of a room, in which to pursue your hobby so that you can lay out your tools without causing inconvenience to others, and without fear of interruption while at work.

The household authorities may not, at first, take kindly to workshop activities within the house, but, if you form the habit of working in an orderly and tidy manner, any objections raised should soon cease when it is seen that you are considerate as well as being intent on your work.

Try, if you can, to get leave to work in the house, as this will make a big difference to the comfort of working in cold weather.

Outside workshops require heating during the colder months, both to make working possible and to prevent rusting of your tools by damp.

However, there may be no facilities for establishing an outside workshop, and assuming that the use of a room for this purpose has been granted, the question arises as to how it shall be fitted up. Obviously, the first requirement will be a good strong bench, big enough to give plenty of room for working. The bench can be either built on to the wall, where the construction of the house allows, or if it is robustly made, it should be steady when standing on its own feet.

To facilitate working, the bench should be placed in the best light, and it is suggested that, to begin with, it should be installed under the window so that the worker faces the light, as shown in Fig. 1, which shows the bench as seen from above.

At the outset, at any rate, the bench will have to serve the novice for all purposes, including a mounting for the vice, as will be described later.

As additional equipment, shelves will be required as well as tool racks and, perhaps, cupboards to house the tools needing greater protection. Fig. 2 shows the workshop as it will now appear with this equipment in place ; the bench seen in the foreground is that illustrated in Fig. 1.

If you are fortunate enough to have the use of a room with

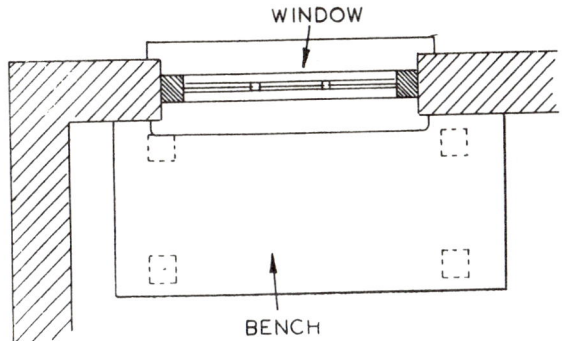

Fig. 1

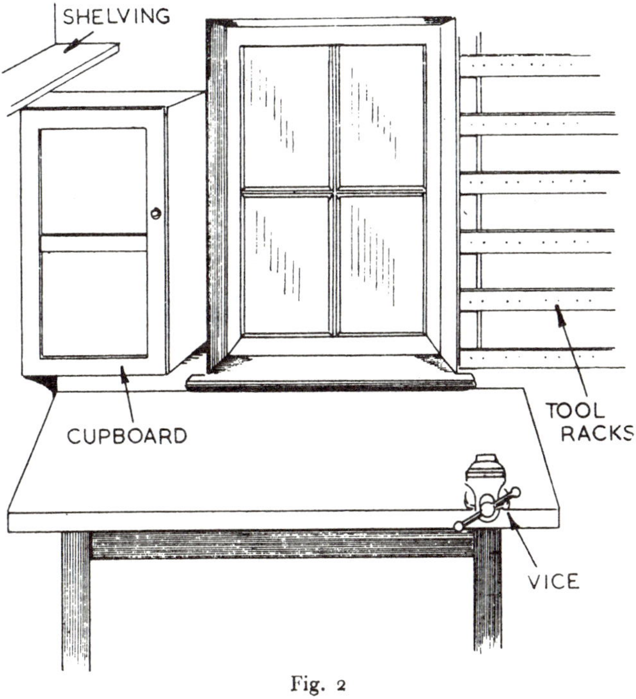

Fig. 2

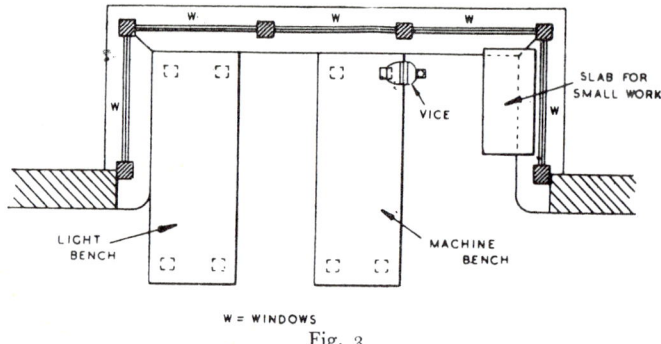

W = WINDOWS
Fig. 3

a large window which is carried outwards and returned on two sides, that is to say a large bay-window, this can be made into an excellent and well-lighted workshop, as illustrated in Fig. 3.

The drawing shows the arrangement in plan, that is to say the bird's-eye view, and it will be seen that two main benches are shown, one for general light work, and the other to carry the vice and the machine tools as they are acquired; in addition, a heavy marble slab, which will be described later, has been fitted into the window corner for doing small work with the best possible lighting.

Admittedly, this is an advanced layout, but it is, nevertheless, well worth bearing in mind as an ideal and as a future possibility; for when arranging the workshop, work, if you can, to a definite plan with a view to acquiring and installing at some future date all the tools needed to fulfil your ambitions. By so doing, constant rearrangement of the workshop can be avoided, and only tools useful for all time will be acquired.

Benches. As has previously been said, the bench should be preferably of robust construction and sufficiently firm on its legs to give steadiness when working. A suitable design is shown in Fig. 4. The legs should be at least 3 in. square, and the top on which the vice is mounted should be made of planks 2 in. thick.

If you have had some experience of woodworking and can obtain the necessary materials, you may be able to make the bench yourself, but if not, it may be possible to buy a bench at a sale or from a furniture store. Failing this, a robust form of kitchen table may be used, at any rate as a start.

In the drawing of the bench shown in Fig. 4 it will be seen that an undershelf is fitted ; this is useful not only as a storage place, but if heavy material is kept there it will help to steady the bench and prevent it moving when heavy filing is undertaken.

As previously mentioned, a slab, as shown at the right-hand top corner of Fig. 3 can be used for doing small work.

I used a heavy marble slab which is fixed to the window sills with wood screws. These slabs form the tops of wash-stands of a type now seldom used, and the complete piece of furniture can often be picked up at a sale for a few shillings ; the woodwork will come in useful for making tool racks and shelves.

Now, as these marble slabs are very heavy, they will form a steady foundation for mounting a small vice of the type that is made with a clamp for attachment to the bench ; in addition, these slabs usually have screw holes for fixing in place.

This little extra bench will be found most useful for doing

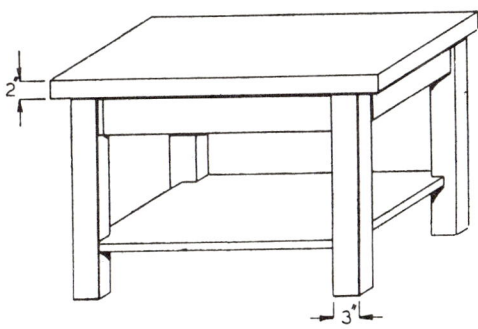

Fig. 4

small work or for making drawings, as in this position it will be well lighted and at a convenient height for working when the operator is seated on a stool of the office pattern.

Storing Tools. As has already been pointed out, if the workshop is fitted out in a living room, any untidiness will almost certainly call for reproof, and, moreover, tools left lying about are easily mislaid or damaged. "A place for everything and everything in its place" is a good rule to follow.

Some workers keep their tools in racks and on shelves near at hand, but however convenient this may be, it has its drawbacks, for the room is not then easily kept clean, and also some of the finer tools may be damaged by exposure to dust.

For these reasons, and perhaps also for the sake of appearance, others may prefer to store the workshop tools in cupboards or in small chests of drawers, where they are out of sight and well protected against damage and casual borrowers.

In the course of time, it is almost inevitable that a great variety of materials and parts such as screws and nuts and bolts will be accumulated in the workshop, and it is very necessary that they should be stored in an orderly and methodical manner, so that, for example, any particular size of screw can be found at once and without having to rummage in a box full of oddments.

Tobacco and cigarette tins are excellent for this purpose, so collect all you can from your friends and keep them in readiness to receive your purchases of screws and other small material.

Glass shaving soap jars with screw tops are also most useful, for as the contents are always visible this may save opening boxes to find what you want. If the lid is attached with wood screws to a beam or batten, as shown in Fig. 5, the jar will take up very little valuable space and can be readily unscrewed to get at its contents.

Cigar boxes, when obtainable, make useful receptacles for storing larger accessories and material.

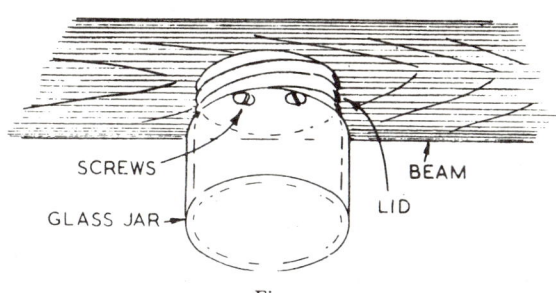

Fig. 5

Although it is hardly necessary to mark glass jars to indicate what they contain, tins and boxes should always be labelled to save time when looking for materials of any particular size.

For this purpose, the titles may be painted on, preferably with cellulose paint which dries quickly and adheres firmly, but it will usually be found sufficient to attach a gummed label, or a piece of sticking plaster, on which is written a list of the contents.

Tool Racks. When the tools are kept in racks, these can be easily made by attaching a leather strap or strip, or a piece of webbing, to a length of wood which is then fixed to the wall or window framing. The design of a simple tool rack is illustrated in Fig. 6.

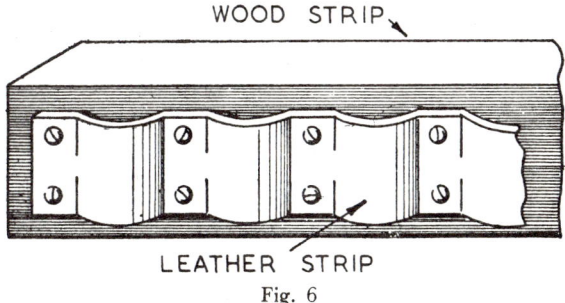

Fig. 6

When attaching tool racks and other workshop fittings to the walls of the room, do not use ordinary nails, as these generally have but little holding power, and when they work loose, as in time they will, the wall will probably be much damaged and hard words may result. On the other hand, if Rawlplugs are properly used, the hold will be firm and the walls will not suffer.

Before using Rawlplugs within the house, it is a good plan to practise a few holes in a place that does not matter, but with ordinary skill, and if reasonable care is taken, no difficulty will be found in fitting these useful fixings.

Shelving. Within the house, built-up shelves like book shelves will generally be used, either standing on a cupboard, or fixed to the wall by means of Rawlplugs ; only in the case of a shed workshop will iron shelf brackets be employed to support lines of shelving. In every case, the shelves must be securely fixed, so that they do not fall when loaded with heavy tools.

Cupboards. Small cupboards are particularly useful, as they afford good protection for the tools and, at the same time, may even enhance the appearance of the workshop. Furthermore, the tools can then be locked up to guard against would-be borrowers.

If possible, cupboards should be placed so that their contents are in full view and can readily be removed when wanted without having to go down on the hands and knees. When large cupboards are fixed to walls it may be necessary to use brackets to give additional support.

Chests of Drawers. Although there are many forms of this article of furniture, one of the most useful is the music cabinet, which usually has some six wide but rather shallow drawers that are ideal for storing files and similar types of tools, where it is important that the tools should not become damaged by being heaped one upon another.

Another form of chest, which can often be picked up quite cheaply at sales, is the Wellington chest. This, again, has six or more drawers placed one above another, but, in this case, the individual drawers, being narrower and deeper, are suitable for holding larger tools and other items of workshop equipment.

With an ample supply of cupboards and chests of drawers all the workshop tools can, if desired, be stored out of sight so as to preserve the good appearance of the room and disguise its real purpose.

Should the air of the room be liable to become damp, this dampness will be absorbed by the woodwork so that tools kept on wooden shelves may be damaged by rust ; this is more likely to occur when the shelves are covered with paper, for ordinary paper readily absorbs moisture. To prevent rusting, therefore, from this cause, all wooden shelves should be covered with some material, such as plastic sheeting, which does not absorb water.

Even this precaution will not safeguard the tools from rusting in a shed workshop where there is no continuous heating, and in this case, the tools should be oiled or greased, preferably with a compound such as Rustveto, which is specially made for this purpose and contains lanoline or wool fat to render the coating impervious to moisture.

Heating and Lighting. In factories a reasonable temperature of the air is maintained not only for the comfort of the workpeople, but also to enable them to do good work and keep up the output. For the same reasons, the heating of the home workshop is equally important, and within the house this should not be a difficult matter, but in the shed workshop it will probably be necessary to use some form of stove if work is to be carried on during the winter months.

As the workshop will probably be largely used after dark, satisfactory artificial lighting is essential if good work is to be done. The general lighting with which the room or shed is equipped will probably not be sufficient for fine or difficult work at the bench, and some form of additional lighting will then be required. For this purpose, a movable form of lamp, such as a reading lamp, will be found an advantage, for then the light can be directed to the exact spot where it is most required. The Anglepoise lamp, manufactured by Messrs. Terry, is made in two sizes, and the larger when standing on the bench is instantly adjustable to cover a wide area, so that it should alone be able to provide all the light necessary for working at the bench, or for using any machine mounted on the bench top.

The Floor. In order not to add to the work of keeping the room clean and tidy, care should be taken to prevent, as far as possible, filings and lathe turnings from falling on the floor ; for not only are these difficult to sweep up, but also, when they are trodden about the room generally, censure is almost sure to follow.

To overcome this difficulty, an old mat should be spread on the floor underneath the vice where it will catch the filings as they fall ; it is then an easy matter to take the mat outside and shake it clean. In the same way, mats can be used to catch the chips that fall from the lathe or drilling machine.

It will be found that chips and filings are easily trodden into lino or soft wood floors and are then difficult to remove, so take special care to protect the floor from damage of this kind.

The bench top should always be brushed clean after working, and the chips, when collected in a domestic dustpan, should either be taken outside at once, or placed temporarily in a box kept for the purpose under the bench.

Methodical Working. Finally, train yourself from the start to follow a tidy and methodical way of working, so that tools are put back in their places as they are used and you do not waste time and temper in searching for them amongst a heap of tools cluttering up the bench. When taking work to pieces, place the screws and other small parts in a tray, such as the lid of a tobacco tin, and you will not then have to search the bench, or possibly the floor, for missing parts when it comes to putting the work together again.

As an example of what is meant by this, when overhauling a motor car engine I used a wooden block drilled with a numbered hole to receive each valve as removed, and set with nails for holding the spring, collar, and cotter belonging to each valve.

In this way, the parts were readily reassembled in their original order, and there was no danger of their not working properly owing to wrong assembly.

Although this was in the early days of motoring when all parts were hand-fitted and not mass-produced, the former method of fitting is still used in some branches of engineering, and nothing is lost, and probably much is gained, by working methodically when overhauling any kind of mechanical work.

CHAPTER TWO

> The Vice—Hand Tools—Files—Hacksaws — Hand Drills — Drills — Screwthreading Equipment—Shears — Chisels—Scrapers—Tools used for Assembling Work — Spanners — Screwdrivers — Pliers — Hammers — Punches — Soldering Equipment—Oil Stones.

The Vice. Before any filing or sawing of material can be undertaken it will be necessary to attach a vice to the bench for the purpose of holding the work securely ; and although

WORKSHOP EQUIPMENT
the vice must, of course, be firmly fixed in place, its weight also helps to steady the work.

It is important, therefore, that the vice should be fully big for its purpose and capable of holding the largest material that is likely to be used.

For general work, a vice of simple design and with jaws not less than 4 in. in width will as a rule be found most suitable.

A well-designed and robust type of vice is illustrated in Fig. 7, and from the cross-section of this appliance shown in Fig. 8 it will be seen that the jaws are closed by means of a square-threaded screw working in a threaded nut attached to the body casting. Although these screw threads are well protected from filings, nevertheless, they should be well oiled from time to time to prevent undue wear taking place and to enable the parts to work freely.

As will be seen, the two jaws carry detachable hardened steel jaw plates which have roughened surfaces to enable them to grip the work more securely, but as it is generally an advantage to have smooth jaws which do not damage finished work, you may be able to get someone to grind these flat for you, or, perhaps, you can buy in the first place a vice with unroughened jaws.

To prevent the surface of finished work being damaged, two strips of sheet lead or copper should be gripped between the jaws and then hammered over to retain them in place when the vice is opened ; these fittings, known as vice clams, are illustrated in Fig. 9. Clams are also procurable made of thick red fibre and fitted with metal clips to hold them in place on the vice jaws. Strips of cardboard will also be found useful as clams when gripping small work.

Fig. 7

The vice is secured to the bench top by means of large wood screws, or preferably with carriage bolts which have a screw-threaded shank and a head to fit a spanner.

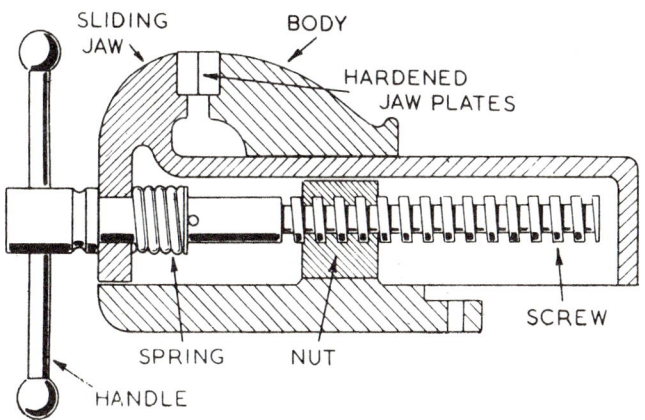

Fig. 8

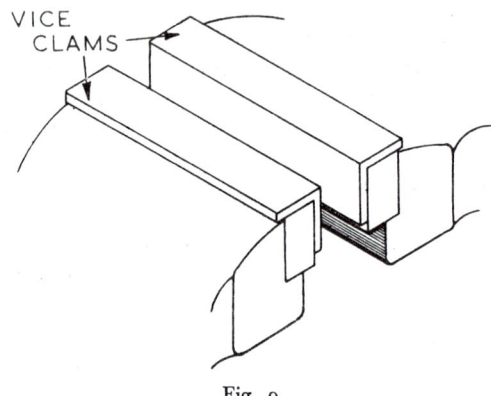

Fig. 9

The latter give a firmer hold and are more readily tightened.

As shown in Fig. 2, Chapter I, the vice is fixed near one of the bench legs in order to give steadiness, but at the same time care must be taken to see that ample room is allowed for standing and for the free working of the arms when filing.

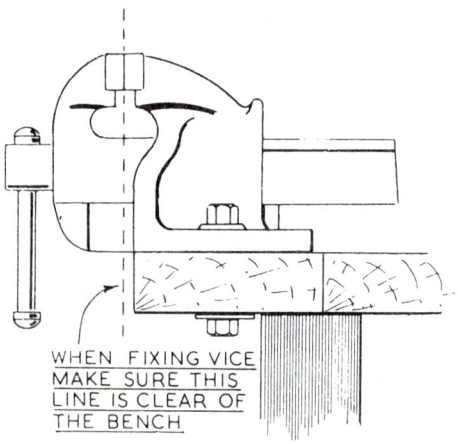

Fig. 10

Furthermore, the vice should be attached so that the fixed jaw projects beyond the edge of the bench, as shown in Fig. 10, otherwise you will not be able to hold long pieces of material in a vertical position between the jaws unless a packing piece is used behind the work.

Fig. 11

If the vice is set at the correct height for working, the top of the jaws should be level with the point of the elbow when the arm is bent, as shown in Fig. 11 ; but if the bench is of the standard height of some 3 ft. and you are not fully grown, you may find that the vice is too high for comfortable working.

In this event, you will find it better to stand on a wooden platform or duck-board when working, rather than to cut short the legs of the bench ; then, in the course of time, as you grow taller the platform can be discarded.

The standard given for the height of the vice is that most suitable for ordinary work, but for fine work the top of the vice can be raised with advantage, in order to bring the work nearer to the eye without the operator having to stoop.

For this purpose, a small vice may be gripped in the bench vice, and if one with a swivelling base can be purchased this will add greatly to its usefulness. The writers use a small " Yankee " vice of this type, and it has proved a great help when dealing with small work.

As has already been mentioned, a small vice can be clamped to the marble slab described in the previous chapter ; if a good quality vice with an efficient clamp is obtained, it will be found that this is a most useful appliance, as it can be fixed where required and readily removed when not needed.

To complete the arrangement of the bench, the bench top should be set level with the aid of a spirit level, and if necessary, thin strips of wood should be placed under the feet for this purpose. This levelling will prevent tools from rolling on the bench top, and may also be helpful, as we shall see later, when using the hand drill in the horizontal position.

Hand Tools. In order to carry out the ordinary workshop operations of filing, drilling, screw threading and soldering, the appropriate hand tools will be required ; these, amongst others, will be first described, leaving an account of their practical use until later.

Clearly, it will be possible to describe only a few of the tools in each class, and the reader is, therefore, advised to consult tool catalogues to make himself familiar with the large variety of types available. Much useful information can also be gained by reading toolmakers' advertisements and by visiting the stands at exhibitions where tools are displayed.

Files. Files are named according to their length, shape, and the coarseness of their teeth. For filing a piece of material to size, where a considerable amount of metal has to be removed, a 10-in. bastard-cut hand file would in many instances be found suitable. This means that the blade of the file, exclusive of the pointed tang, is 10 in. in length. Bastard-cut signifies that the file has rather coarse teeth for taking a heavy cut; the other grades of teeth in common use are second-cut, smooth and dead smooth. A hand file is one which, as illustrated in Fig. 12A, has a flat parallel blade with a smooth or safe-edge along one side for use when filing against shoulders.

Other shapes of files in general use are the flat, square, triangular, round and half-round, as depicted in Fig. 12 B, C, D and E respectively.

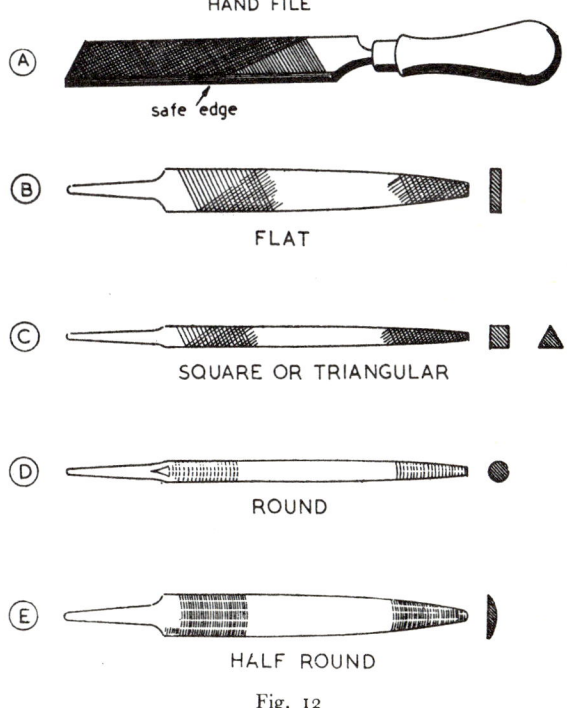

Fig. 12

In addition to these forms, there are many varieties intended for special purposes and less commonly used ; these are usually illustrated in tool merchants' catalogues, and further information about them and about files in general can be found in "The Amateur's Workshop," (Argus Books Ltd.), where the subject is fully discussed.

Before a file is put into use, it is essential that it should be fitted with a handle, both to enable proper guidance to be given to the blade when filing and also to protect the hand from damage by the pointed tang. For this purpose, the file is secured just below the shoulder of the tang between clams in the vice, and the handle is driven home with light blows from a wooden or raw-hide mallet ; if a mallet is not available, a piece of wood should be held against the handle and struck with a hammer.

It is important that a handle large enough to give a comfortable hand-hold should be fitted, and in addition, the handle must be driven on so that it lies in a straight line with the blade of the file, as shown in Fig. 13.

Always buy your files from a reputable tool merchant, for then you will avoid getting poor quality tools that will give you little satisfaction.

The length of the files you should buy will depend largely on the size of the work to be dealt with, and if you keep adding to your stock as required, rather than buying a large number of files at the outset, in time you will acquire a good selection suitable for all ordinary purposes.

For cutting brass and similar alloys, the file must be quite sharp or it will tend merely to skid over the surface of the work ; a file that has been used to file steel will not cut brass as it should, but, on the other hand, a file used on brass will be perfectly satisfactory for filing steel.

To get satisfactory results, therefore, either the files can at first be used solely for brass and then given over to steel, or a duplicate set of files can be bought in the first instance, or, as a further alternative and as a measure of economy, one side of the file can be marked with yellow paint indicating that it is to be reserved for use only on brass, and the other side is then kept for filing steel.

Saws. For sawing metal, a tool termed a hacksaw is used ; this consists of a frame to hold and strain the narrow saw blade which is furnished with teeth after the manner of a wood saw.

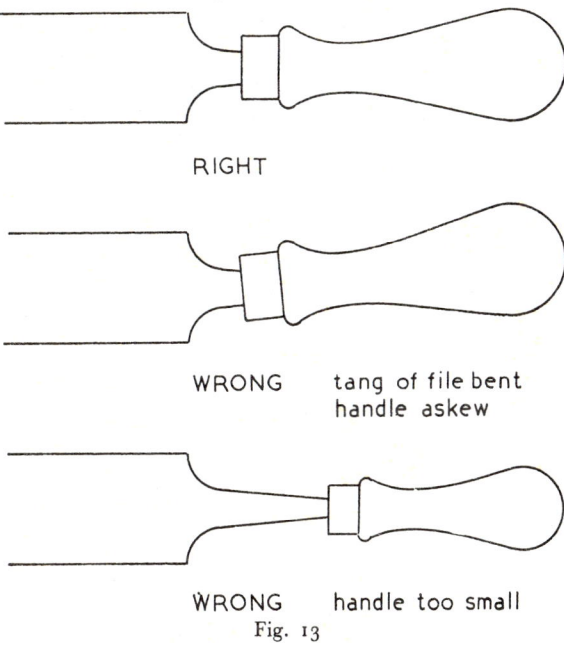

RIGHT

WRONG   tang of file bent handle askew

WRONG   handle too small
Fig. 13

As this tool is used almost exclusively for cutting up all the materials used in the small workshop, it is important that it should be of good construction, and that blades suitable for this purpose should be available.

Although a hacksaw frame adjustable for various lengths of blades is shown in Fig. 14, on the whole I would recomend a simple non-adjustable pattern to take 10 in. (254 m.m.) blades; for not only is the latter type cheaper, but the short blades used are more readily kept on a straight path when sawing and are not so easily broken.

As in the case of files, a coarse tooth is used for the rapid cutting of heavy material, and a blade of fine tooth pitch is more suitable for small work ; moreover, a blade that has been used on steel will not readily cut brass.

If we are to use the right blade for the job, two courses are open to us : either to change the blade as required, or to keep several frames fitted with different types of blades.

The former course is apt to be tiresome and often results in using any blade that happens to be in the frame, although it is unsuitable for the work in hand and may have its

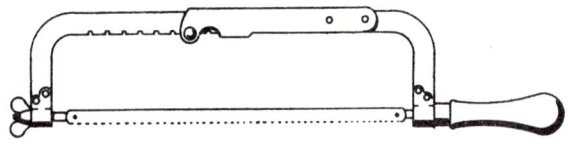

Fig. 14

teeth broken in the attempt. If, on the other hand, the simple type of frame recommended is used, several frames can be bought quite cheaply and, when used with the correct blades for the work, the teeth will not be damaged and better work and a considerable saving in saw blades will result.

If much heavy sawing has to be undertaken, there is no reason why a large or an adjustable frame fitted with a 10-in. blade should not be kept for this purpose. " Eclipse " hacksaw frames are available in many patterns suitable for use in the small workshop.

Saw blades for these frames are made with teeth ranging from 14 to 32 per inch. These blades can also be obtained hardened throughout, or with only the teeth hardened and the backs of the blades left soft ; the latter are recommended for the use of the beginner as they are much less easily broken if the blade is inadvertently bent when sawing.

The Eclipse light pattern saw frame, illustrated in

Fig. 15, holds narrow 6-in. blades with fine teeth. This little saw will be found invaluable in the workshop for all kinds of small work.

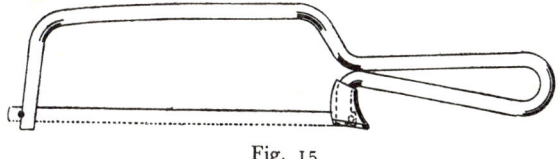

Fig. 15

The small saw shown in Fig. 16 is made with a stiff back of either brass or steel which is folded over the blade and gives it support throughout its length. The blade, with its fine teeth, is useful for slotting the heads of small screws and also for cutting thin tubing and slitting sheet metal.

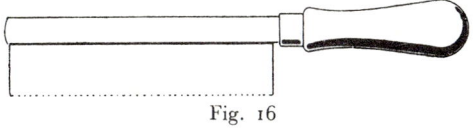

Fig. 16

The piercing saw illustrated in Fig. 17 is in many respects similar to the ordinary fretsaw and, as will be seen, the tension of the blade is adjusted by setting the frame and springing it while the blade is clamped in place.

The 5-in. blades are made in various widths; the narrower

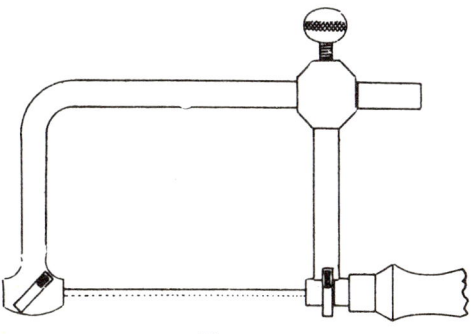

Fig. 17

are used, as will be described later, for cutting internal holes and shapes in metal sheet and plate, whilst the broader blades are more suitable for slitting and cutting off light sections of material.

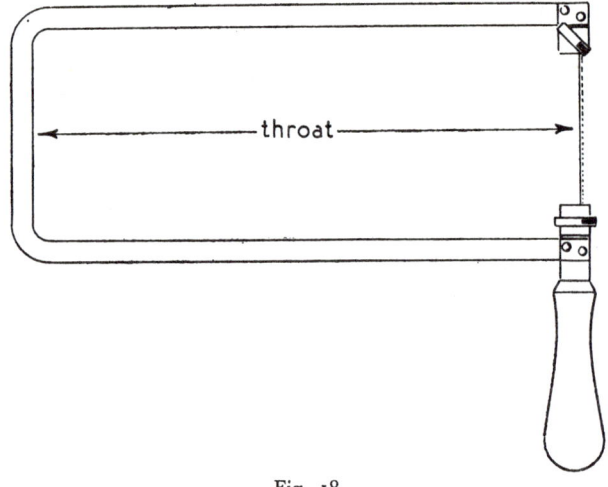

Fig. 18

The familiar fretsaw of the pattern shown in Fig. 18 will be found useful for cutting sheet metal, for the great depth of the throat enables large sheets to be dealt with or patterns to be cut out as in ordinary fretwork. Special blades made for cutting metal should be used ; these have a very rapid cutting action, and, if reasonable care is taken, they are not so easily broken as might be supposed.

Another special form of hacksaw is the Abrafile, shown in Fig. 19 ; this frame carries a blade of circular section, somewhat like a slender round file, which can be threaded through a hole in the work and then used to cut out a larger hole or any other pattern desired.

Hand Drills. We are here concerned only with hand drills, for power-driven drilling machines as well as the methods used in operating them will be described in the Part Two of this book.

Fig. 19

The light type of single-geared hand drill shown in Fig. 20 is fitted with a small chuck that will usually hold drills up to $\frac{1}{4}$ in. in diameter. The heavier pattern drill, illustrated in Fig. 21, is termed a breast drill, as it has a curved plate at its upper end against which the chest is pressed during drilling, thus leaving the hands free to work and guide the tool.

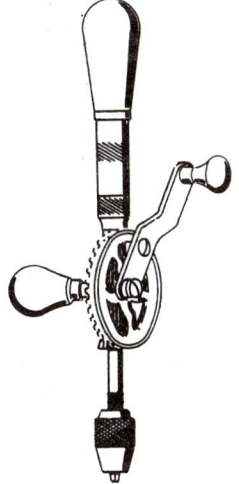

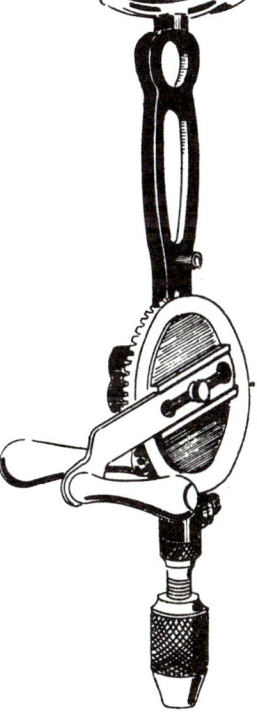

Fig. 20

Fig. 21

In this case, a larger chuck capable of holding up to ½ in. is fitted, and an easily-engaged two-speed gear is incorporated in the machine. It will also be seen that the operating handle can be adjusted to give greater leverage when drilling large holes with the slow-speed gear engaged.

Drills. As to the actual drills themselves, twist drills will be found to cut more easily than other types, and, in addition if care is taken when drilling, holes equal to the nominal size of the drill can be bored with considerable accuracy. For drilling sheet metal, the straight-flute type of drill is recommended ; these drills are similar to twist drills except that the flutes are straight instead of being formed on a spiral path.

It should again be stressed that drills of good quality will prove the most satisfactory, and these can be bought either in sets or as individual drills, according to requirements.

One disadvantage, perhaps, of these drills, when used in the small workshop, is that owing to their special form they are not readily resharpened with that degree of accuracy which is essential for doing good work. You may, therefore, have to ask a friend who has a grinding device to do this work for you.

The classification of twist drills up to ½ in. diameter is as follows :—

Number sizes.

From No. 80 (0.0135 in. diam.) to No. 1 (0.2280 in. diam.), advancing in steps of a few thousandths of an inch.

Fractional Inch sizes.

From 1/64 in. (0.0156 in. diam.) to ½ in. diam., advancing by 1/64 in.

Letter sizes.

From A (0.2340 in. diam.) to Z (0.4130 in. diam.), advancing in steps of several thousandths of an inch.

Metric sizes.

Many readers will be aware that the metric measurement system is in the process of universal adoption. It follows therefore that the three classes of drill mentioned will be phased out in course of time. Meanwhile, drill manufacturers have been increasing the range of metric sizes they produce. The sizes available are now very finely graduated, as may be inferred from an inspection of the tables at the end of the book.

Screw-Threading Tackle. Screw threads are cut by hand by means of taps and dies. The tap is screwed into a hole drilled to the correct tapping size, as it is termed, to form an internal thread, and the die is screwed on to round material, again of the correct diameter, to cut an external thread ; with the result that the two parts so threaded can be screwed together, as is seen in the case of a bolt and its nut.

Taps and Dies. These are referred to both as to the outside diameter of the work they are intended to thread, and to the pitch or number of threads per inch, written t.p.i., that they cut.

The pitch of a thread is the distance measured between two of its crests, so that when a thread is described as 16 t.p.i. it means that the distance from the top of one thread to the top of the next is $\frac{1}{16}$ in., and it is said to be of $\frac{1}{16}$ in. pitch.

In addition, the shape of the actual thread itself is always of some standard form, such as the well-known Whitworth thread ; but we need not here go further into this, except to point out that nuts and bolts used together must have the same form of thread, as well as being of the same diameter and pitch.

The question of the form of the thread and the size of the tapping hole required will be dealt with in a later chapter, when the actual screw threading operations are described.

When buying screwing tackle, you must decide what standard of thread pitch will best suit the work you have to do.

For wireless components and other small equipment of this sort, the British Association, or B.A. standard of pitches and diameters is generally used, and this will also be found suitable for model engineering and other similar work.

B.A. sizes are denoted by numbers, the largest, No. 0, being rather less than $\frac{1}{4}$ in. in diameter and the smallest you will probably need, No. 10, has a diameter of a little more than $\frac{1}{16}$ in.

To begin with, you will probably find that the alternate sizes from No. 0 to No. 10 will be all that you need, and any intermediate sizes can then be bought later as required.

The standard Whitworth sizes above $\frac{1}{8}$ in. have too coarse a pitch for small work such as model engineering. The British Standard Fine, or B.S.F. sizes, although of finer pitch, are still rather coarse for small engineering and instrument work.

The Standard Brass thread of 26 t.p.i. in all sizes up to $\frac{1}{2}$ in., and more, is suitable for threading the larger components used in model engineering work.

To meet the special needs of the model maker, *The Model Engineer* many years ago very wisely introduced a standard of 40 t.p.i. for all sizes up to $\frac{1}{4}$ in. in diameter, and having 32 t.p.i. for $\frac{5}{16}$ in. and $\frac{3}{8}$ in., and 26 t.p.i. for $\frac{7}{16}$ in. and $\frac{1}{2}$ in.

Following this, taps and dies of 40 t.p.i. are now available in all sizes up to $\frac{1}{2}$ in. or more. These fine threads are especially useful to the model engineer for threading thin-walled tubes and piping.

From what has been said it will be apparent that fine threads are tending to replace the older forms of coarse threads for small engineering work, and this has been made possible by the accurate methods now used in making taps and dies which produce a well-cut thread that gives a secure hold.

When buying screwing equipment, it is also most important to choose the best quality obtainable, and moreover, it is a good plan to buy a set of tackle, provided that it is exactly what is required, for then a box will be included for storing the equipment and protecting it from damage.

Taps. In the smaller sizes two taps are usually provided for each size, that is to say a taper tap for starting the threading operation and a second tap for completing the thread.

A third form known as a plug or bottoming tap is used, particularly in the larger sizes, for cutting the thread to the bottom of a hole. These three forms of taps are illustrated in Fig. 22.

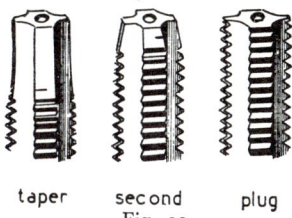

taper   second   plug
Fig. 22

Dies. For all small work these are now made of the circular pattern shown in Fig. 23, and it will be seen that the die is split so that it can be adjusted for wear, either by means of a setting screw or by being pinched in the die holder.

Tap and Die Holders. If you buy a set of screwing tackle, a tap holder and a die holder will probably be included. The tap holder illustrated in Fig. 24 is adjustable to fit taps of different sizes, and when secured to the squared portion of the tap's shank it is used as a turning wrench.

When applied to small taps, this type of wrench may be found rather difficult to use and somewhat cumbersome, and in that case the holders shown in Figs. 25 and 26 may be more convenient.

Fig. 23

These holders have a two-jaw chuck which is contracted by means of the knurled sleeve to grip the squared end of the tap.

The die holder depicted in Fig. 27 is provided with a set screw for holding the circular die in place, and some patterns of die holders, and by far the most useful, have guides for holding the die truly in line with the work. A

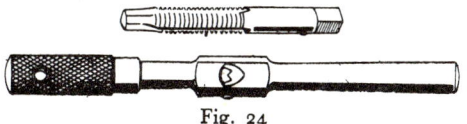

Fig. 24

holder of this type is shown in Fig. 28, and it will be seen that below the die is a housing in which a circular guide collet is retained by means of a set screw. Needless to say, a collet of the correct size must be used to fit the work being threaded, but there is no difficulty in this, as sets of collets are supplied with die holders of this type.

Some standard American die holders are of this pattern, but at present some difficulty may be experienced in obtaining these tools.

Another form of die collet is shown in Fig. 29 ; here, the die fits into a housing which itself forms the collet or guide for the work.

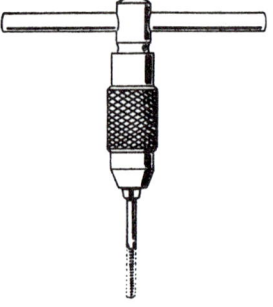

Fig. 25

Shears. For cutting sheet metal, the tool generally used

Fig. 26

is the hand shears or tinman's snips, and both the straight and the curved pattern are illustrated in Fig. 30.

The straight form is used for all straight-line work and for cutting out large diameter circles, whilst the curved pattern is suitable for cutting out circles of small diameter and for all internal curved work.

Fig. 27

As in the case of ordinary scissors, only thin material can be cut owing to the limited leverage available. Where thick sheet metal has to be dealt with, greater cutting pressure is required, and for this work a bench shearing machine of the type illustrated in Fig. 31 is generally used.

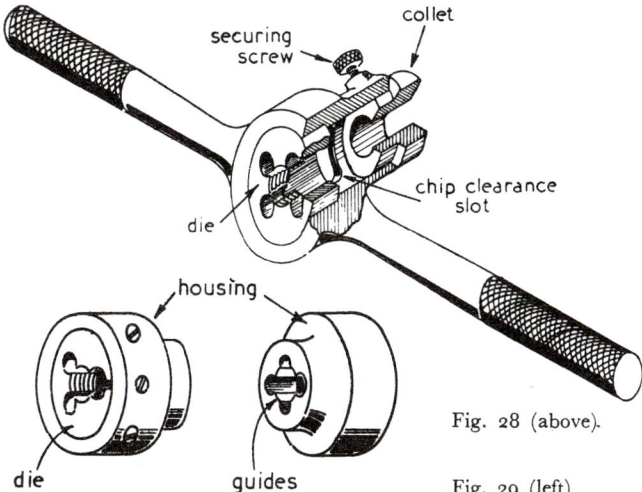

Fig. 28 (above).

Fig. 29 (left)

As will be seen in the drawing, the system of linkage employed provides great leverage and this is further increased by using a long handle to work the machine.

Although this machine is undoubtedly useful in the small workshop, its purchase would seem hardly justified unless much sheet metal cutting is undertaken.

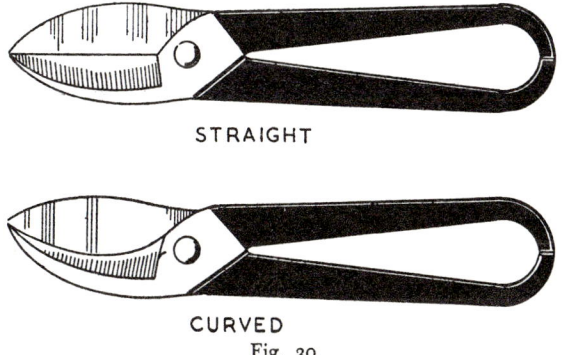

Fig. 30

When dealing with the use of the hand shears in a later chapter, some ways of increasing the cutting power of the tool and making it more easily operated will be described.

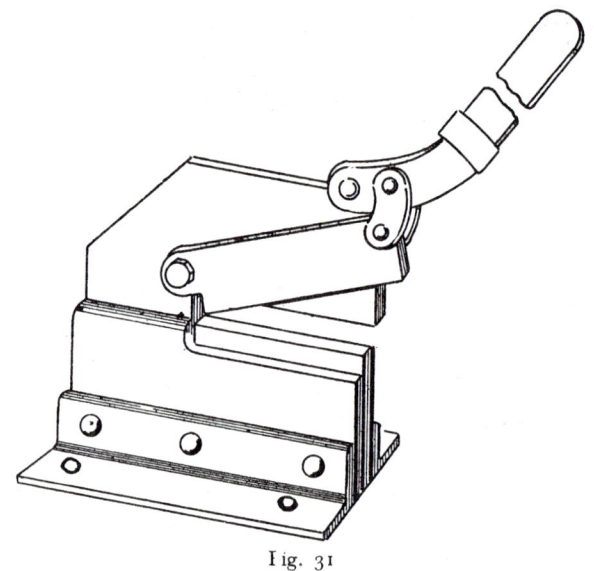

Fig. 31

Chisels. The four forms of metal-cutting chisels in common use, or cold chisels as they are called, are illustrated in Fig. 32 ; and of these the flat type is often used by the model engineer for cutting metal in awkward places where other tools, such as saws and files, cannot easily be brought to bear.

The other three forms are used for special work, that is to say for cutting heavy metal plate and keyways, forming oil grooves in bearings, and clearing out the corners of cast work respectively.

These chisels are usually forged from octagon tool steel and are then hardened and tempered to enable the cutting edges to withstand the shock of the hammer blows used to drive the tool along the work.

In addition to this pattern, Messrs. Moore & Wright

manufacture a range of flat rectangular section chisels, made of a special nickel alloy steel, which have superior cutting properties and are more readily resharpened when blunted.

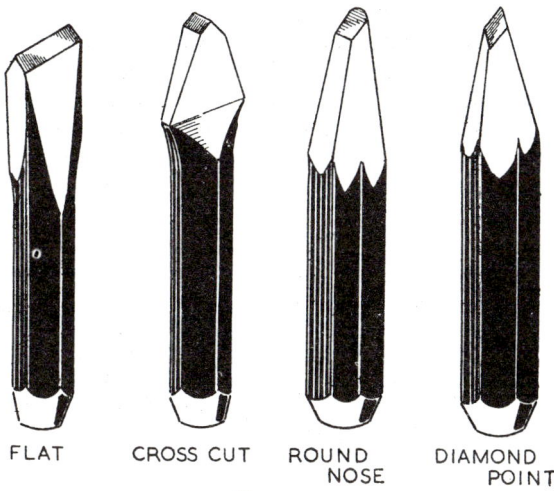

FLAT   CROSS CUT   ROUND NOSE   DIAMOND POINT

Fig. 32

Scrapers. Although scrapers are made in a variety of forms adapted for different purposes and for working on flat and curved surfaces, a single flat scraper of the pattern illustrated in Fig. 33 will be found sufficient for most purposes in the small workshop. The scraper is a most

Fig. 33

useful tool for removing small amounts of metal when fitting parts together, and, unlike the file, it will readily remove the metal in exactly the place required.

Scrapers can be bought from the tool merchant, but mechanics usually prefer to make them from a discarded flat file, as files of good quality are made from steel which is most suitable for this purpose. So if you have a friend who is willing to make you a scraper, so much the better.

The method of using and sharpening the scraper will be described in a later chapter.

Tools used for Assembling Work. Although the size of these tools will, of course, vary with the character of the work undertaken, their actual form will be substantially the same in all cases. For assembling models and other small work, you will find it a good plan to keep a selection of these tools in a box or drawer apart, so that they are always ready for use and do not have to be collected from various places in the workshop.

Spanners. The open-ended type shown in Fig. 34 can be obtained, to fit all sizes of nuts from 10 B.A. up to the very

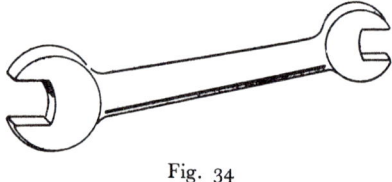

Fig. 34

largest, and their size is always denoted by the size of the nut they are intended to fit, and not by the width apart of the jaws.

Spanners of the open-ended pattern have the disadvantages that they are apt to slip when in use, and also they

Fig. 35

engage with only two of the flats on the nut at a time, whereas the types shown in the subsequent drawings make contact with all six of the nut faces and thereby obtain a better hold with much less liability to slip or damage the nut. If a spanner slips when turning a nut, it may cause unsightly damage which will spoil the appearance of a well-finished piece of work.

The spanner shown in Fig. 35 is known as a ring spanner and is largely employed for turning nuts which are in frequent use, such as those on the adjustable parts of machine tools.

Fig. 36

Messrs. Terry make useful sets in thin material of both open-ended and ring spanners to cover the range required for all ordinary work.

The box spanner, Fig. 36, is generally used for heavy

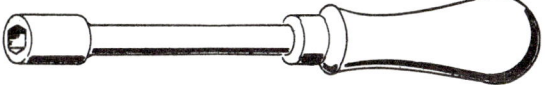

Fig. 37

work, but it can also be obtained in small sizes suitable for wireless and other similar work. As will be seen, the tubular portion is cross-drilled to take a round tommy bar to give the necessary leverage for turning the nut.

A more highly-finished form of box spanner is shown in Fig. 37; here, the recess to receive the nut is machined and the shank is fitted with a plastic or wooden handle. These spanners will be found much the most useful form for light assembly work.

For heavier work, this type of spanner is fitted with a metal cross-handle, as illustrated in Fig. 38, and is then known as a T-spanner.

Where nuts have to be fully and securely tightened the socket wrench illustrated in Figs. 39 and 40 may be used with advantage, for both a firm hold and good leverage are readily obtained.

These spanners comprise a set of sockets, which for storing are threaded on to the turning bar and retained in place by means of the spring detent shown on the left of Fig. 39.

When buying spanners make sure that you select only those of good quality and of sizes suitable for the work you intend to do, bearing in mind that you can always add others later on as the need arises.

Screwdrivers. Three forms of screwdrivers are illustrated in Fig. 41 ; the first is the type commonly used by the woodworker ; the second is the machinist's screwdriver which is fitted with a fluted handle to give a firm hand-hold and is the pattern generally used by metalworkers. The third form is smaller in size and has a blade adapted for turning the small screws used in model engineering and instrument work. When using these tools, the tip of the forefinger is placed in the recess of the swivelling top and the handle is turned with the tips of the thumb and second finger.

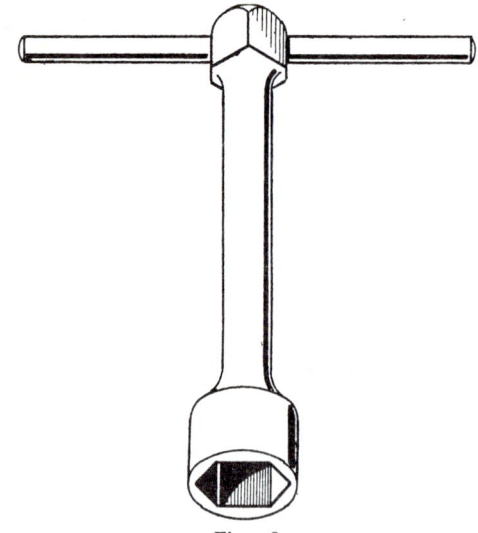

Fig. 38

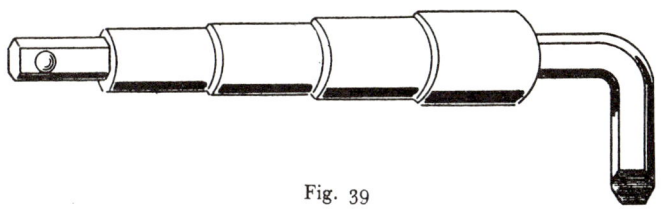

Fig. 39

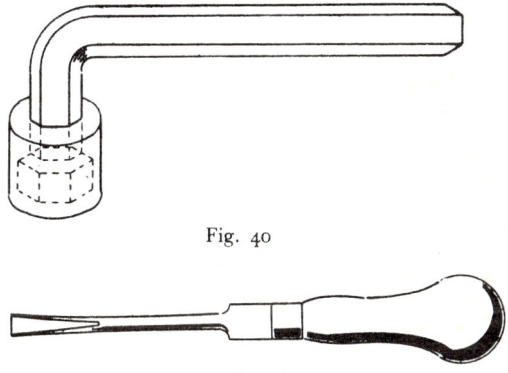

Fig. 40

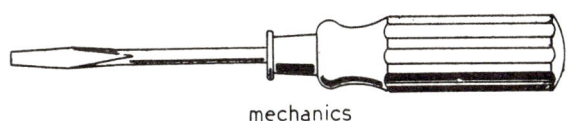

woodworkers

mechanics

watchmakers
Fig. 41

These screwdrivers can be bought in sets to fit the screw heads of a wide range of small screws.

It is important that not only should a screwdriver be used that fits the screw head, but, at the same time, the tip of the blade should be kept in good condition, so that it does not tend to slip out of the screw's slot and thus, perhaps, mar the appearance of a carefully-finished piece of work.

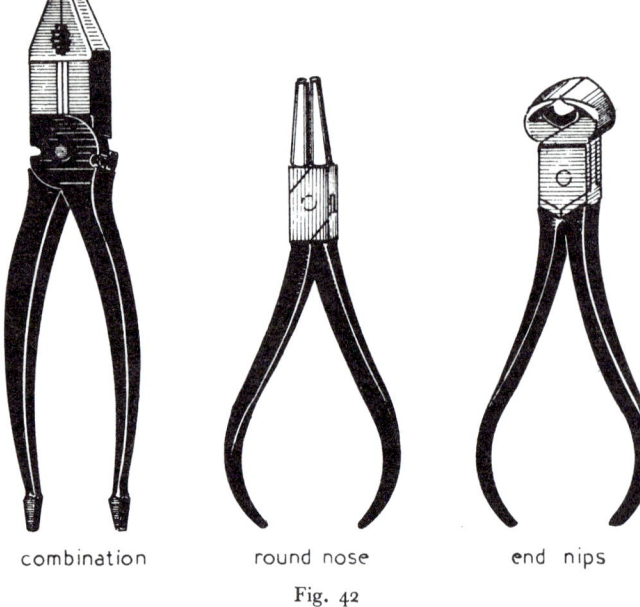

combination   round nose   end nips

Fig. 42

Those wishing for further information on this point should consult " Sharpening Small Tools," published by Argus Books Ltd.

Pliers. Inspection of a tool merchant's catalogue will show the great variety of pliers made for general use and also for special purposes. There is, however, no need to buy a large selection of these tools in the first place, as a pair of combination pliers will probably be found sufficient for all ordinary work. Nevertheless, a pair of round-nosed pliers and also a pair of end- or side-cutting pliers, as illustrated in Fig. 42, will form a useful addition to the tool kit.

When buying, it is important to select tools of good quality, as shown by the pliers being polished all over and having a firm but smooth-working joint ; in addition, the jaws should be well finished, so that they meet accurately.

Formerly, parallel-jaw pliers of American make could be

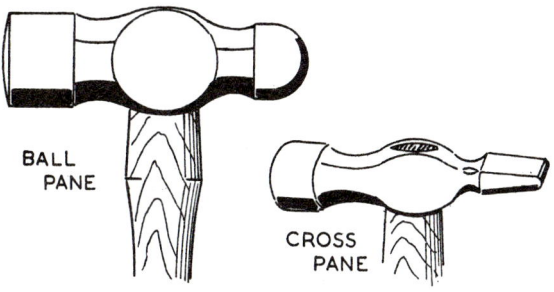

Fig. 43

obtained at any good tool store. These tools were of good quality with a fine finish, and as they were well designed and accurately made of high-class materials, they gave good and long service in the hands of a careful user.

Hammers. Two patterns of hammers are shown in Fig. 43.

The ball-pane or rounded face is used in the metal workshop for setting and rounding over the heads of rivets and pins. For general use, a hammer of some ¾ lb. weight will be suitable, whilst for light work a small hammer with a 2 to 3 oz. head will be required.

The cross-pane hammer is mostly used in woodworking shops where the cross-pane is essential for setting and driving nails in awkward places.

Best quality hammers have a finely-finished and polished head, and the shaft is made of straight-grained hickory ; in addition, the perfect balance can at once be detected when the hammer is taken in the hand.

Pin Punches. These tools, which are usually purchased in sets, are used for driving out pins when taking machines and other mechanisms to pieces. The drawing in Fig. 44 shows that the punch has a long parallel working portion and a knurled shank to provide a good grip for the fingers.

Fig. 44

Soldering Equipment. For ordinary soldering operations quite simple equipment will suffice. This consists of one or more soldering irons with a means of heating them, and, in addition, a supply of solder and fluxing material.

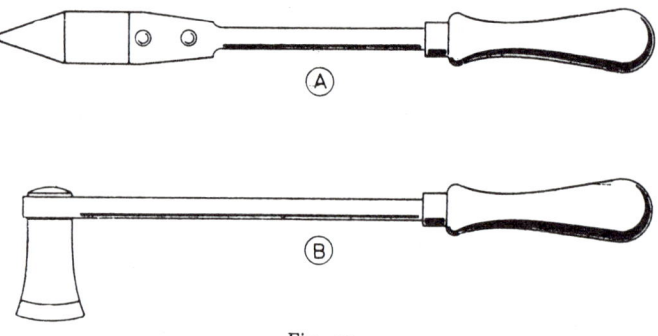

Fig. 45

A soldering iron, as shown in Fig. 45, consists of a copper bit, as it is termed, riveted to an iron shaft which is fitted with a wooden handle. The bit illustrated in Fig. 45A is pyramidal in form, and that in Fig. 45B is hatchet-shaped for use when soldering seams and for penetrating into awkward places.

Soldering irons are made in various weights, but for general work a bit weighing from 6 to 12 oz. will be found suitable.

Gas, when available, may be used with a Bunsen burner or gas ring for heating the iron, which in the former case can be supported on an ordinary laboratory tripod, as shown in Fig. 46.

Self-contained gas-heated soldering irons can also be obtained, and although this is a convenient method of heating the iron, the attached gas pipe may be found rather a nuisance.

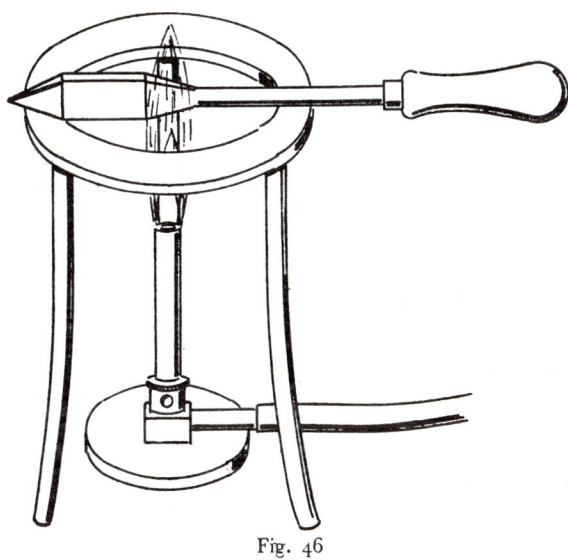

Fig. 46

When a coal or coke fire is used for heating, the iron is apt to become coated with ash; also, it is more difficult to control the heat and this may result in the bit being overheated.

As an alternative to heating the bit with a gas burner, an electrically-heated soldering iron may be used.

This has many advantages, for the iron is then kept clean and, as a result of the special manner in which the iron is wound, there is little danger of overheating the bit.

The question of solders and fluxes will be dealt with in a later chapter, where soldering operations will also be described.

Oilstones. For sharpening tools, such as chisels, scrapers and pointed tools, in addition to any woodworking tools you may use, you will need an oilstone or, perhaps one stone for rapid cutting and another for giving the final fine finish to the cutting edge.

Oilstones are of two kinds : the artificially produced carborundum stone, and the natural form, such as the Arkansas which consists of almost pure quartz.

For restoring the damaged edge of a tool, an artificial stone will remove the unwanted metal quickly ; and it will be found that the India stones manufactured by Messrs. Norton Abrasives are not only excellent for this purpose, but their hard texture prevents them from becoming unevenly worn or scored if reasonable care is taken.

To produce a highly-finished cutting edge, the sharpening operation is usually completed on a natural stone like an Arkansas or Washita. The former is rather expensive, but as it is extremely hard it will resist wear and should last almost indefinitely. If a soft stone is purchased, it will be found that the surface is easily scored and is apt to wear unevenly, so that in time it becomes unfit for sharpening tools accurately.

It is best to buy bench stones of the standard size, that is to say they should be 8 in. long, 2 in. wide and 1 in thick.

Smaller stones usually make tool sharpening more difficult, especially in the case of the larger tools, such as scrapers, wood chisels and plane blades, which usually have a place in the small workshop.

Read the makers' instructions carefully and carry out their recommendations as to upkeep, in order to ensure good and lasting service from your oilstones, for the quality of your work may in part depend on their efficiency.

Those who require further information about the selection and use of oilstones should consult " Sharpening Small Tools," published by Argus Books Ltd.

CHAPTER THREE

> Callipers — Rulers — Micrometers — Depth Gauge—The Protractor—Drill Gauge — Marking-out — Equipment required—Marking-out Sheet Metal Work —Witness Lines — Marking-out Solid Objects—Marking-out a Bearing Bracket —Marking-out the Centre of a Shaft— Reading Machine Drawings.

IN all mechanical work, where parts are machined or formed with hand tools to fit together, some means of making measurements will be almost essential both for maintaining accuracy and for saving loss of time.

EQUIPMENT FOR MEASURING AND MARKING-OUT

For example, if we have to fit a shaft to a small bearing, we could go on gradually removing metal from the shaft until it fitted in place, but clearly a better method would be to measure the bore of the bearing and then to machine the shaft to exactly this diameter, less, of course, a small allowance to give a working clearance.

How then are we to make these exact measurements?

In commercial practice the bearing may be made in one factory and the shaft in another, yet when the parts are assembled in a third factory they are found to fit together perfectly.

This result is obtained by the use of very accurate and expensive gauges, but these methods are hardly suited to the type of work usually undertaken in the small workshop, where a single model only may be constructed and the parts are then made and fitted together individually.

Callipers. Let us again consider the shaft and its bearing.

What we are really concerned with here is the diameter of the shaft *relative* to the bore of the bearing and quite irrespective of the *actual* size of the parts measured in inches.

The bore of the bearing can be gauged by means of the inside callipers shown in Fig. 47. The legs are set with the fingers to make contact with the bore and the final fine adjustment is made by tapping the callipers on a piece of wood. To open the legs, the callipers are held with the

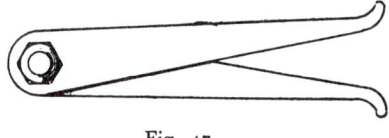

Fig. 47

points uppermost and the jointed end is tapped on the wood, whilst to close the callipers the legs themselves are lightly struck against the wood.

The adjustment is continued until a slight resistance only is felt as the tips of the calliper legs are moved to and fro in the bore.

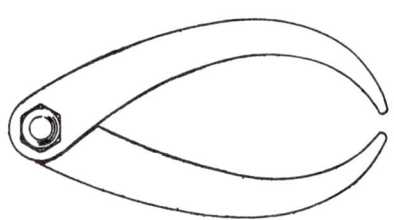

Fig. 48

The next step is to set the outside callipers, shown in Fig. 48, exactly to the inside callipers, using the method of setting already described, but great care must be taken when doing this not to upset the adjustment of the inside callipers.

The points of both callipers must be held quite square to each other when testing the setting, as shown in Fig. 49, otherwise a false reading will be obtained ; in addition, the process will be made easier if the points of both callipers are rested on a flat surface when testing the setting.

The outside callipers can now be used as a gauge to determine the diameter of the shaft required to make it a sliding fit in its bearing, and, moreover, it will be apparent that only simple tools are needed when this method is used.

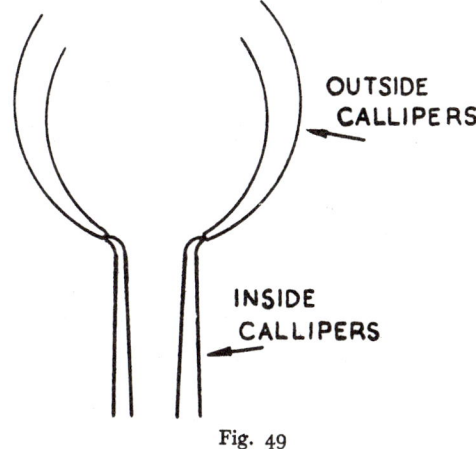

Fig. 49

As to the accuracy of the method, the writer found that, when making a series of measurements, errors of one thousandth of an inch could quite readily be detected, but some practice will be needed before this degree of accuracy of working is acquired.

The work of setting the callipers will be made easier if the screw-adjustable pattern is used ; these are illustrated in toolmakers' catalogues and also in Fig. 56, where the dividers of this type are illustrated.

If desired, the setting of the inside callipers can be measured against a rule and the outside callipers then adjusted to the same mark on the rule, but in this case quite large errors are almost sure to arise and this method is not recommended except for making rough measurements.

As an alternative method, instead of the inside callipers, a piece of metal rod can be used to gauge the bore, and the outside callipers are then set to this.

For this purpose, the shank of a drill which exactly fits the bore can be used, or a tapered cotter pin such as is used for assembling machinery will make a useful gauge. The latter can be inserted in the bore of the bearing and marked with a pencil at the line of contact, as illustrated in Fig. 50;

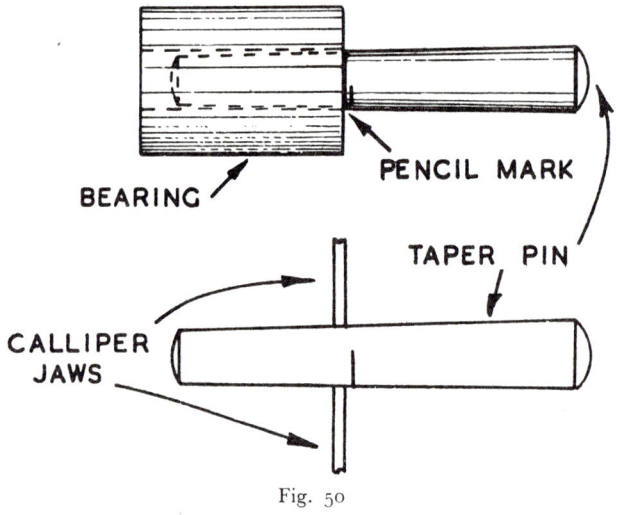

Fig. 50

the outside callipers, when set on the gauge piece just short of the pencil mark, can then be used for determining the size of the shaft required to fit the bore.

The Rule. So far, we have considered only the relative sizes of components without giving their actual size such as we could state numerically, or could show in a mechanical drawing.

When actual linear dimensions are required they can be measured, although not really accurately, by means of a rule of the pattern familiar to all workers.

These rules are made of steel and the graduations are machine engraved to ensure the accuracy of the markings.

Tempered steel rules are best, as they resist wear and are not so liable to become rusted from handling.

A large rule of 1 ft. or 6 in. in length will be required, and in addition, a short 3-in. or 4-in. rule will be found handy for small work.

Rules are generally made with several sets of graduations ranging from $\frac{1}{8}$ in. to 1/100 in., and although the latter fine divisions may be useful at times, they are difficult to read accurately and confusion may easily arise.

Micrometers. For the accurate measurement of length in the workshop, that is to say in terms of a thousandth of an inch, it is usual to employ a micrometer, which consists of a steel bow fitted with a fine measuring screw ; or a sliding gauge with a vernier attachment may be used for this purpose.

These rather expensive instruments are usually graduated to read in thousandths of an inch.

The micrometer of the form in general use has a range of only 1 in., and separate instruments are required for making inside and outside measurements, as well as for determining the depth of holes and dimensions of height.

The vernier slide gauge, on the other hand, has a long graduated scale which enables a single instrument to make both inside and outside measurements up to a length of 12 in. or more.

Those who, at this point, require further information about these tools should refer to " The Amateur's Workshop," published by Argus Books Ltd., whilst particulars of the patterns in general use will be found in toolmakers' catalogues.

The Depth Gauge. The gauge shown in Fig. 51 is used for measuring the depth of a hole or shoulder, as indicated by the rule when the base piece is in contact with the surface of the work.

The narrow rule fitted is usually graduated in 1/64 in. on one side and in 1/100 in. on the other.

To use the gauge, the base piece is pressed against the work and the rule is pushed downwards until it meets the bottom of the hole whose depth is being measured ; the clamping screw is then tightened to enable the gauge to be handled without fear of upsetting its adjustment.

The Protractor. This instrument, which is illustrated in Fig. 52, is used for measuring and marking-out angles.

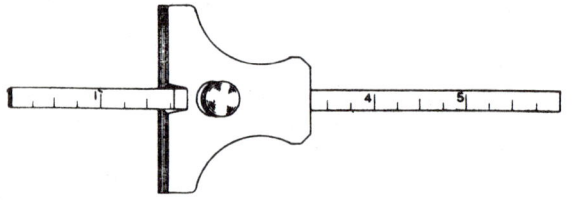

Fig. 51

The rectangular stock or base is graduated in degrees from 0 to 180 deg. at either end.

When the protractor has been set as required, the movable blade is locked to the stock by tightening the central clamping screw.

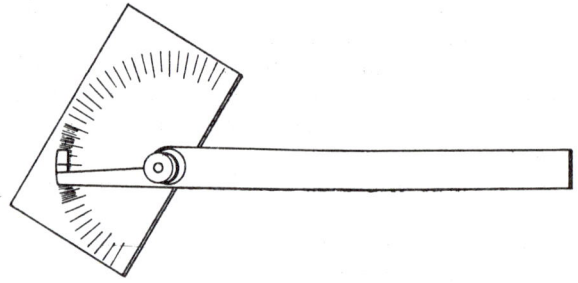

Fig. 52

The Drill Gauge. As will be seen in Fig. 53, one form of this gauge is made with a series of holes ranging from $\frac{1}{16}$ in. to $\frac{1}{2}$ in. in diameter and advancing in steps of 1/64 in.

These gauges are accurately made of hardened steel, and, as far as the hole sizes allow, can be used for determining the diameter of shafts and other components in addition to their normal use for gauging the size of drills.

Besides the fractional inch gauge illustrated, a similar pattern can be obtained with holes indicating the diameters of the number-size drills from No. 1 to No. 60, that is to say from 0.040 in. to 0.228 in., advancing in steps of a few thousandths of an inch. These drill gauges are also marked with the decimal inch equivalents of the drill sizes.

In addition to its use for measuring the size of drills and other small components, this gauge, as will be described later, can be employed for determining the size of the tapping holes required for small taps used to cut screw threads.

Marking-out. Marking-out is, briefly, the process of drawing lines on the surface of the work to indicate its finished size and, at the same time, marking the centres of any drill holes required, and scribing reference lines as an aid to setting the work for machining.

Marking-out flat work or sheet metal is very much the same as making a mechanical drawing, and, here, at any rate, you will be able to make use of any geometry you have learnt.

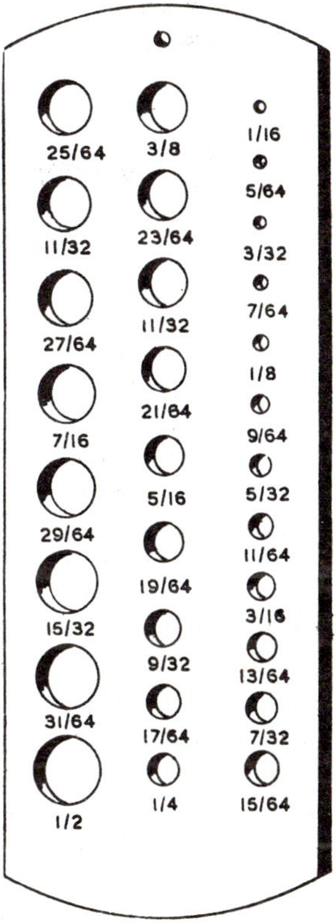

Before any marking-out work can be undertaken a few simple tools and materials will be needed, and these will now be described.

Fig. 53

In the first place, it is essential that the marking-out lines drawn should be clearly visible to act as a guide when later the work is being formed to shape.

If the material used is sheet copper or brass, the lines will probably show up clearly, but in the case of steel the surface will have to be painted with a *marking fluid* to ensure this.

Blue-coloured, quick-drying, marking fluid can usually be purchased from the tool merchant, but if there is any difficulty about this, some French polish or spirit varnish with a little blue dye, such as methylene blue, added will make a good substitute.

Fig. 54

For scratching the lines on the surface of the work a *scriber*, as shown in Fig. 54, is used ; this tool has a hardened-steel sharp point and a knurled handle to give a good finger-hold.

To cover the usual range of work when drawing lines at right angles to a base line, one or more *squares*, as illustrated in Fig. 55, will be required.

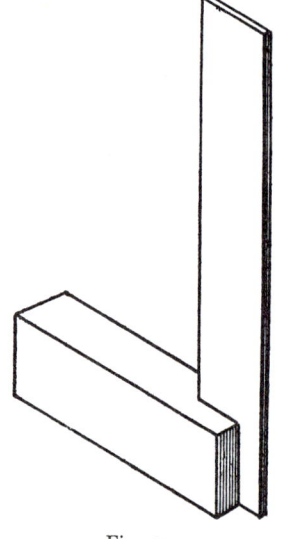

A 6-in. square should be ample for larger work : a 3-in. square will be found most generally useful : and it is an advantage to have a 1-in. square for small work and for checking the squareness of edges when filing. Messrs. Moore & Wright make a full range of accurate squares suitable for use in the small workshop.

For laying off distances and for scribing circles a *pair of dividers* is essential. The pattern illustrated in Fig. 56 is adjustable by means of a screw and is greatly superior to the plain type. To set the dividers,

Fig. 55

one point is placed in an inch mark on the rule and the other point is then adjusted until it lies exactly in the graduation line required.

When lines have to be scribed at a fixed distance from the edge of the work, the *jenny callipers* shown in Fig. 57 are used.

The legs are set to the required distance apart by placing the point in the required graduation on the rule, and the

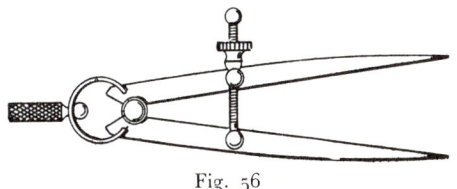

Fig. 56

other leg is then pressed inwards until it makes contact with the end of the rule.

To use the callipers, the curved leg is pressed against the edge of the work and the sharp point is used as a scriber, but care must be taken to maintain the callipers at right

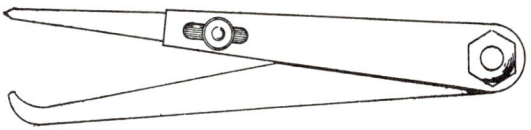

Fig. 57

angles to the work, otherwise the line marked will not be at the correct distance from the base throughout.

When the point of intersection of two scribed lines is used to denote a drilling centre, this point is marked with a fine-pointed *centre punch*, as illustrated in Fig. 58.

Fig. 58

As an aid to locating the punch exactly at the required point, a magnifying glass can be used with advantage, and the punch, while held vertically, is then struck a light but firm blow with a small hammer.

Marking-out Sheet Metal Work. As a practical example of marking-out let us take the sheet metal packing-piece or

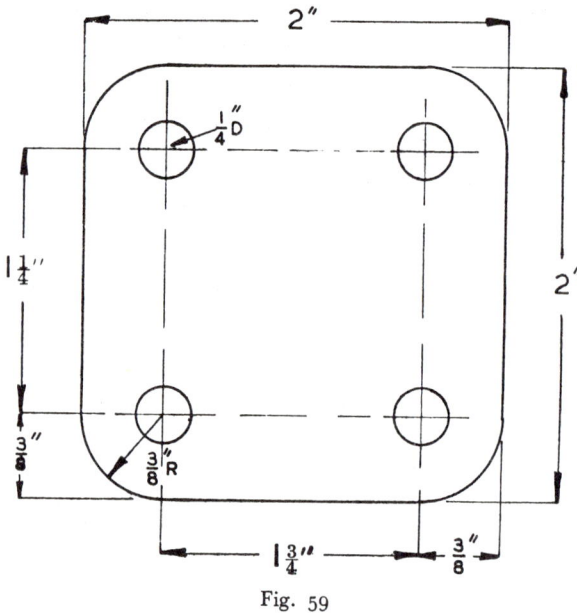

Fig. 59

cover plate shown in the drawing in Fig. 59 ; its thickness does not matter for our purpose, as we are concerned only with its shape as seen from above.

The drawing represents a square plate with rounded corners and having four holes equally spaced at a given distance apart.

The drawing also shows the exact dimensions required, that is to say the length and breadth of the plate, the position and size of the holes, and the radius of the rounded corners.

To make a start, take a suitable piece of flat sheet metal and with a rule and scriber draw a straight line along one edge, as indicated in Fig. 60.

The edge of the sheet is then cut and filed exactly to this line as will be described in detail in the next chapter. The straight edge so formed is called the datum edge, as from it the dimensions of the work are marked-out in accordance with the drawing.

Apply the square to the datum edge and scribe a line, AB, Fig. 61, at right angles to it to represent one side of the square; then set the dividers to exactly 2 in. and scribe an arc of a circle, CDE, from a point on this line.

Apply the square again to the datum edge and draw a vertical line, FG, through the extreme edge of the arc to mark the opposite side of the square.

Set the jenny callipers to exactly 2 in., and with the curved leg against the datum edge mark off the line, GB, to complete the square. The next step is to mark the lines HJ and KL with the jenny set to $\frac{3}{8}$ in. Set the dividers to $\frac{3}{8}$ in., and with one point placed at the intersection of the lines FG and HJ mark off the distance HM, and also LN, in a similar manner.

With the square against the datum line, draw the two vertical lines OP and QR through the points M and N respectively.

Set the dividers to $1\frac{1}{4}$ in., and from M and N scribe arcs to cut OP and QR at S and T. Mark the points M, N, S and T with the centre punch to denote the drilling centres of the four holes.

When doing this the centre punch must be held exactly vertical, otherwise the centres will be drawn over to one side and the holes will be drilled out of their correct position.

The appearance of the work will now be essentially as shown in Fig. 62, and it only remains to complete the marking-out in the following manner. Set the dividers to $\frac{3}{8}$ in. and mark off the radius of each corner as shown; then reset the dividers to $\frac{1}{8}$ in. and scribe the dimension lines of the four holes. The final step is to scribe and

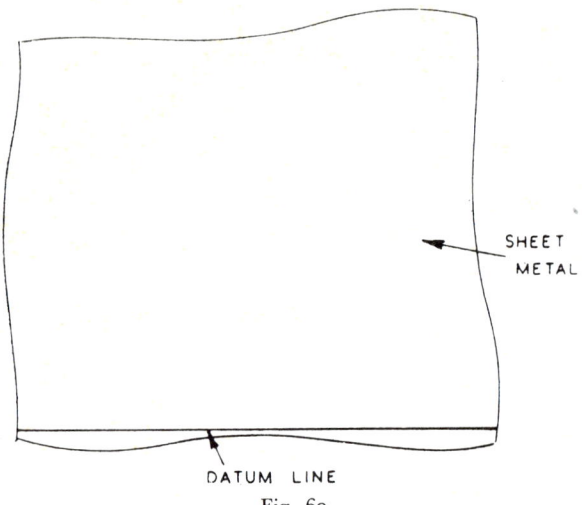

Fig. 60

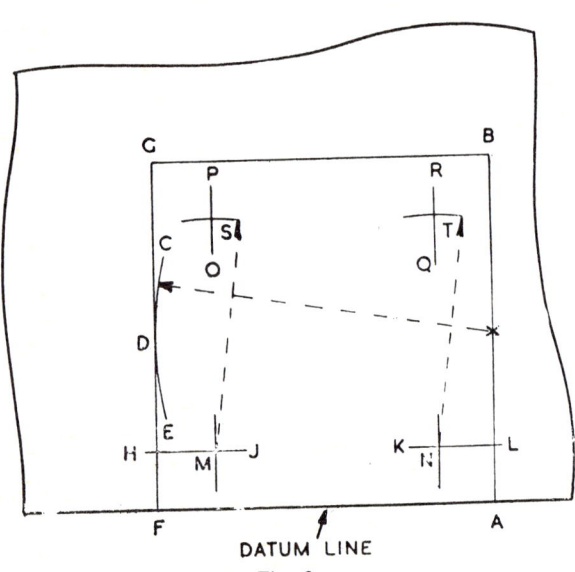

Fig. 61

punch-mark what are described as the witness lines.

Witness Lines. When small holes are being drilled, the circle scribed to show the diameter of the hole will clearly indicate if the drill at starting is at all off-centre, but in the case of larger holes, one or more witness or guide circles should be scribed within this circle to make any error of drilling more readily apparent as the work proceeds.

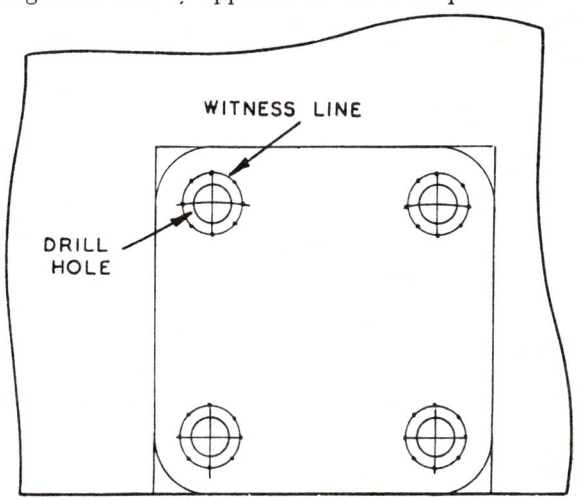

Fig. 62

A witness line, outside the circle indicating the hole diameter, as shown in Fig. 62, may be found useful as a check on the final accuracy of the drilled hole, and will also serve as a guide should the position of the hole have to be corrected later by filing.

To make sure that these lines do not become obliterated until they have served their purpose, they may be lightly marked with a centre punch as shown in the drawing.

When marking-out a piece of work in which holes of various diameters have to be drilled, you will find that mistakes can be avoided if the size of each hole is marked opposite to it with the scriber.

The work is now marked-out in accordance with the drawing and is ready for drilling and cutting to shape.

Marking-out Solid Objects. So far, we have considered only flat work, but when we come to marking-out solid objects some additional equipment will be required.

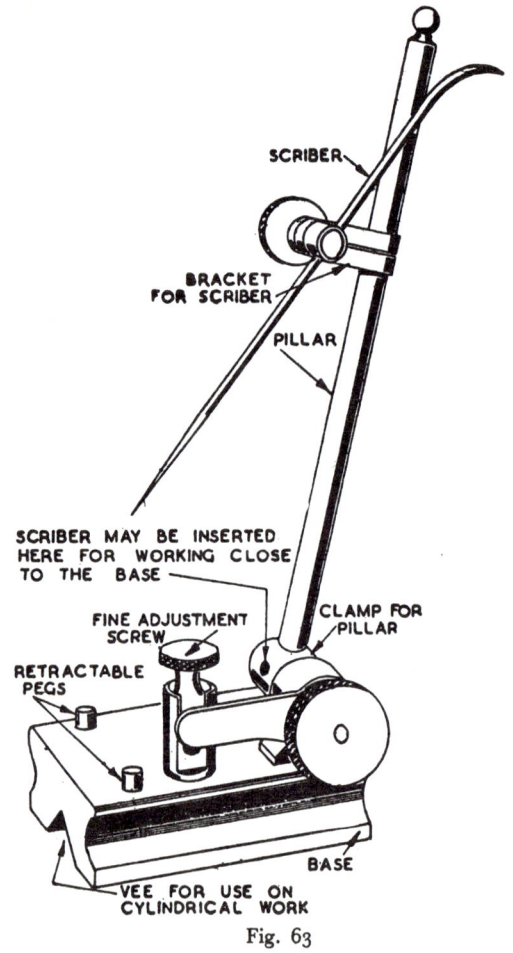

Fig. 63

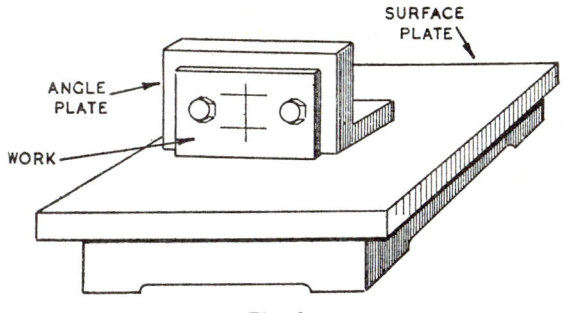

Fig. 64

In the first place, a flat surface on which the work can stand must be provided, and for this purpose a *surface plate*, as illustrated in Fig. 64, is generally used, but a sheet of plate glass makes a satisfactory substitute.

The surface plate is a heavy rigid iron casting whose upper surface has been machined and finally hand-scraped to a high degree of flatness, but a machined casting will be sufficiently accurate for ordinary marking-out purposes and has the advantage of being very much cheaper.

For scribing lines on the work at a given height above the base, the *surface gauge* is used instead of the jenny callipers.

The surface gauge made by Messrs. Brown & Sharpe is illustrated in Fig. 63, and it will be seen that the pointed scriber can be set in any position required and also adjusted for height by sliding on the pillar. In addition, the height of the scriber point can be set by swinging the pillar itself, whilst the final exact setting is made by means of the fine adjustment screw shown.

The retractable pegs fitted to the base can be pushed downwards to guide the gauge along a reference surface, such as the machined edges of the surface plate.

The height of the scriber point is set against a rule, held truly vertical to the surface of the marking-out table either by being pressed against a rectangular block or *angle plate*, Fig. 64, or by being clamped in a special *rule holder* or stand.

Full directions for making a simple but efficient rule stand are given in Chapter Five.

When cylindrical work has to be marked-out on the surface plate, it is usually held in position by means of a *V-block*, as shown in Fig. 69, or two similar blocks may be used to support long work.

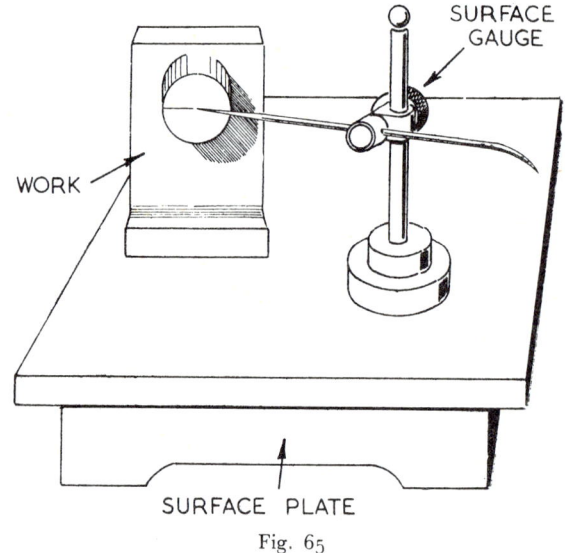

Fig. 65

To denote drilling centres, as in the case of sheet material, two lines are scribed at right angles, and to facilitate this, the work, where it will not stand firmly and evenly of its own accord on the surface plate, may be secured to an angle plate as shown in Fig. 64.

Marking-out a Bearing Bracket. Now that the tool equipment required has been briefly described, let us take the bracket shown in Fig. 65 as a simple but practical example of marking-out a solid object on the surface plate with the aid of the surface guage.

The problem here is to mark-out the boss so that it can

be drilled and bored to receive a bearing bush or liner; the centre line of the bearing must be exactly 2 in. above the base line in order that the shaft it carries will be truly aligned in the machine to which the bracket is attached.

In the first place, the under surface of the foot piece must be made flat, as will be described in the next chapter, so that it will stand on the surface plate without rocking.

This surface, corresponding to the datum edge of the work in the previous example, is called the datum surface,

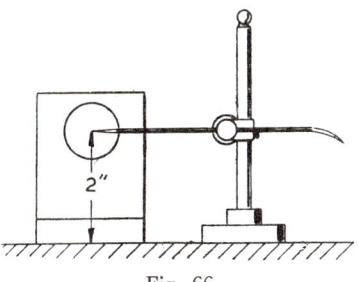

Fig. 66

and it is on this that the bracket is finally bolted in place in the machine of which it forms part.

Accordingly, the centre line of the bearing is scribed 2 in. from the datum surface.

After the face of the boss has been painted with marking fluid, the casting and the surface gauge are placed on the surface plate as illustrated in Fig. 65.

The next step is to set the point of the scriber exactly 2 in. above the base line, as shown in Fig. 66. This is done by holding the rule in a truly vertical position against an angle plate, or by clamping it in a rule holder, and then setting the scriber point to the 2-in. mark by using the fine adjustment screw for the final setting.

When set, the scriber should lie horizontally, or nearly so, for in that position not only will it mark better, but it will be less liable to deflection when meeting any irregularities on the surface of the work.

Now, grasp the base of the surface gauge and move the scriber point right across the surface of the boss so that a clear, even line is marked; when doing this, the scriber should be allowed to trail somewhat, otherwise it is apt to dig into the work and form an irregular marking.

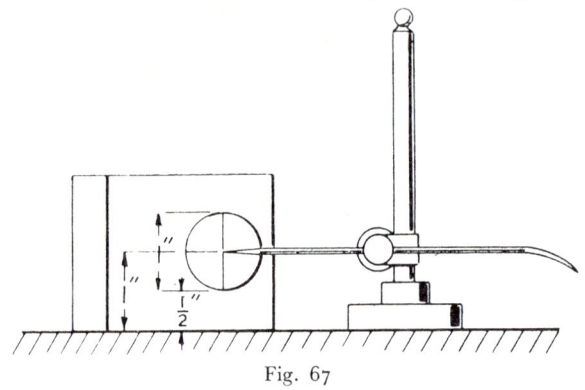

Fig. 67

To scribe the cross-centre line, the casting is placed on its side as shown in Fig. 67. The diameter of the boss was found to be 1 in., and its outer diameter lay $\frac{1}{2}$ in. from the edge of the casting; the scriber point is, therefore, set to 1 in. against the rule, and the cross-line is scribed across the centre of the boss.

As in the case of the sheet metal component already referred to a centre punch-mark is made at the intersection of the two cross-lines, and from this centre both the bore diameter and the inner witness lines are scribed with the dividers.

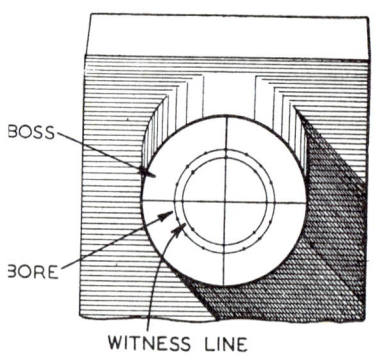

Fig. 68

The marking-out is completed by dotting the circumferences of these two circles with the centre punch, in order to ensure their remaining visible throughout the subsequent machining operations.

The appearance of the finished work will then be as depicted in Fig. 68.

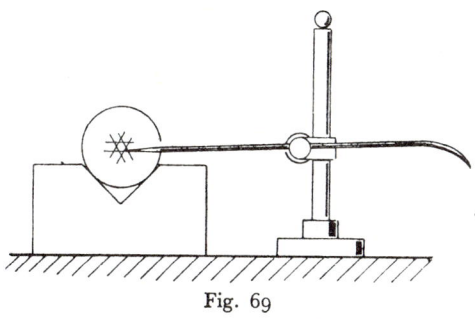

Fig. 69

Marking-out the Centre of a Shaft. An operation commonly required in the workshop is to mark-out the centre of a round shaft. For this purpose, the shaft is placed in a V-block, or in a pair of similar blocks, on the surface plate as shown in Fig. 69.

The point of the scriber is set to the approximate centre height and a short line is scribed across the centre; the shaft is then rotated some sixth of a revolution and a second line is scribed; this procedure is repeated until the shaft has been completely turned.

It will be found that the marking lines now enclose a small central space, and if the scriber point is reset to the centre of this area, the cross-centre lines can be readily marked-out. If the two centre lines are required to be exactly at right angles to each other, the horizontal centre line alone is marked with the surface gauge, and the vertical centre line is then scribed from a square standing on the surface plate.

Those who desire further information will find the whole subject more fully dealt with in "Marking-out Practice" published by Argus Books Ltd.

Reading Machine Drawings. Machine drawings are issued as a guide to enable workers to make mechanical parts in the workshop.

These drawings usually comprise a general arrangement drawing giving a picture of the work as a whole, and, in addition, detail drawings showing the form and dimensions of the several parts.

In the general arrangement drawing the appearance of the component is represented separately in the three planes in space as illustrated in Fig. 70 ; that is to say the plan view as it is seen directly from above, the front elevation as viewed from in front, and the end elevation showing the component as seen end-on.

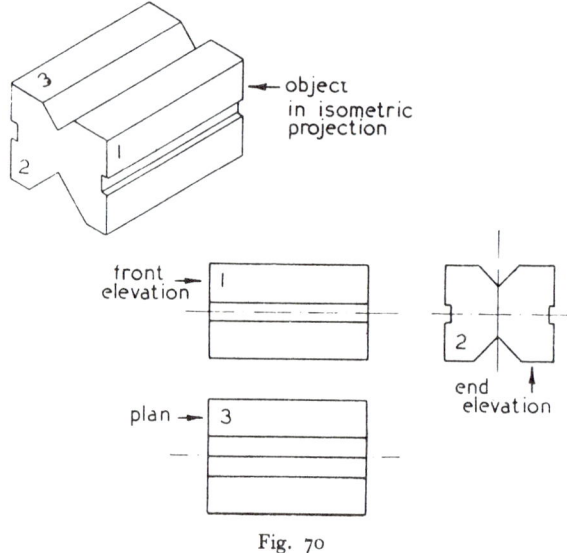

Fig. 70

Those who are familiar with mechanical drawings are able to combine these three drawings in the mind's eye, as it were, and to visualise the object as it would actually appear ; but for the benefit of those who are unable to do this, the modern method of isometric projection combines these three drawings in a single view, as seen in Fig. 70, which shows clearly exactly what the object is like and thus prevents any mistake being made as to its real form.

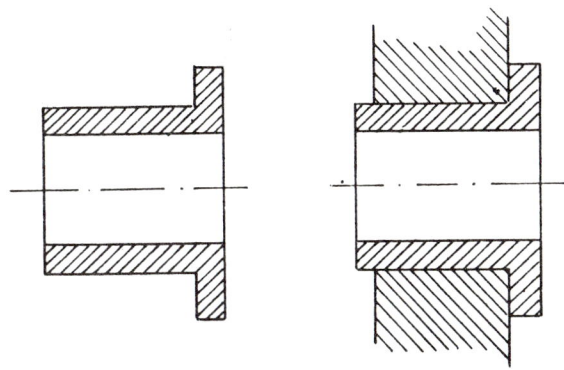

Fig. 71

Another form of drawing, which is often used to show the internal construction of mechanical work, is the sectional drawing. These drawings are not only a great help to the mechanic when dealing with complicated work, but they also lessen the work of the draughtsman by simplifying and reducing the number of drawings required to show all the details of construction and the position of the individual parts.

A typical example of sectional drawing is given in Fig. 71. which shows in section a bush inserted in a housing.

Unless otherwise indicated in the drawing, these sections are always taken through the centre line of the component; and in order to make the relation of the parts clear, the bush is hatched with a series of parallel lines, whilst the shading lines on the housing are drawn at right angles to those on the bush.

Conventions Used in Drawings. For the sake of uniformity, certain methods of drawing have been adopted and are now in general use; as a guide to their interpretation the more common conventions are now described.

Screw Threads. In Fig. 72 the various ways of representing both external and internal screw threads are illustrated; those shown at A and D are detailed drawings of the thread form, and the shading is added to improve the appearance

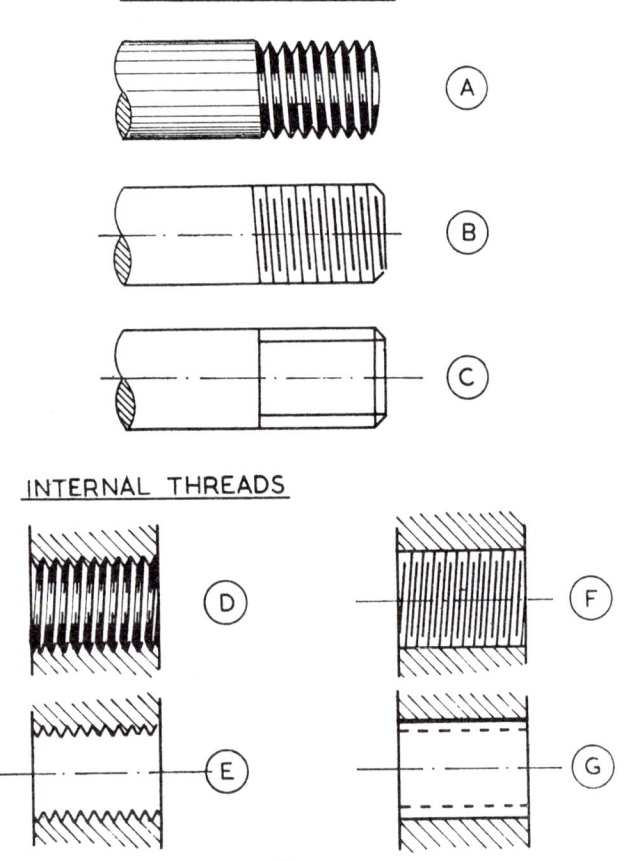

Fig. 72

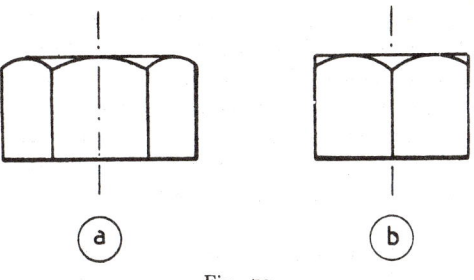

Fig. 73

and to make the drawing suitable for reproduction in the Press.

Of the remainder, C and G are the simplest, and, as they

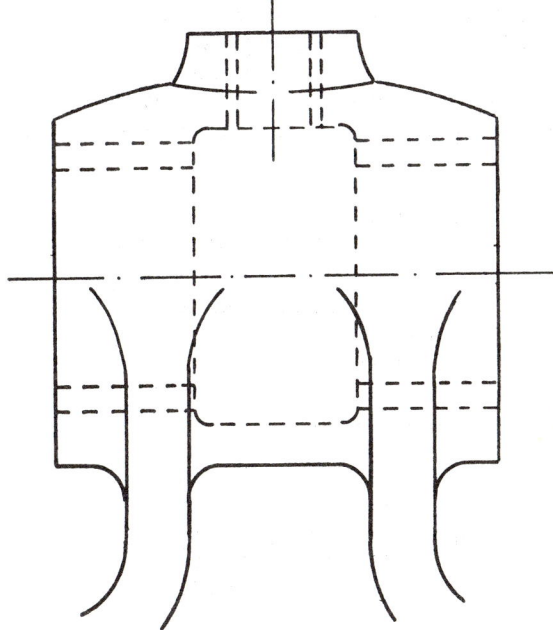

Fig. 74

take but little time to draw, this method is now largely used in the drawing office to save valuable time.

Nuts and Bolt Heads. These are always shown in solid form unless a sectional view is necessary for some special reason, and the full diameter of the nut across its corners is represented as in Fig. 73A; but where the nut has to be shown at right angles to the former position it is drawn as in Fig. 73B.

Centre Lines. In all drawings the centre line of each component is shown by a chain-dotted line.

These lines are important to enable measurements of dimensions to be taken readily. For example, the centre lines of the cylinders of a petrol engine are drawn so that the exact distance between the cylinders can be measured in the workshop.

Hidden Parts. These are represented in the drawing by broken lines as shown in Fig. 74, which depicts a bearing bracket fitted with three inset bushes. The use of this convention saves much work, as otherwise several drawings might be required to show the exact relation of the parts.

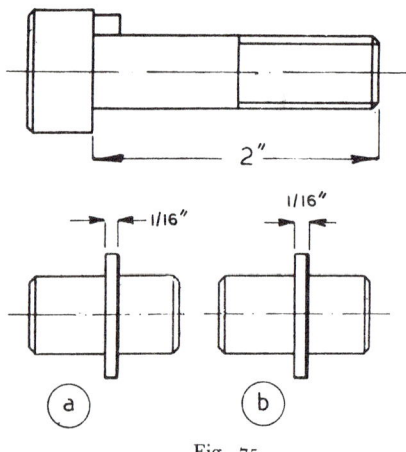

Fig. 75

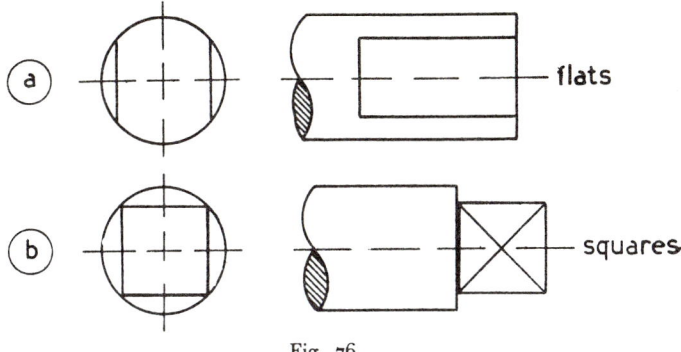

Fig. 76

Dimensions. As shown in Fig. 75, these are indicated in inches, and parts of an inch, by figures between arrows pointing to the lines which show the limits referred to. Where space is restricted, the position of the arrows and figures may be arranged as illustrated in Figs. 75A and 75B.

Flat Surfaces. When a flat surface is formed on a shaft this is indicated as shown in Fig. 76A, and in addition, the surface of the flat is sometimes drawn with the diagonals, as when a square formed on a shaft is denoted in the manner illustrated in Fig. 75B.

CHAPTER FOUR

Filing — Pinning — Draw Filing — Filing Aluminium — Scraping — Sawing Metal — Marking-out the Work — Using the Hacksaw — Sawing Curves — Cutting Metal — Cold Chisels — Hand-Drills — The Drilling Operation — Polishing — Reaming — Screw Threading — Cutting Threads — Soldering — Hardening and Tempering.

USING HAND TOOLS

" CLEANLINESS in the workshop is the first essential, and is the basis of accuracy and efficiency. Without it good work can only be produced with difficulty, if at all. A clean workshop inspires good work ; a clean machine and a clean work bench produce it." These words are taken from the Introduction to a handbook on engineering workshop practice published in the early part of the recent war ; they were intended for the host of inexperienced but willing people who were, at the time, flocking into our munition factories.

Nevertheless, this good advice has lost none of its force even today, and its import should be borne in mind by amateur and professional worker alike.

Beginners should cultivate the right way of working from the start, so that in time the maintenance of tidiness and cleanliness in the workshop becomes a fixed habit.

As it is almost impossible to keep the wooden bench top perfectly clean while working, spread newspaper where you put down your work or fine tools, and change it frequently so that you can be sure that it is always clean and free from filings or emery dust. Keep some trays or old saucers handy in which to put small parts when taking work to pieces.

Filing. I have already described the forms of files in common use and have pointed out the necessity of fitting a proper handle to the file. Further the importance of having the vice firmly secured to a rigid part of the bench has been stressed.

The question of using different files for various types of metals has also been dealt with.

When it comes to the actual filing operation, the method used varies somewhat for heavy or light filing.

When a bastard-cut file, for example, is used for the quick removal of a large amount of metal, not only must considerable downward pressure be exerted to keep the file in cut, as it is termed, but the heavy work entailed is carried out largely by putting one's back into it rather than by using the arms alone, for the arm muscles, particularly in the case of the casual worker, quickly tire, whereas the powerful muscles of the back are better adapted for prolonged heavy work.

The file is held as shown in Fig. 77 and the palm of the left hand is used to apply the downward pressure required ; the feet should be well apart with the weight taken on the left foot, which is advanced and the left knee slightly bent, as illustrated in Fig. 78.

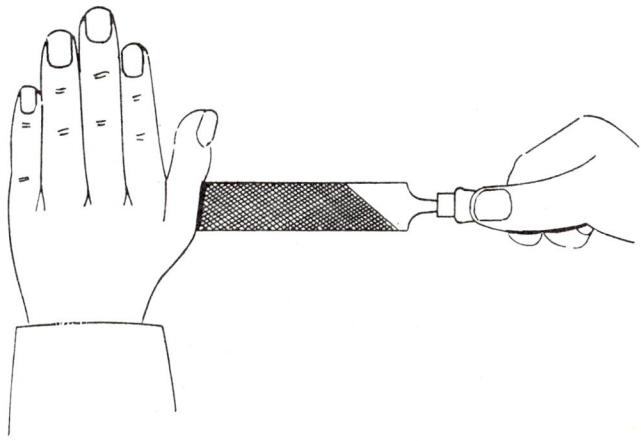

Fig. 77

Clearly, for heavy filing one must be well above the work so that the downward pressure can be maintained and the body movements given full play ; if there is any difficulty about arranging this, you will find it a great help to stand on a slightly raised platform.

Fig. 78

The chief difficulty the beginner finds when filing is to file the work flat, for he tends to press the file handle downwards at the beginning of the stroke and to press too hard with the left hand towards the end of the stroke. This results in what is called fiddling, after the manner of using a violin bow.

It is only with long practice that the art of filing with an even flat stroke is acquired.

It is important that on the return stroke the downward pressure should be relaxed in order to prevent damage to the file teeth, but the file should, nevertheless, be kept in light contact with the work surface so that the sense of direction is not lost.

For light filing and for finish filing the work, the body is kept more upright, the feet should be closer together, and the work is done almost entirely with the arms ; in addition, the work can with advantage be held higher, and not below the level of the elbow.

The file is then best held with the tips of the fingers of the left hand, as this gives more delicate control.

When filing, the stroke should always be in the direction of the long axis of the blade, as shown in Fig. 79, and not across the axis of the file, as shown in Fig. 80, as this will tend to roughen the surface of the work.

To maintain an even surface, it is helpful to change the direction of filing from time to time, as shown in Fig. 79 ; the fresh file marks then show up clearly and indicate exactly where the metal is being removed.

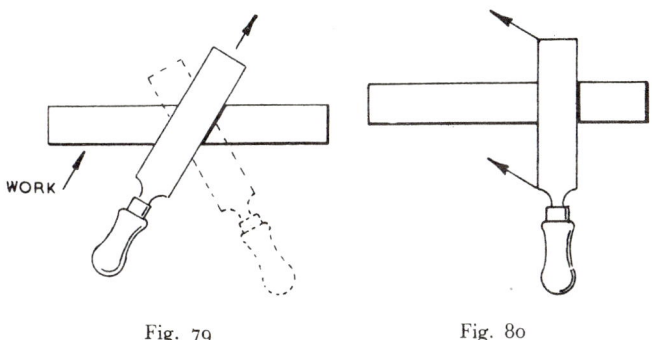

Fig. 79　　　　　Fig. 80

The flatness of the surface should be frequently checked with a straight-edge or a rule, whilst its squareness can be tested with a small try square.

The work should always be held so that it does not project more than is necessary above the vice jaws, otherwise it will tend to vibrate, after the manner of a tuning fork, and a screaming noise will be produced, accompanied by a ridged finish on the work.

When metal is filed in the ordinary way, a rough, burred edge will be formed on the side away from the worker; this should be removed with a fine file to form a slightly chamfered edge.

Pinning. It may be found, particularly when using a fine file on steel, that the teeth become clogged or pinned, as it is termed, and in consequence the surface of the work is scored.

This can, to some extent, be prevented by chalking or oiling the face of the file, and reducing the downward pressure applied.

The clogged teeth should be cleaned by means of a wire brush, such as a strip of file card glued and screwed to a wooden backing, as illustrated in Fig. 81.

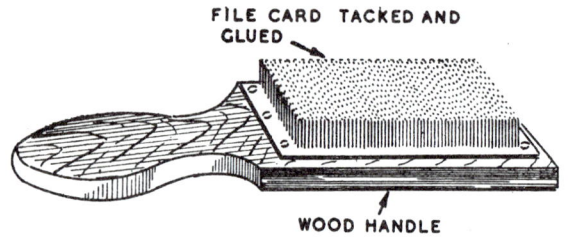

Fig. 81

Where particles of metal, called pins, become firmly wedged between the file teeth, they must be removed with a pointed piece of mild steel rod, otherwise deep scores will be formed on the surface of the work.

Draw-filing. This method of filing is used for filing flat surfaces and also to remove the marks formed by the ordinary diagonal filing. In this operation, the file, held

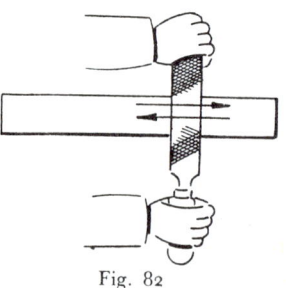

Fig. 82

evenly in the two hands, is worked to and fro along the surface as depicted in Fig. 82.

Care should be taken to keep the file level and not to allow it to rock or the surface of the work will become rounded.

Draw-filing is particularly useful for accurately finishing long narrow surfaces, for it is a scraping rather than a true cutting action, but it is, however, difficult to apply to

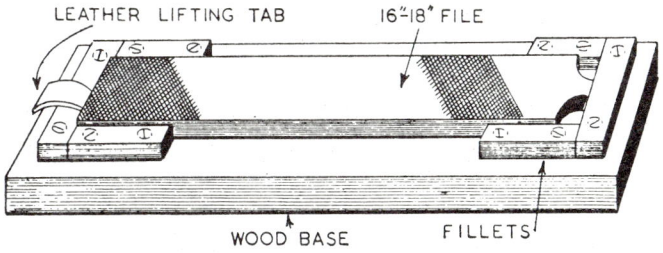

Fig. 83

short work as the length of the stroke is then too limited.

Hollow-curved surfaces can also be finish-filed in this way by using a half-round file, or in the case of very small work a round file will be found more suitable.

Another method of draw-filing, largely used by instrument makers, is to place a large flat file on the bench and to move the work to and fro along it whilst maintaining firm but even downward pressure. The file should be brushed clear of filings at frequent intervals to prevent the work being scored. A large file will be found most suitable for draw-filing, as it allows the whole surface of the work to be kept in contact with the blade. For the sake of convenience, the tang should be nicked on the grinding wheel and then broken off; the file is securely mounted on a wooden base, as shown in Fig. 83, and a leather tag is fitted to enable the file to be easily raised and turned over when the reverse side is needed.

One side of the file should be marked with yellow paint

to indicate that it is to be used only for brass, whilst the other side is reserved for filing steel.

Filing Aluminium and its Alloys. Now that the model engineer is making ever-increasing use of aluminium alloys, particularly for small engine parts, some hints on filing this material may be found useful.

Owing to its rather soft nature, aluminium tends to clog and pin the teeth of an ordinary file.

To overcome this difficulty, special files known as milling files have been introduced, and of these the best known is, perhaps, the Dreadnought file illustrated in Fig. 84.

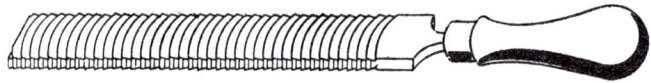

Fig. 84

As will be seen, the cutting surfaces of this file are quite different from the teeth of an ordinary file, for, here, a series of curved cutting edges are widely spaced so that the intervals between them allow the filings to escape and not become wedged between the teeth.

This method of construction not only effectively prevents pinning, but also promotes free and rapid cutting.

However, to obtain a good finish on aluminium parts, an ordinary file should be used, and to lessen the tendency to pinning only light downward pressure should be employed when filing ; in addition, turpentine may be found helpful when applied to the teeth of the file.

Scraping. When components such as lathe beds and slides are machined by milling or planing, their surfaces are left slightly irregular, and also the parts may be somewhat distorted when clamped in place during machining.

To correct these errors a process of hand scraping is employed, by which small amounts of metal are removed from any high places, and in this way very accurate flat surfaces are formed suitable for use in the highest class machines.

This work is carried out with a scraper of the pattern illustrated in Chapter Two, or a tool made from a discarded file, as illustrated in Fig. 85, may be used.

The first step is to make the surface as nearly flat as possible by filing or machining, as it is important that the work should not rock on the surface plate if a clear picture of the high spots is to be obtained.

The work is then lightly rubbed on a surface plate, or sheet of plate glass, which has been smeared with a thin coat of marking compound ; the high spots are then shown up clearly by the marking compound transferred to them.

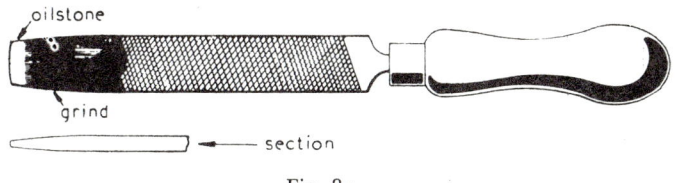

Fig. 85

The blue marking compound, which can usually be obtained from a tool merchant, is best applied to the surface plate in a thin, even coat by means of a piece of wash-leather glued to a flat wooden strip.

To remove these high spots, the work should be secured in the vice and the scraper, held firmly in the two hands, is used to pare away the metal, at the blued areas only, with a well-controlled but decisive thrusting motion.

The correct angle at which the scraper should be held, so that it cuts freely and without digging into the surface of the work, will soon be found with a little practice.

In the first stage of the operation the scraper should be worked in one direction only, and, after re-applying the work to the surface plate and taking a second set of rubbings, the scraper is worked across the previous line so that the two series of scraper marks are formed roughly at right angles to each other.

This process of taking transfer marks, and then scraping

them down, is continued until the blue marking is found to be evenly distributed over the surface when the work is applied to the surface plate.

Although at first this may take a considerable time, with practice it will be found easier to estimate exactly where and how much metal should be removed to make the surface flat without undue waste of effort.

When the scraper is used on hard cast iron it may be found that it is soon blunted, and on no account should the work be continued if increased pressure has to be used to make the tool cut, for this will only result in forming an irregular and unsightly surface on the work.

To sharpen the scraper, it should be worked to and fro along the oilstone after the manner of sharpening a woodworking chisel and as illustrated in Fig. 86. When both sides of the blade have been stoned, the end of the blade is applied in a vertical position to the stone, as shown in the drawing, and the scraper, while firmly held, is moved to and fro along the stone with a slight rocking motion to conform with the curvature at the end of the blade.

In time, as the tip of the blade becomes worn down with stoning, it may be found necessary to have it reground to restore the original form of the cutting edges.

Sawing Metal. The various forms of metal-cutting saws and saw blades commonly used in the workshop have been described in Chapter Two.

Before starting the actual sawing operation you must make sure that the saw blade is suitable for the work in

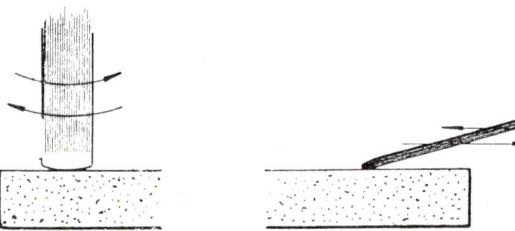

Fig. 86

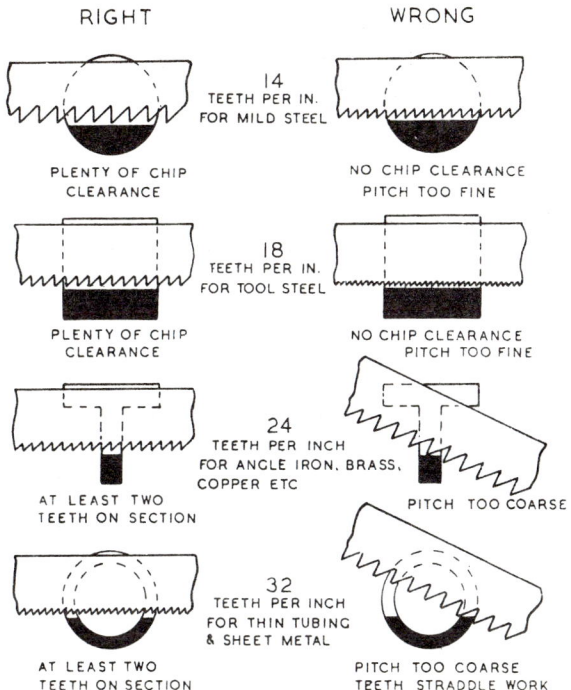

Fig. 87

hand, and reference to Fig. 87 will show that there are two main essentials : first, the pitch of the teeth, whether it be 14, 18, 24 or 32 teeth per inch, must be sufficiently coarse to allow the chips to escape and not clog the saw ; the broader the work surface the coarser the pitch should be. The second and more important point is that the pitch of the teeth must be such that the tips of at least two teeth are always in contact with the work.

If this is not the case, all the cutting pressure may fall on a single tooth, as represented in the drawing, with the result that this tooth will probably be broken off and the blade ruined. The narrower the work surface, the finer, therefore, should be the pitch of the teeth.

Marking-out the Work. The next step is to mark-out the work to enable the sawing to be accurately carried out, that is to say the cut must not encroach on the finished size of the work nor should an excess of metal be left behind,

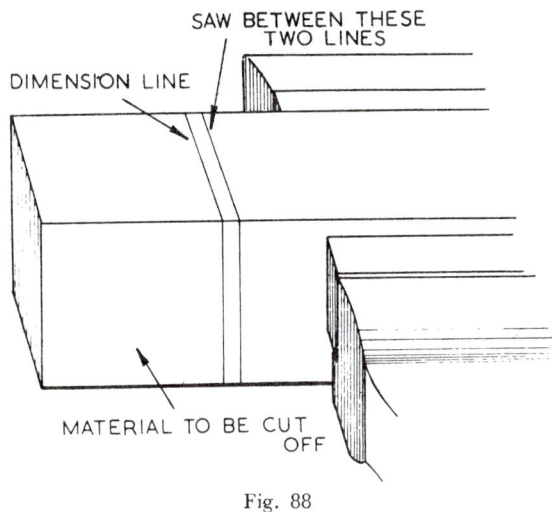

Fig. 88

for this will later have to be removed by what may amount to a laborious filing operation.

To denote the exact position and direction of the cut, therefore, two lines should be scribed on the upper and front faces of the work, as shown in Fig. 88.

The distance apart of these two lines should be a little greater than the breadth of the saw cut, which should be kept close to the outer line but just clear of the inner dimension line indicating the size of the finished part.

Some mechanics prefer to saw along a single witness or guide line, but in this case the line is obliterated as the work proceeds and it may, at times, be necessary to disengage the saw to see the direction the cut is taking.

Using the Hacksaw. As shown in Fig. 89, the saw should be started against the edge farthest from the operator, otherwise contact with the vertical face of the work at its near edge will probably break off the saw's teeth.

Deliberate, even strokes should be made at the rate of some 60 a minute and, at the same time, the saw must be well controlled so that the blade travels in a straight line and does not jam in the cut, as this often leads to breakage of the blade.

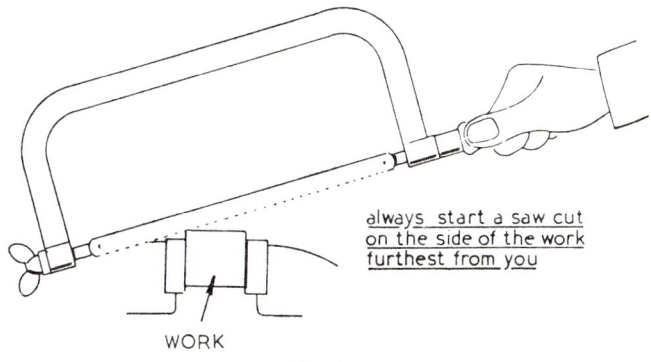

Fig. 89

To prevent uneven wear of the teeth, use the whole length of the blade and not merely its middle portion.

When sawing heavy section material, tip the saw from time to time so as to lessen the work surface in contact with the teeth ; this will enable the saw to cut more freely.

Pressure must be relieved on the return stroke to avoid blunting the teeth, but the saw must not be actually lifted in the cut.

Should a blade be broken while cutting, the new blade should be started in a fresh place, as the previous cut will be narrower than that made by a new blade. This is due to the fact that the teeth are set, as it is termed, that is to say alternate teeth are bent outwards, as shown in Fig. 90, but with use this set is worn away so that an unworn blade will tend to jam in the cut and will have its set worn away unduly quickly.

Sawing Curves. The hacksaw, owing to the width of its blade, is not well adapted for cutting on a curved path, and for this purpose either an Abrafile or a fretsaw is generally used.

Fig. 90

The Abrafile, described in Chapter Two, has a slender blade of circular section and will readily follow a curved line marked-out on the work.

If the figure to be cut is enclosed on all sides, a preliminary hole is drilled through which the blade is threaded and then again secured in the saw frame.

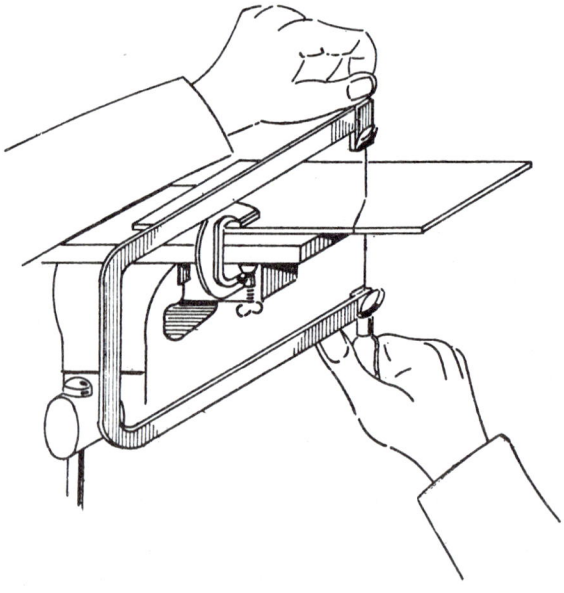

Fig. 91

The work is gripped in the vice so that the cut is made in a downward direction and with the saw blade held horizontally.

For larger work the fretsaw, with its deep throat, will be found more suitable.

In this case, the work should be secured with G clamps to a wooden table held in the vice by means of a projecting tenon.

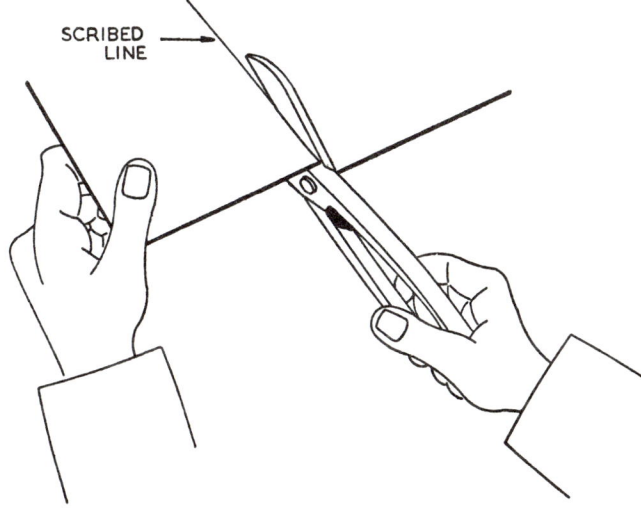

Fig. 92

The blade is mounted in the frame so that it cuts on the downward stroke, as illustrated in Fig. 91.

Cutting Metal. Apart from the various types of saws which have been described, the cutting of metal, as far as bench work is concerned, is carried out with shears and cold chisels, all of which have been illustrated, together with a short description, in Chapter Two.

Shears are used in exactly the same way as scissors, and the cut is usually made with reference to a guide line, as shown in Fig. 92, where the work is viewed during the operation from the side, but when the shears used are of the pattern shown in Fig. 93, that is to say with the upper blade placed to the left side, cutting is more easily controlled if the work is viewed directly from above.

When cutting deeply into sheet metal, it may be found that with some shears the cut edges of the work tend to get

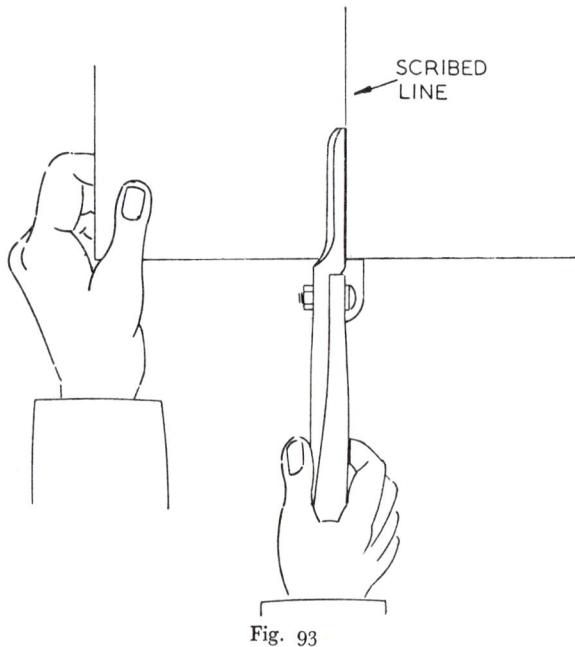

Fig. 93

in the way of the hand, but when the blades are of the cranked form illustrated in Fig. 94, this difficulty is largely overcome.

For cutting out curved work in flat sheet metal, either the shears with curved blades illustrated in Chapter Two are used, or a special type of shears with narrow blades, known as alligator shears, can be employed.

The curved-blade shears can also be used for such work as trimming the edges of a sheet-metal cylinder.

The chief difficulty in shearing heavy-gauge sheet material is to obtain sufficient cutting pressure, but this can, to some extent, be overcome by gripping one leg of

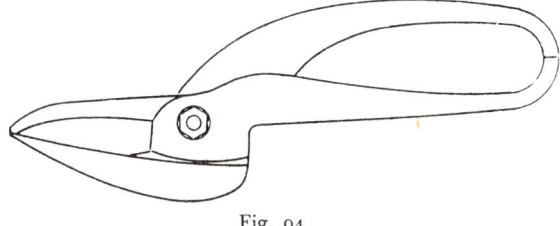

Fig. 94

the shears in the vice, as shown in Fig. 95 ; this allows the full weight to be applied to the other leg and, in addition, better control of the work is then obtained.

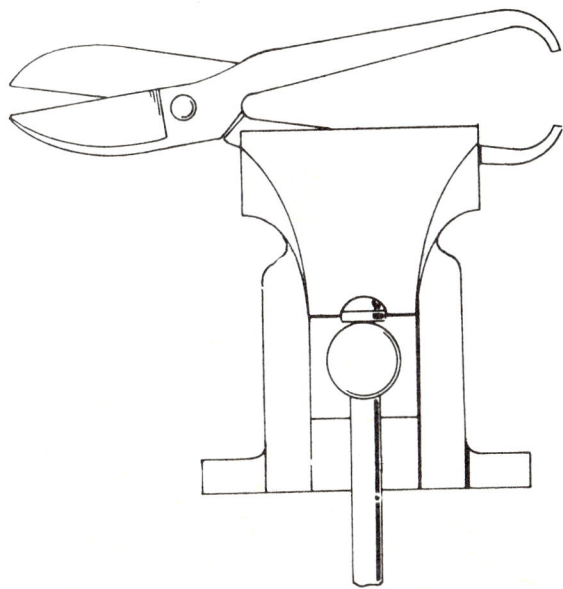

Fig. 95

The ordinary tinman's shears are made with one long leg to afford greater leverage, but if an extension, such as a length of tubing, is fitted to the workshop shears in order to obtain increased leverage, care must be taken not to strain the joint and so upset the contact between the cutting edges of the blades.

When cutting sheet metal, the points of the blades must not be allowed to close fully, as this will make an unsightly mark on the cut surfaces of the work.

Using Cold Chisels. In the small workshop the cold chisel is used mainly for cutting sheet metal and trimming castings.

Although the various forms of cold chisels in common use have been described and illustrated in Chapter Two, it should be pointed out that for cutting sheet metal, supported on a block, the edge of the chisel should be curved, as shown in Fig. 96A ; further, the cutting edge should be formed to the correct angle of some 60 deg., as shown in the drawing, for if the cutting angle is too acute the edge will be easily broken, and if too obtuse the chisel will not cut freely.

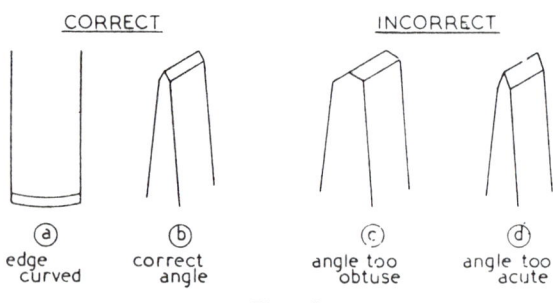

Fig. 96

Cold chisels are supplied by the makers with the edges correctly ground, and when blunted they can be re-sharpened on a carborundum bench stone, but when the chisel becomes badly worn, regrinding will be necessary.

After much use, the top of the chisel will become burred over as shown in Fig. 97, and the sharp fringes so formed are apt to cut the hand, or metal particles detached by the hammer blows may endanger the eyes; this end of the

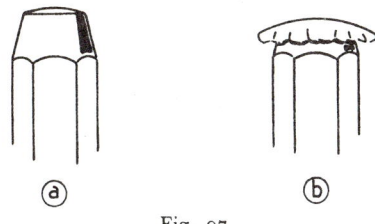

Fig. 97

chisel should, therefore, be kept smooth either by grinding or filing away these rough edges.

For cutting sheet metal two methods are in common use.

In the first, as illustrated in Fig. 98, the work is supported on a heavy iron block, and, with the chisel inclined away from the operator, the cut is made towards the body.

A succession of cuts is made in this way until the chisel

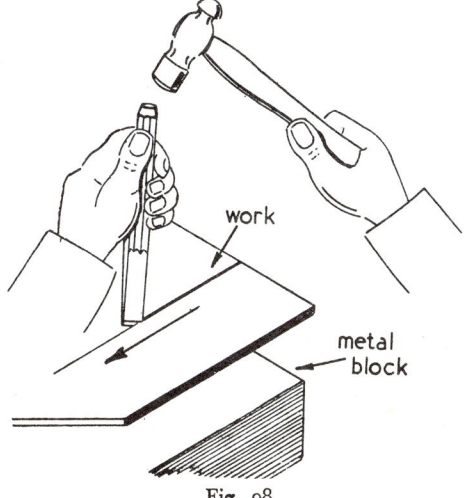

Fig. 98

breaks through all along the scribed line and the work is parted off.

It should be pointed out that considerable distortion of the metal is caused both by the hammer blows and by the wedging action of the chisel point ; in addition, this distortion will be increased if an attempt is made to cut through thick sheet metal at a single passage of the tool, or if the work is not well supported on a rigid cutting block.

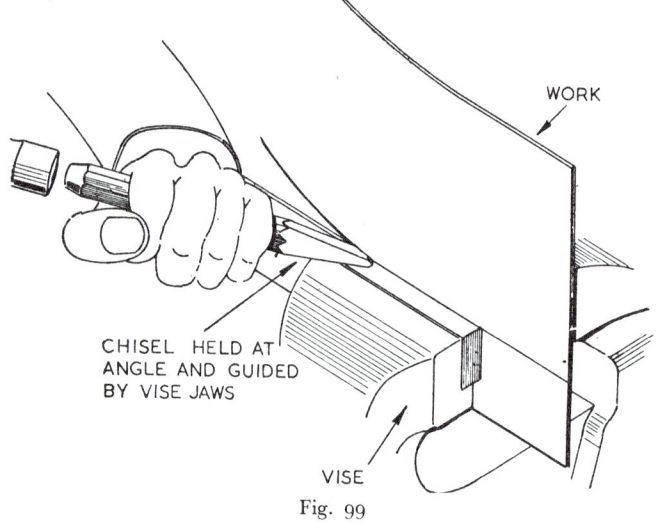

Fig. 99

For this reason, when it is important to maintain the flatness of the material, it is better to use the hacksaw for cutting thick sheet metal.

In the second method, the work is held in the vice, as shown in Fig. 99, and the vice jaws are then used to guide the cutting edge of the chisel. The chisel should be held at an angle to the work, so that it advances along the line of the cut when struck with the hammer.

Although the material held between the vice jaws will remain straight, the upper strip, particularly if it is narrow, will be distorted by the chisel and will tend to curl up into a spiral, which when straightened out will have curved sides and so will be of little use where a straight-sided strip of metal is required.

When surfaces, such as those on a casting, have to be rendered flat by means of a cold chisel, the work must be first marked-out on its sides to indicate the exact level of the surface throughout.

The chisel is then worked across the surface, using a part only of the cutting edge to enable the chisel to be driven by light hammer blows ; following this, a second series of cuts is taken crossing the first diagonally.

Do not carry the chisel right to the far edge of the work or the metal will break away, but work from the edges towards the centre.

When the chisel is used on large surfaces, preliminary cuts should be taken across the work in two directions with a narrow cross-cut chisel, and this is followed by cutting down to the grooves so formed with an ordinary flat chisel.

Drilling with the Hand Drill. A drilling machine is constructed to drill holes truly vertical to the surface of its work table, but when a hand drill is used this alignment has to be maintained with one hand whilst the other turns the drill.

Usually, the drill is aligned with the aid of the eye alone, but some of the larger hand drills are fitted with a spirit level to enable the drill to be held horizontally.

When small drills are used, the hand drill is best held in the vertical position, as the weight of the tool itself may then impart sufficient pressure for drilling, and, moreover, fine drills are less liable to be broken when used in this way, especially if they project for only a short distance from the chuck.

As a check on the position in which the drill is held, a small square may from time to time be applied to the work surface and held in contact with the drill.

It is important that the hand drill should be held steady, otherwise a bell-mouthed hole will be formed and there is an added risk of breaking the drill.

With larger drills it is better to use the hand drill in the horizontal position, for this allows greater pressure to be exerted by pressing the body against the breast piece, and at the same time it is easier to maintain the proper alignment.

It may be remembered that it was suggested that the bench top should be set horizontally with a spirit level; if this is done, the spirit level attached to the drill can be used to align the drill truly with the work held in the vice.

Where the hand drill is not fitted with a level, the writer has, on occasion, used a small circular spirit level borrowed from an old camera and attached to the shank of the hand drill by means of a metal clip.

The Drilling Operation. The location of drill holes is usually marked by the point of intersection of two crosslines, scribed when the work is being marked-out for machining.

A punch mark should be made exactly at this point, and from it the circumference of the hole is scribed with the dividers, as was described in Chapter Three, and as is shown in Fig. 100.

Now, it will be clear that, if the drill is not held truly vertical to the work surface, its point will wander in the direction in which the drill points, but as soon as the drill has entered up to its full diameter this wandering will be checked by the sides of the drill itself. If, therefore, a

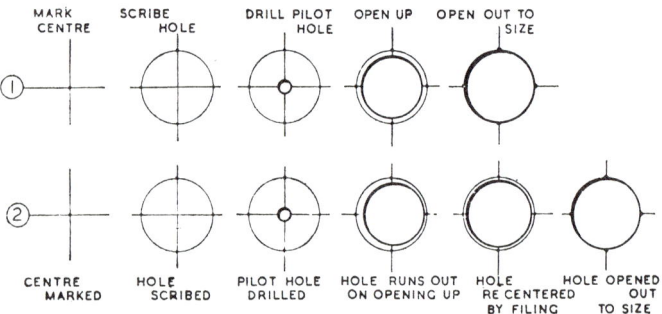

Fig. 100

Fig. 101

centre drill of the type shown in Fig. 101 is used to start the hole and is entered up to the full diameter of the shank, or nearly so, the drill following will be much less liable to wander, as its cutting edges will have much greater support.

Except in the case of small holes, the centre drill should be followed by a pilot drill, as represented in Fig. 100, and the hole formed is, in turn, opened out with a larger drill, but one rather smaller than the size of the hole required.

It will then be clearly seen if the drilling is so far concentric with the marked-out hole, but if this is not the case, the hole must be trued by filing, before the final drill is used.

However, this procedure should, as far as possible, be avoided by trying to ensure that the drilling is accurately carried out from the start.

When drilling blind holes it is very important to start the drill correctly, for, in this case, the farther the drill has entered the more difficult it will be to correct any error of centring; but if it is found that the drill has started off-centre, then the shallow hole must be corrected, by

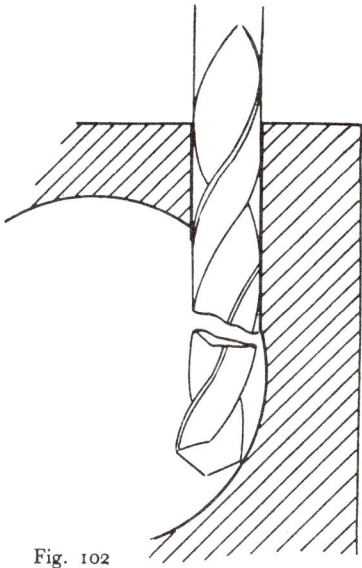

Fig. 102

means of a small round-nosed cold chisel, to make it truly central with the scribed circle denoting the true position.

Avoid drilling in to the side of another hole, as shown in Fig. 102, for this will almost certainly break off the point of the drill ; but when this has to be done, fit a metal plug into the cross-hole to support the point of the drill as it breaks through.

When drilling a hole in an inclined surface, as shown in Fig. 103, it may be possible to avoid the hole running down the incline if a small centre drill is first used, but it is better to form a flat surface for the drill, either by filing or by cutting out a step with a small cold chisel.

Drilling Sheet Metal. Two difficulties commonly arise when drilling sheet metal. First a burr tends to form on the under-side of the sheet, as illustrated in Fig. 104, and interferes with the assembly of the work at a later stage. This can usually be overcome by supporting the work on a piece of metal instead of wood.

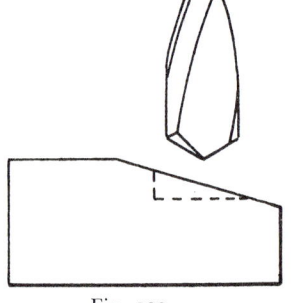

Fig. 103

Secondly, the work is apt to spin and the hands are not free to prevent it ; but if a clamp of the pattern shown in Fig. 105 is used to secure the work to the bench, the sheet will be firmly held, and, moreover, this will at the same time stop the work from riding up on the drill and thus causing a burr to be formed on its under surface.

As will be seen in the drawing, this clamp has a V notch for the passage of the drill, and the two limbs of the V hold the work securely, close to the drill hole.

Polishing Work with the Hand Drill. The ends of rods, the heads of screws, and other small parts can be polished when secured in the drill chuck by revolving them against a piece of emery cloth. The cloth should be supported on a piece of wood to allow the end of a rod, for example, to

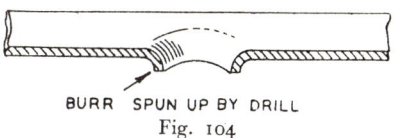

BURR SPUN UP BY DRILL
Fig. 104

centre itself by indenting the surface of the abrasive material

Reaming. This is the process of truing holes and making them to the exact diameter required by means of a reamer. The hand reamer, shown in Fig. 106, is made of hardened

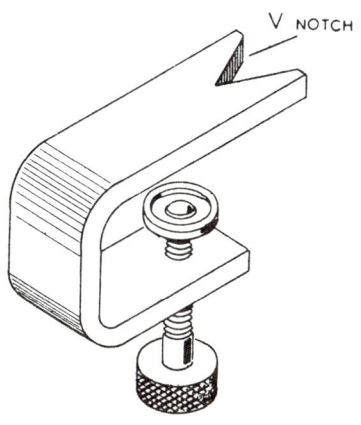

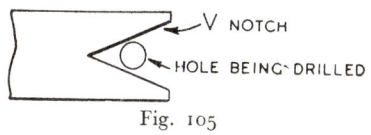

Fig. 105

steel and has a number of flutes with accurately ground cutting edges; in this case the flutes are straight, but more commonly they are of spiral form. The nose of the reamer

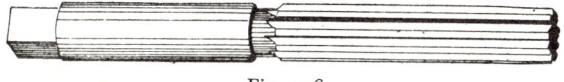

Fig. 106

is slightly tapered for a short distance to allow it to enter under-sized holes.

This tool is intended to be used for the removal of only very small amounts of metal, that is to say to bring to the full diameter holes which have been drilled a few thousandths of an inch under the required size.

To use the reamer, the squared shank is gripped in a tap wrench, or other form of holder, and the tapered tip is inserted in the hole ; the tool is then turned in a clockwise, or right-handed, direction until it has passed fully into the hole.

The reamer is withdrawn from the hole by still turning it in the same direction so as not to blunt the fine cutting edges.

On no account should the reamer be forced into the hole or otherwise roughly used, for this may result in blunting or chipping the cutting edges.

When steel is reamed, a plentiful supply of lubricant is essential. When reaming a long hole, the reamer should be withdrawn from time to time, and after the chips have been cleared from the flutes, it should again be lubricated before the work is continued.

Screw Threading. Screw threading consists in forming a thread either on the external surface of a rod or shaft, that is to say a male thread, or in the interior of a hole when it is termed a female thread.

As ready-made screws are usually purchased, the tapping of holes to receive them is more commonly required in the small workshop than cutting external threads, and so will be first considered.

Cutting Internal Screw Threads. From the drawing of a screw thread shown in Fig. 107 it will be seen that the outside diameter of the thread is equal to the diameter of the rod, and corresponds with the nominal size of both the tap and the die used for cutting this particular thread. Further, it will be apparent that the diameter of the rod at the bottom of the threads, or core diameter, is considerably less than the overall size of the rod.

This core diameter will vary with the coarseness or pitch of the thread used ; so to find the right size of drill to form the hole for the tap, a table must be consulted which takes into account both the outside diameter of the rod and the pitch of the screw thread.

The hole to receive the tap is drilled somewhat larger than the actual core diameter, both to provide working clearance for the tap and to allow for the spreading and upsetting of the metal which takes place during the tapping operation.

If the tapping sizes given in the tables are used, it may be found that, except in the case of very fine threads,

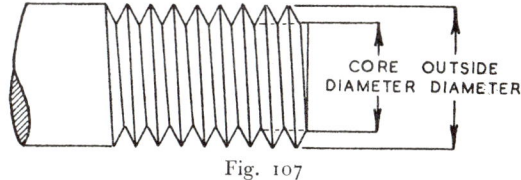

Fig. 107

considerable difficulty is experienced in tapping the hole, for the tap has to be worked in very slowly and carefully to avoid breaking it.

If, however, the hole is drilled rather larger than the size given, the tap will cut much more freely and without risk of breakage ; in addition, it will be found that the tap can be more readily kept on a straight course in the larger hole.

It matters little if the crests of the threads of the tapped hole fall short of the roots of the external thread, for the tips of a screw thread have but little strength.

An easy method of finding the right size of tapping drill to use is to insert the tip of the taper tap into the holes in the drill gauge ; and when a hole is found which admits the tap as far as the bottom of the threads at its tip, this hole denotes the size of the tapping drill.

If you have any doubt in this matter, drill some trial holes of various sizes in a piece of scrap metal and tap them, you can then select a hole which allows the tap to cut freely and at the same time shows that a full, or almost full, thread has been cut. When you have found satisfactory sizes of tapping drills for the taps you commonly use, make a table of these for future reference.

When the tapping size hole has been drilled, its mouth should be opened out, for a depth equal to about one and a half threads, with a drill at least equal to the outside diameter of the tap.

The appearance of the work is then as shown in Fig. 108, which also illustrates the result of tapping a hole without drilling a preliminary counterbore. Should an attempt be made to enlarge the mouth of a tapped hole with a full-sized drill, the counterbore formed will be found to be off-centre, as shown in Fig. 108.

The next step is to tap the hole, using the taper tap at the start. A tap wrench suitable for the size of the tap should be used, for if too much leverage is obtained the tap will be easily broken.

The tap must at all times be kept truly vertical to the

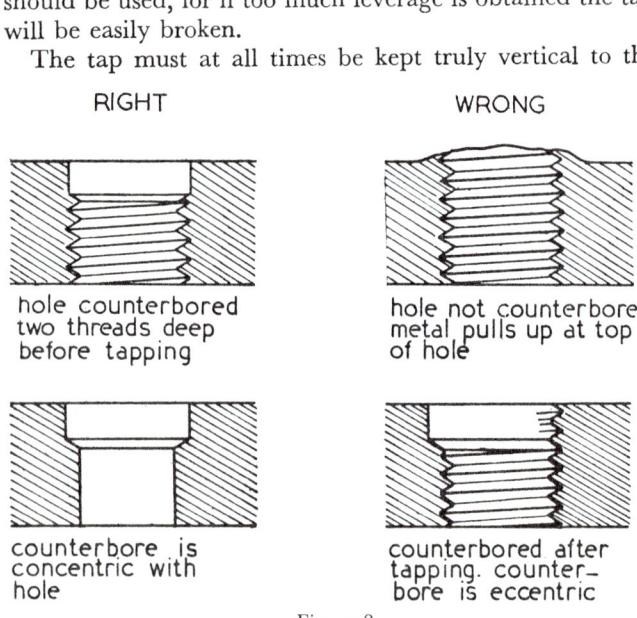

Fig. 108

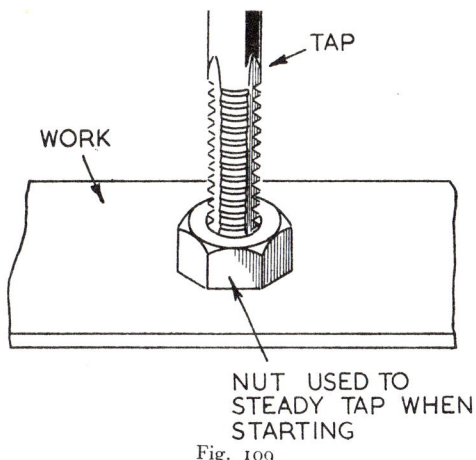

NUT USED TO STEADY TAP WHEN STARTING

Fig. 109

work surface, and this is facilitated by using a nut on the tap to act as a guide and to maintain an even bearing, as shown in Fig. 109.

A check can also be kept on the alignment of the tap by applying a small square to the surface of the work.

Thin material can usually be tapped to the full thread diameter by the passage of the taper tap alone, but in the case of thick metal parts, or when tapping deep holes, the taper tap is worked in slowly by advancing it half a turn at a time and then turning it back for a turn to clear the chips.

After the taper tap has been entered for some distance, it should be withdrawn and the second or plug tap is worked down until resistance is felt; this process is then continued until the hole has been tapped for the required depth.

Always keep the flutes of the tap clear of chips and use plenty of oil when tapping steel; cast-iron and brass do not require lubrication. Furthermore, when a blind hole is being tapped the chips must be cleared from the hole, otherwise it may be thought that the full depth has been reached when the point of the tap bottoms on a pad of cuttings.

Should a tap be broken off in the work, it can be removed with a pair of pliers if a hold can be obtained ; but if the tap has broken off short, it may be possible to unscrew the broken portion by carefully driving it round with a small pin punch.

In the case of large taps, a pair of fine-pointed pliers, or a tool specially made for the purpose, may be used to grip the flutes and unscrew the broken fragment. If these methods fail, the tap must be heated until it is softened and then drilled out.

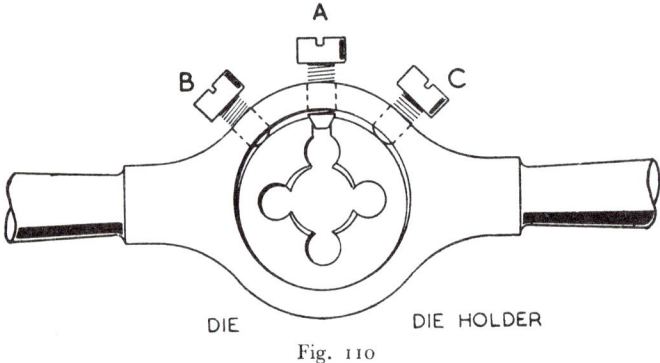

Fig. 110

Cutting External Threads. For all the work undertaken in the small workshop the circular split die of the pattern shown in Fig. 110 is generally used. Formerly, these dies were made with an adjusting screw, by means of which the die could be set and correction made for wear.

The die is held in the holder as shown in the drawing ; the central screw, A, is engaged with the slot in the die and the screws at either side, B and C, are then tightened to secure the die in place and lock it against the central screw.

The size to which the die cuts can be adjusted over a small range either by expanding it by means of the screw A, or by contracting it with the screws B and C.

The chief difficulty in cutting a thread with this type of

die and holder is to form the thread exactly in line with the axis of the work.

The end of the rod to be threaded should be well tapered with a fine file to give the die a lead and to enable it to grip the work without excessive downward pressure having to be used.

Care must be taken to hold the dieholder truly square with the work when starting the thread; this can, if desired, be checked by means of a small square.

These dies are designed to cut the thread to the finished size at a single passage over the work; the chip holes should be kept clear of cuttings, and when steel is being threaded plenty of oil should be applied to the work surface and the cutting edges of the die.

Formerly, dieholders could be obtained fitted with detachable guide collets which ensured that the thread was cut squarely, and also, when required, a collet of the correct size could be fitted to engage the stepped part of a shaft when threading a portion of smaller diameter at its end.

In Part II of this book full instructions will be given for making dieholders and collets of this type.

Soldering. Soldering consists in joining together metal parts by means of a solder, that is to say an alloy of lower melting point which in part combines with the metallic surfaces.

In addition to the solder, a flux must be used to prevent the formation of metallic oxides which would interfere with the process.

The best known flux is, perhaps, what is known as killed spirits, that is hydrochloric acid, or spirits of salts, to which metallic zinc has been added until all chemical action ceases; there are also various proprietary liquid fluxes of this type such as the well-known Baker's Fluid. These liquid fluxes are best applied to the work by means of a tool formed from a piece of copper wire with a flattened end as illustrated in Fig. 111.

The other class of fluxes usually have a resinous or fatty base, and these generally have the merit that, unlike the former, they do not cause corrosion when used for soldering fine wires and other parts used in instrument work.

As the makers of some electrically-heated soldering irons advise that their products should not be used with an acid

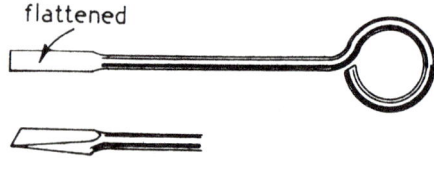

Fig. 111

flux, care must be taken in such a case to select a flux which does not damage the connections of the heating coils within the iron.

As to the actual solder, the variety known as blowpipe solder will be found most generally useful for all ordinary work ; this has a high percentage of tin, which causes it to run well and prevents it from tarnishing.

The compounds consisting of a combined solder and flux mixture are now largely employed for special work, as they

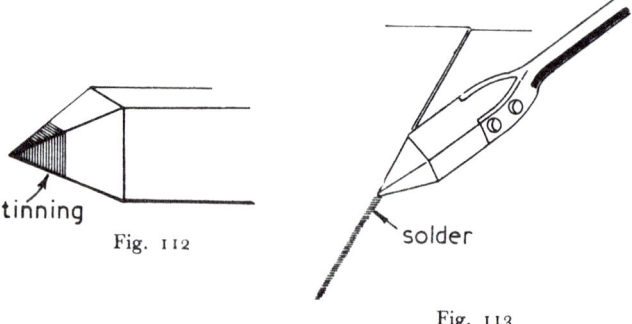

Fig. 112

Fig. 113

are easy to use and some at least are free from corrosive action.

These can be obtained in the form of either a liquid paint or a paste. In addition to these, solder is available as a wire with one or more cores composed of a non-corrosive fluxing material.

When an iron is used for the soldering operation, its tip must first be tinned, as it is termed, that is to say covered

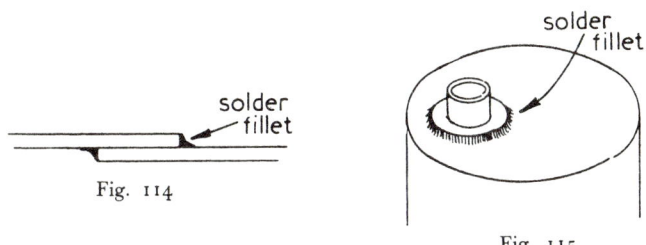

Fig. 114

Fig. 115

with a coating of solder. After heating the iron to a temperature sufficient to melt the solder, it is dipped in the flux and then applied to the stick of solder ; the solder should run over and adhere to the surface of the iron, but if it does not readily do so, the tip of the iron should be cleaned with an old file to remove the film of oxide and a further trial made.

In this way all four faces of the tip should be tinned as shown in Fig. 112 and the iron is then ready for use.

Should the iron be subsequently overheated, the tinning will be burnt off and retinning will be necessary.

After the work to be soldered has been thoroughly

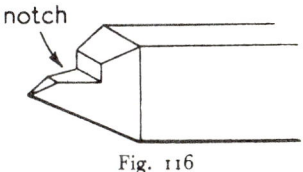

Fig. 116

cleaned and rendered quite free from grease or surface corrosion, it is painted with liquid flux and the iron, with the solder adhering to its tip, is applied to the work and slowly moved along its surface, as represented in Fig. 113.

The same procedure is adopted when, for example, soldering a bushing into a tank.

This should result in the application of a thin, even layer or fillet of solder, as illustrated in Figs. 114 and 115, but some practice will be required before this can be done neatly.

For soldering wires or Bowden cables, an iron with a notch formed at its tip, as shown in Fig. 116, will be found most convenient, as the solder will lie in the notch and is then readily applied to the work.

Some combined solder-flux compounds can be used in a similar manner with the soldering iron, but of these some are better adapted for this purpose than others.

A process which is much more easily carried out than soldering with an iron is known as sweating. This consists either in coating the parts with a layer of solder, or merely in applying to the surfaces concerned a solder-flux paint, or paste, and then heating the parts while they are pressed together, until the solder melts.

Sweating carried out in this way forms a neat joint, as no superfluous solder is used, and, moreover, hardly any skill is needed to obtain a good result.

Hardening and Tempering. The mild steel used generally in the workshop for constructional work cannot be hardened in the ordinary way, but tool or carbon steel from which the workshop tools are made can be readily hardened.

The essential difference between the two types of steel is that mild steel has a low carbon content, whereas tool steel has much more carbon combined with it.

Silver steel is a form of tool steel which can be easily hardened, and it is, therefore, most useful for making small tools and other components which need to be hardened.

To harden tool steel, it is heated to a bright cherry red colour and then quickly dipped in water. This leaves the steel dead hard but rather brittle, so that where toughness is required, as in the case of cutting tools, the work must be tempered after being hardened, before it can be used effectively.

To temper the steel, it must first be cleaned with a piece

of emery cloth until it shows a bright surface ; it is then carefully heated at a place well away from the cutting edge and the flow of colour formed is closely watched. The first colour noticed will be a pale yellow, and, as the work is heated further, this will be succeeded by a play of colours ranging from a dark straw to a deep blue.

For ordinary metal-cutting tools a straw colour will give about the right degree of hardness, and blued steel will generally be found much too soft.

When the straw tint has spread to the cutting edge from the heated portion of the work, the tool is again quickly dipped in water.

Nowadays, metal-cutting tools are largely made of high-speed steel, which contains tungsten or other scarce metals ; this steel is hardened and tempered by a special process of heat treatment, and no attempt should be made to soften or harden tools made of this material. Short lengths of this steel, suitable for making tools, are supplied by the manufacturers properly hardened and ready for grinding to the shape required.

Although, as has been said, mild steel cannot be hardened as can tool steel, it can, however, have its outer surface hardened, whilst the centre portion remains soft, by a process known as case-hardening.

This consists of heating the steel, while in contact with a case-hardening compound, so that extra carbon becomes combined with the surface layers of the steel and, in effect, converts this portion into tool steel.

This outer layer of tool steel can then be hardened in the manner already described, but for most purposes subsequent tempering is unnecessary as the inner portion of the steel remains soft and retains its full strength.

CHAPTER FIVE

A Simple Depth Gauge—A Rule Stand.

Now that we have considered most of the ordinary workshop operations carried out with hand tools, it is time to put this to useful account in making some small articles of equipment that may be helpful in the workshop.

TOOLS TO MAKE

A Simple Depth Gauge. The illustration in Fig. 117 gives a general view of the gauge and shows the main points of its construction and design.

You should notice two things : one, that the drawing is three-dimensional, that is to say it represents the device in three planes in space and shows its length, breadth, and thickness in one view. The alternative to this is to make three separate drawings, showing the plan view, as seen from above, and, in addition, an end and side elevation to represent the end and side views respectively. Moreover, from the single drawing you will be able to see at a glance exactly what the gauge is like, just as though it were actually before you ; you are, therefore, saved the trouble of trying to build up in the mind's eye a picture of the object from three different drawings.

A drawing of this type is termed isometric, and you will see that, unlike an artistic drawing, all side and end lines are parallel and do not converge to represent a perspective view.

Secondly, you will see that all the parts are numbered, and these same numbers are used in all subsequent drawings whenever the parts are shown. When you do any machine drawing or sketching for yourself, try to adopt this methodical way of working in order to save confusion and loss of time when making components from drawings.

The gauge is used in the same way as the depth gauge described in Chapter Three, that is to say, the base block is held against the work while the spindle is pushed to the bottom of the hole to be measured, and the clamp screw is then tightened.

Although the spindle is not graduated, as in the former case, it has the advantage that it can be used in very small holes.

To record the actual depth, the length of the spindle projecting below the base is measured with a rule.

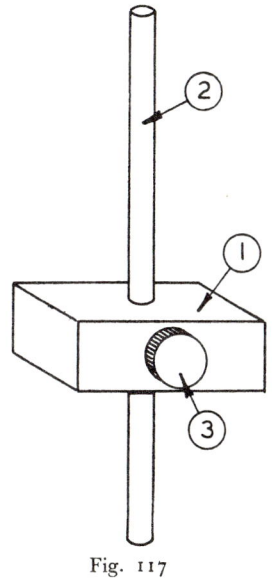

Fig. 117

The base block, part No. 1, is best made of steel, both to resist wear and to look more workmanlike; it is formed by cutting off a piece 1 in. in length from a bar ½ in. wide and ⅜ in. thick, or it can be sawn out with a hacksaw from a larger piece of material.

When the base has been cut to shape, the edges are filed straight and square and the surfaces are finished with a fine file to give a good appearance; all edges are then chamfered with the file to remove their sharpness.

The upper and lower surfaces are best made flat by rubbing the work on the bench file as previously described.

The under surface, where it will come in contact with the work being measured, must be made quite flat by using the scraper in conjunction with the surface plate. The next step is to paint the upper surface and one side with marking fluid to enable the drill hole centres to be marked-out.

For this purpose, the jenny callipers are set to ¼ in. and,

as shown in Fig. 118, a line is scribed along the upper surface, and then on the front face with the callipers reset to $\frac{3}{16}$ in.

With the callipers set to $\frac{1}{2}$ in., the cross centre lines are then scribed on these two faces, as shown in the drawing.

The points of intersection of these centre lines are marked with a centre punch, and the upper hole is drilled $\frac{1}{8}$ in. right through to take the spindle, but if you happen to have a $\frac{1}{8}$-in. reamer, drill this hole with a No. 31 drill and ream it to the finished size. The two ends of the hole should be

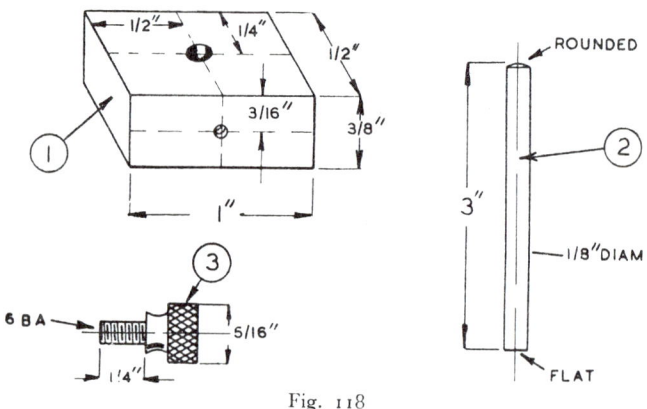

Fig. 118

very lightly countersunk with a centre drill to remove the sharp edges.

The hole at the side of the block is drilled with a No. 42 drill through into the previous hole; it is then tapped to receive the 6-B.A. clamp screw.

After the drilling and tapping have been completed, any burrs which may have been formed are removed with the scraper, and the base block is then finished and ready to receive the spindle.

The spindle should be made from a length of $\frac{1}{8}$-in. diameter silver steel, as this material is usually straight and accurate as to size. Three inches will probably be sufficient for the length of the spindle, but, if desired, it can be made to the full standard length of 6 in.

When the spindle has been cut to length, the ends are filed flat with the aid of a square, and the upper end only is rounded off and then polished by using the hand drill as previously described.

The clamp screw can quite well be made from a knurled terminal screw, preferably of brass, as this will not damage the spindle.

The diameter of the head of the screw must not be greater than $\frac{3}{8}$ in. or the base block will not lie flat on the work when measurements are being made.

The threaded portion of the screw should, if necessary, be cut short so that the screw itself does not project unduly and spoil the neat appearance of the finished gauge.

A Ru'e Stand. This easily-made form of rule holder is used, as previously described, to hold the rule in the upright position on the surface plate when setting the scriber point of the surface gauge. The stand described was made to take rules up to $\frac{1}{16}$ in. thick and $\frac{5}{8}$ in. wide, but it will also accommodate rules of other sizes.

The general, isometric, view is shown in Fig. 119, and the component parts are illustrated in Fig. 120.

The base block is made from a $1\frac{3}{4}$-in. length of $\frac{3}{4}$-in. square steel bar, and, as will be seen, all the drilling work is confined to the front face.

The steel block, part No. 1, should be carefully filed square and to a good finish ; the edges are then chamfered with a fine file to remove the sharp corners.

As it is essential that the holder should stand evenly on the surface plate and without rock, its under surface must be scraped true so as to form a good seating surface.

When this work has been completed, the front face is painted with marking fluid and then marked-out as shown in Fig. 120.

The hole to receive the 6-B.A. screw, used to fix the spring clip, is marked-out with the jenny callipers $\frac{5}{8}$ in. from the left-hand end of the block and on the centre line of the front face, that is to say $\frac{3}{8}$ in. from either the upper or the lower edge.

The holes for the register pins are marked-out $\frac{9}{16}$ in. from the right-hand edge and $\frac{1}{16}$ in. from the upper and lower surfaces respectively. All these centre points are then marked with a centre punch, and the screw hole is drilled with a No. 42 drill to a depth of $\frac{1}{2}$ in. and afterwards tapped

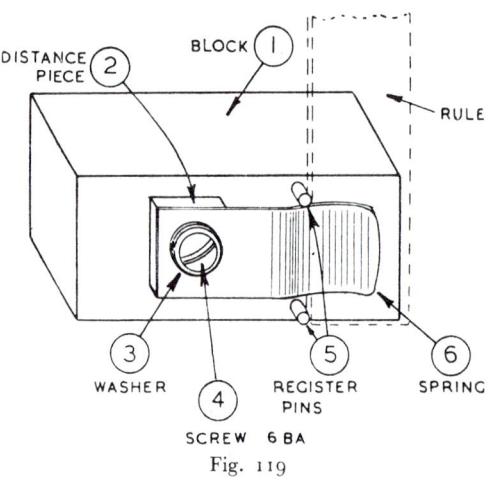

Fig. 119

for a depth of some $\frac{5}{16}$ in. The register pin holes are drilled with a No. 53 drill to a depth of $\frac{1}{4}$ in.

To complete the work on the base block the register pins, No. 5, have to be fitted. These are made from $\frac{1}{16}$ in. diameter silver steel, but as the diameter of the drilled holes is some three thousandths of an inch less than the diameter of the rod, the silver steel will have to be slightly tapered at its end before it can be fitted. An alternative method is to use a piece of 16-gauge bicycle spoke and drill the holes with a $\frac{1}{16}$-in. drill; as in this case the difference between the diameters is only one and a half thousandths, the spoke can be pressed into the holes once it has been started by slightly tapering its end.

Tapering the rod is best done by supporting its end in a notch filed in a piece of brass secured in the vice, and then turning the rod with the fingers while it is filed with a fine file. In any case, before fitting the pegs to the block, it is a good plan to make a preliminary trial on a piece of scrap metal to find out how much taper is needed to allow the pins to be pressed into place.

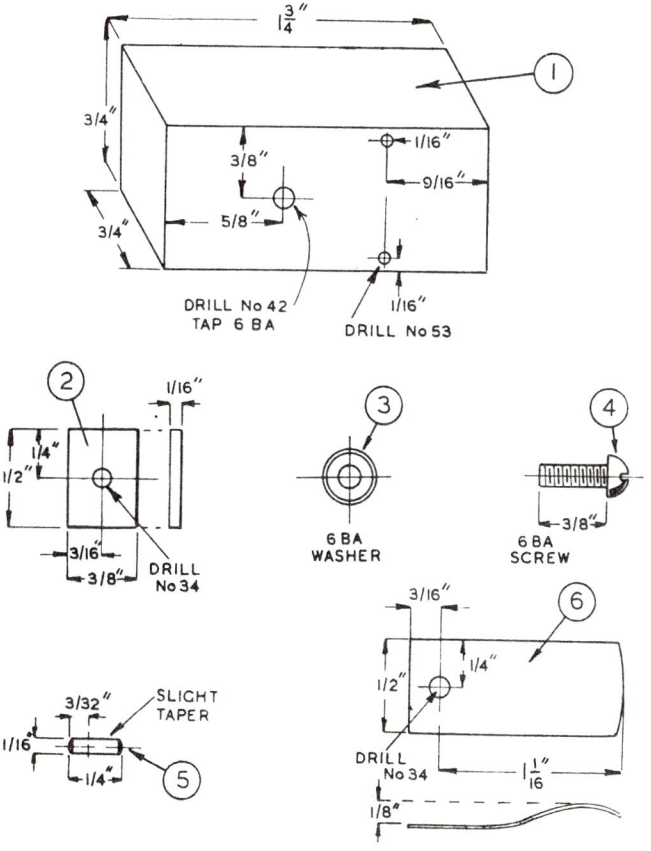

Fig. 120

After two pins have been suitably tapered and cut off to ¼ in. in length, their heads are rounded off and polished as previously described. Press the two pins into the block, using finger pressure only, and check their vertical alignment with the square either resting on the surface plate, or applied to the under surface of the block.

If your drilling has been accurately carried out, the two pins should stand vertically one above the other, but if this is found not to be the case, any error must be corrected by filing a flat on one pin.

When all is in order, the pins should be pressed home in the vice, leaving 3/32 in. of their ends projecting.

The next step is to fit the leaf spring, No. 6, that holds the rule in position. This is made of 26-gauge spring brass, as this material will not scratch the rule as would steel clock spring ; and, moreover, it is much more easily drilled and cut to shape.

The brass is painted with marking fluid, and after it has been marked-out with the jenny callipers, a strip ½ in. wide is cut off.

In order to afford a better hold of the material while it is being drilled, it is not cut to length until after the No. 34 drill hole shown in the drawing has been marked-out and drilled.

The end portion of the strip is then polished with a piece of fine emery cloth, and the free end is made slightly curved with a fine file. When the strip has been cut off to a length of 1¼ in., it is given a double curve, as shown in the drawing, by bending it with the aid of the round-nose pliers, or it can be formed equally well by bending against a piece of rod held in the vice.

A distance piece, No. 2, is fitted behind the spring to allow the latter to bear evenly on the rule when in position. This component is cut out from a piece of brass $\frac{1}{16}$ in. thick, and after it has been marked-out in accordance with the drawing, it is drilled with a No. 34 drill to form a clearance hole for the screw.

To complete the list of components, a 6-B.A. brass,

chamfered washer and a 6-B.A. round-headed, brass screw, ⅜ in. in length, are required, that is to say parts 3 and 4.

The rule holder can now be assembled ; and it should be noted that the register pins serve the double purpose of aligning the rule and at the same time holding the spring in position, for the spring should fit closely between the projecting ends of the pins.

The rule should now be sprung into place, and if it is found that the hold is too firm, or too light, the spring should be removed and reset accordingly by means of the round-nose pliers.

INTRODUCTION PART II

WE have now finished considering workshop premises, the furniture needed in them as well as the hand tools desirable if a full range of activity is to be pursued.

The time has now come to review the machine tools required if the beginner is to extend both his facilities and his skill.

CHAPTER ONE

> Lever-feed and Rack-feed Types — Electric Drilling Machine—Driving the Machine—Drilling Speeds—Machine Vice—Table V Blocks—Work Clamp—Drill Chuck—Table Stop—Depth-drilling Stop and Gauge—Drilling Operations—Drilling into a Cross-hole—Drilling on an Inclined Surface—Cross-drilling Shafts—Drilling for Tapping—Tapping in the Drilling Machine—Countersinks—Counterbores and Pin Drills.

THE drilling machine, as opposed to the hand drill, has the great advantage that it can be relied on to bore holes truly at right-angles to the surface of the work and with great accuracy as regards size and position.

THE DRILLING MACHINE

This is ensured by mounting both the headstock of the machine and the work table in accurate alignment on a rigid column; further, the high speed obtainable with a power drive makes successful drilling possible with even the most slender drills.

Types of Machines. The smaller drilling machines are usually of what is termed the sensitive type, that is to say the lever mechanism that feeds the drill is so designed that the pressure on the drill can be readily felt by the hand, as distinct from the feed pressure which is applied by a screw mechanism as in the lathe tailstock or in the cruder forms of drilling machine.

In the simplest form of machine the feed lever is connected directly to the drill spindle, which carries the chuck holding the drill and is moved downwards when pressure is applied to the hand-feed lever.

A well-designed machine of this type, illustrated in

110

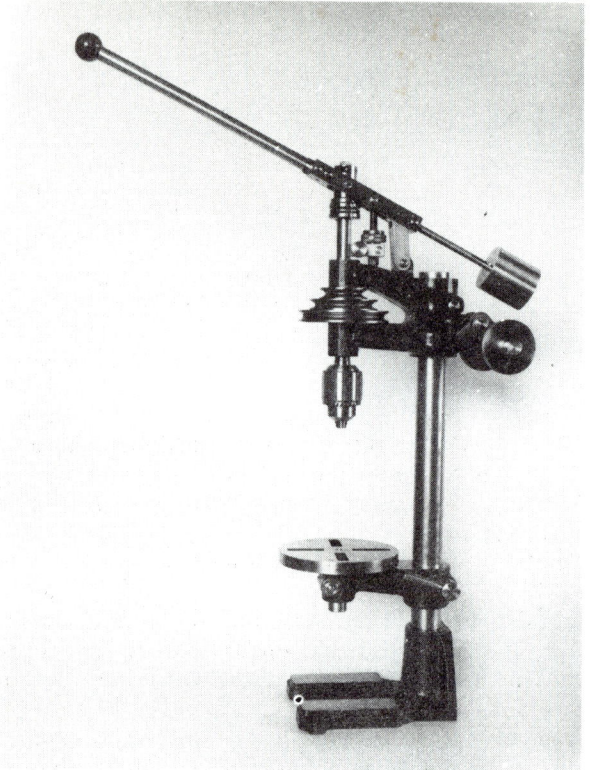

Fig. 1

Fig. 1, is the "Model Engineer" Drilling Machine which takes drills up to ¼ in. in diameter.

Although this machine cannot be purchased, as the design hardly lends itself to economic commercial production in view of the number of small components required and the accurate hand-fitting of the bearings rightly recommended; nevertheless, castings of good quality are readily obtainable, and from them an accurate, high-class machine can be built by those possessing the necessary skill and equipment; moreover, the machine has been so designed that all the machining can be carried out in a lathe of 3½ in. centre height.

The writer built one of the machines several years ago and, as a result of careful hand-fitting, no wear has become

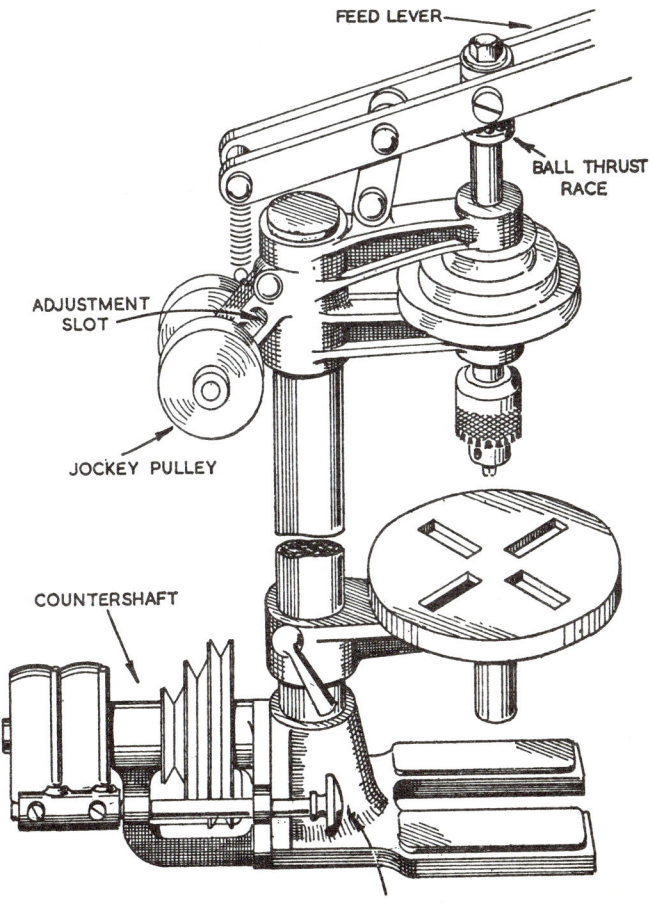

Fig. 2

apparent and the machine's accuracy has been maintained in spite of prolonged use.

Reference to Fig. 2, depicting the general construction of the headstock, will show that a ball bearing is fitted to the spindle to take the thrust of the feed lever, which is returned to its upper position by means of a spring ; a counterweight can, however, be used for this purpose to ensure a very delicate and highly sensitive feed motion. The three-step drive pulley, in conjunction with the adjustable jockey pulleys, provides for a wide range of speeds and correct tensioning of the driving belt.

The Rack Feed Machine. When the larger sizes of drills are used in machines fitted with a lever feed acting directly on the drilling spindle, it will be found that considerable hand pressure has to be applied to the feed handle to make the drill cut ; those who have used a hand drill will be well aware of the heavy pressure needed in this case. Although the leverage, and with it the pressure on the drill, can be increased by lengthening the feed lever, it is not usual in small machines to provide a leverage greater than about four to one if a lever of reasonable length is to be used.

To overcome this difficulty and to provide adequate drilling pressure together with a sensitive feed, a more complicated mechanism consisting of a rack and pinion feed is generally employed.

The headstock mechanism of a drilling machine of this type is illustrated in Fig. 4, and it will be apparent that, when the feed lever is depressed, the pinion attached to it will rotate, thus causing the rack of the spindle sleeve, or quill, to move downwards and feed the drill against the work.

The leverage obtained in this way is usually some sixteen to one ; a great advance on the limited leverage provided in the more simple type of machine.

The sleeve on which the rack teeth are cut is known as the quill, and machines so constructed are called quill machines to distinguish them from the previous type.

Fig. 3

The quill does not, of course, rotate but moves upwards and downwards in the headstock under the control of the feed lever. Further, it will be seen that the feed lever is returned to its starting position by means of a coil spring contained in a housing enclosed by a cover plate.

The drawing in Fig. 4 represents the working parts of

the Champion drilling machine, illustrated in Fig. 5.

This machine, once popular for many years, took drills up to ¼ in. diameter. A ball thrust bearing was fitted at the lower end of the spindle and at its upper end the three-step driving pulley was mounted on a sleeve in order to relieve the spindle from side pressure due to the pull of the driving belt.

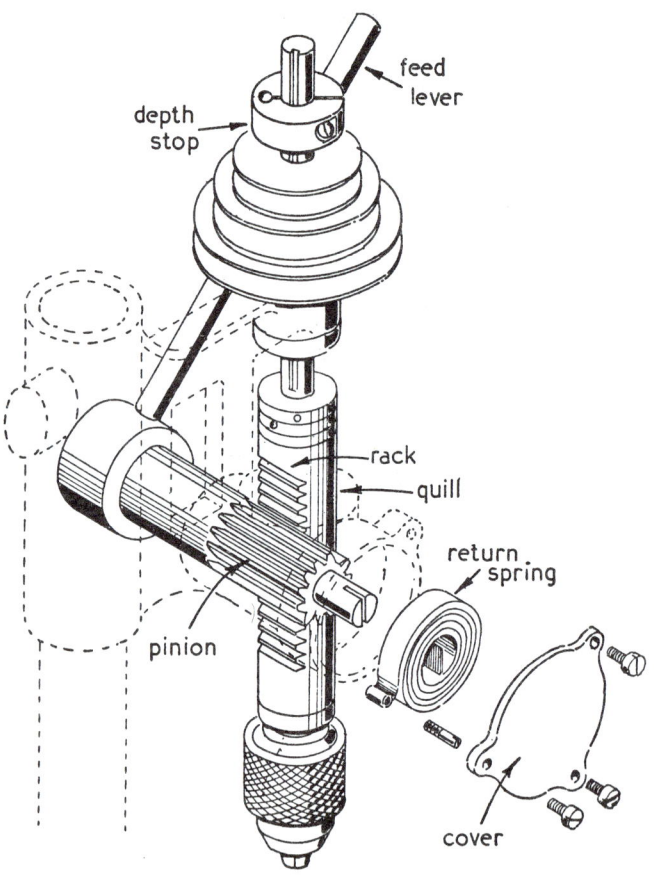

Fig. 4

Fig. 5

A 4 in. diameter canting work table was fitted and was provided with a graduated angular scale and register pin for setting the table to the exact horizontal position.

The great length of the sliding headstock casting where it engaged the column made for rigidity and ample provision was made for adjusting the belt tension by means of a sliding bracket carrying the jockey pulleys. An adjustable stop as illustrated in Fig. 4 could be clamped to the spindle to regulate the depth of drilling. It is to be hoped that someone will be found to market the machine again, for it is one eminently suited to the needs of the amateurs workshop.

The particular "Champion" drill illustrated was modified by the author in order to provide a readily obtainable range

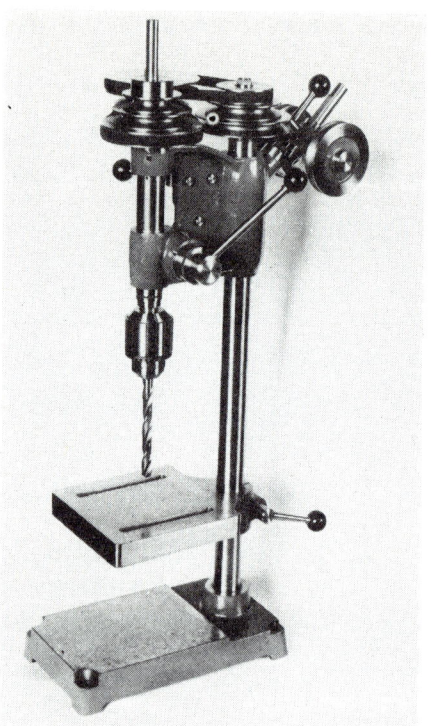

Fig. 6

of spindle speeds in conjunction with a motor fitted with a 2-step pulley.

The Cowell drilling machine, illustrated in Fig. 6 is designed for those who require a rather larger machine of ⅜ in. drilling capacity and with a work table 5 in. in diameter.

This machine is essentially of similar construction to the preceding model, but has certain detail modifications.

As before, the spindle runs in a quill operated by a rack and pinion gear, and the mounting of the drive pulley on a sleeve ensures that the spindle is not subjected to the strain of the pull of the driving belt. A neat form of return mechanism for the feed lever is enclosed in the housing of the pinion gear.

The rotating work table is of the fixed type and not tilting as in the previous machine; this overcomes the difficulty that is sometimes experienced in resetting a tilting table accurately after the machine has had much use. The jockey pulleys slide on an inclined shaft so that

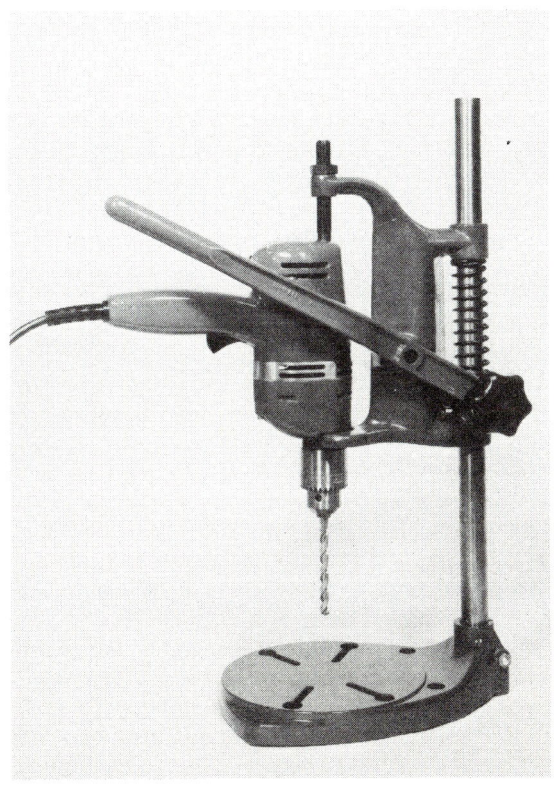

Fig. 7

the belt can be aligned correctly with any of the steps of the driving pulley when the speed is changed.

The ball handles fitted to the feed lever and the table setting clamps make for easy handling and add to the appearance of the machine as a whole. As with the "Champion" drilling machine, the Cowell drill depicted has also been modified by the author to provide a suitable range of spindle speeds.

Self-contained Electric Drill. The drilling machine shown in Fig. 7 is the Black and Decker hand drill mounted on a drilling stand specially designed for the purpose. The drill itself can be readily detached from its stand and used as a portable drill in the workshop or garage ; moreover, it can be employed to mount a grinding wheel, a polishing buff, or a wire brush for decarbonising.

Although this type of drilling machine has the advantages enumerated above, it will be apparent that the limited speed range, as compared with a separately-driven machine, detracts from its utility as a general purpose machine in the small workshop, where slow or moderate speeds are sometimes essential.

Driving the Drilling Machine. Drilling machines are usually driven by means of a belt, for this provides a drive that is both quiet and flexible and, at the same time, the drilling speed is readily varied to suit the occasion by moving the belt from one step of the driving pulley to another.

In small machines, such as those described, the drill spindle is driven by a round belt which is maintained in line with the driving pulley by means of a pair of jockey or guide pulleys.

The belt tension can be adjusted either by altering the position of the jockey pulleys or by raising or lowering the headstock on the column of the machine.

In some instances a countershaft is incorporated to enable the machine to be driven by a flat belt from the workshop lineshaft. The "Model Engineer" machine is designed to carry a countershaft should this be required, and in this case a belt-shifting gear is fitted to move the belt on the fast and loose pulleys when starting and stopping the machine.

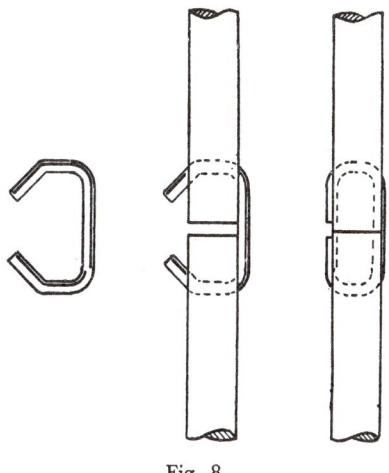

Fig. 8

Small high-speed drilling machines can be driven by means of a sewing machine belt, but it is important, when using these round belts of small cross-section, that the fastener should be properly fitted to prevent its tearing out.

The correct method of fitting a steel U fastener is shown in Fig. 8; it will be observed that the cut ends of the belt are butted closely together, and the lower part of the U projects but little below the belt to ensure that the fastener is kept well clear of the bottom of the V in the pulleys.

When fitting fasteners of this type, the ends of the belt should be drilled exactly centrally with a $\frac{1}{16}$ in. drill, and at the correct distance from the joint to allow the final closure of the fastener to bring the ends of the belt firmly together.

Fasteners fitted in this way should be noiseless in action, and proof against tearing the belt provided that excessive belt tension is not used. For those who wish to avoid using belt fasteners, endless round belts are now obtainable in lengths suitable for driving small machine tools.

Probably, the most convenient method of driving a small drilling machine is to employ a direct belt drive from a motor installed near the drill, as illustrated in Fig. 9. Although only a single driving pulley is shown, the speed range of the machine will be correspondingly increased if a two- or three-step pulley is fitted to the motor shaft. The simplest form of installation is depicted in Fig. *A*, and it will be seen that all that is required is to fix the motor to the bench and fit the belt.

In this case, the motor occupies valuable space on the bench and is not protected in any way. Method *B* affords some protection for the motor, is more compact and, in the case of a low bench, raises the machine to a more convenient working position.

The arrangement shown in Fig. 9c is widely used, for the bench top is then but little encumbered and the motor is well protected from metal cuttings. When the motor is installed in this way below the bench, it can be attached to a wooden base sliding in strips secured to the underside of the bench top ; this allows the motor to be easily removed for periodic cleaning and oiling.

When much fine drilling has to be undertaken, the raised position of the drill, as in Fig. 9B, will be found a great convenience in affording the operator a comfortable working position without excessive stooping being required to bring the eyes close to the work. Before leaving the subject of driving the drill, it must be emphasised that a switch should be fitted close at hand to enable the machine to be stopped instantly in an emergency.

Drilling Speeds. When planning the drive of a drilling machine, account should be taken of the size of the drills to be used, for although a heavy machine must be capable of driving large drills at comparatively slow speed, a

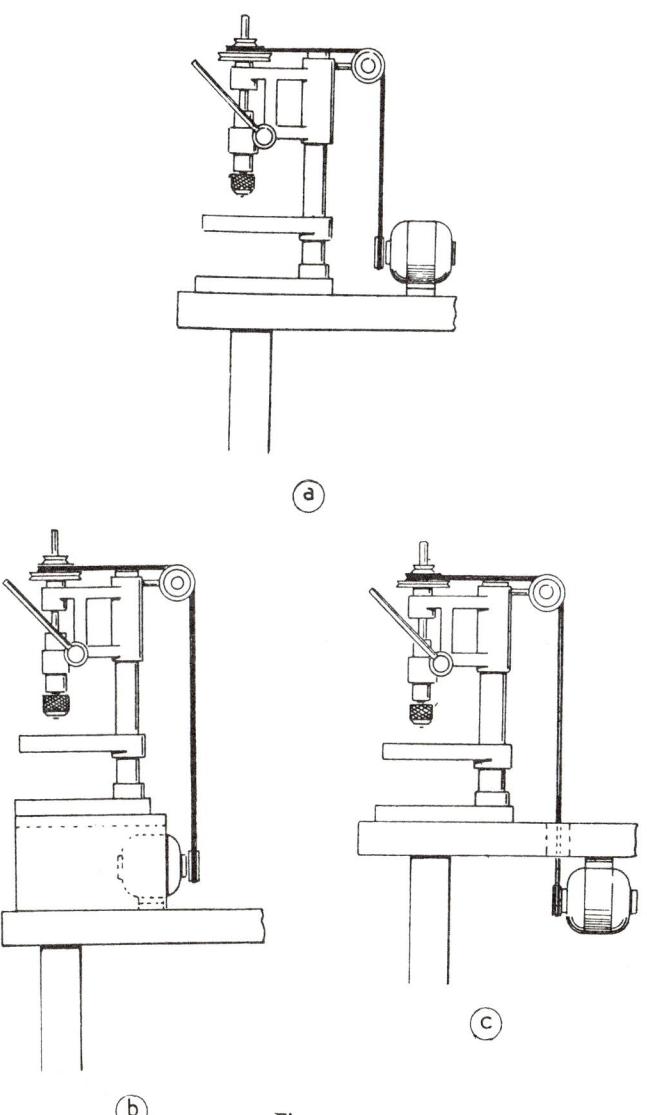

Fig. 9

sensitive type of machine used for light drilling with fine drills will need to be driven at high speed.

The following table gives the speeds recommended by drill manufacturers for drilling mild-steel for commercial purposes, but in the small workshop, where the rate of production is of less importance, these speeds may be reduced.

Drill diam. in in.	High-speed Steel Drills r.p.m.	Carbon Steel Drills r.p.m.
1/16	4,000	1,800
1/8	2,000	900
3/16	1,500	600
1/4	1,100	450
5/16	900	340
3/8	750	280
7/16	650	240
1/2	550	210

These speeds may be doubled when drilling brass and aluminium.

Although the figures given above are by no means absolute, they will serve as a guide when arranging the details of the drilling machine drive from an electric motor.

It will be apparent that high-speed steel drills can be driven at much higher speeds than carbon-steel drills, and for this reason they are to be recommended for use with high-speed self-contained electric drills ; moreover the former retain their sharpness for a longer time and are much less easily broken.

When drills are driven too fast the cutting edges may become quickly blunted, and overheating will arise which will draw the temper and soften the drill point. The speed should be reduced when drilling cast-iron otherwise the cutting lips may become worn and the drill will then tend to bind in the hole.

It is important where high drilling speeds are used that the cutting edges of the drill should be maintained in a really sharp condition in order to ensure free-cutting and avoid rapid blunting of the drill point ; it may, therefore, be advisable to restrict the speed until some experience has been gained.

Drilling Machine Equipment—Drills. These have been described in Part I where a list of the sizes manufactured will also be found.

Machine Vice. For supporting the work on the machine table when drilling, a machine vice will be found essential both to align the material correctly and to prevent it from turning with the drill and damaging the fingers.

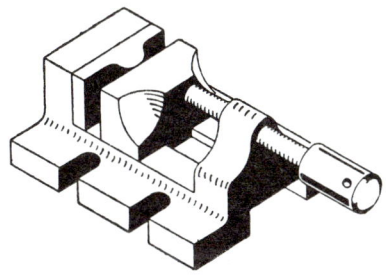

Fig. 10

A small, accurate machine vice, manufactured by Messrs. Myford and well-suited for use in connection with the small drilling machine, is illustrated in Fig. 10. It is essential for accurate drilling that the work held in the vice should lie parallel with the drilling machine table and at right-angles to the drilling axis ; to ensure this the work surface of the vice must be parallel with the underside of the sole plate, and the fixed jaw must stand at right-angles to this surface.

When these conditions are satisfied, any work secured in the vice will automatically be truly aligned in the drilling axis.

As will be seen in the drawing, a loose, swivel jaw-piece is included for holding tapered or irregular work, and

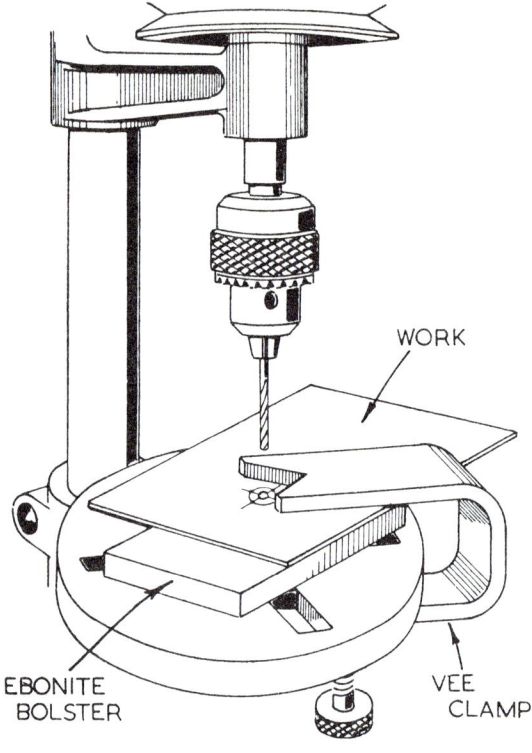

Fig. 11

bolting slots are provided for securing the vice to the work table.

Heavier vices of greater holding capacity and suitable for use with larger drilling machines are also obtainable, but it is advisable to check the accuracy of any vice, not of reputable make, before putting it into use.

Table V Blocks. A V block or a pair of V blocks is used for holding round shafts and other parts on the work table of the drilling machine. The Eclipse V blocks, illustrated in Fig. 12, will be found especially serviceable as they can be readily clamped to the work table as illustrated in Fig. 19. The work itself is secured in place in the block by means of the screw-clamp supplied with each set of two blocks.

Another useful appliance for this type of work is the Myford saddle or table V block, illustrated in Fig. 13.

The sole plate can be drilled, as required, for bolts to secure the device to the work table and, if necessary, clamping strips can be fitted to the upper surface of the blocks to hold the work in place.

Work Clamp. For securing work, such as sheet metal, which cannot be held in the vice for drilling, a work clamp of the pattern illustrated in Fig. 11 will be found useful.

As will be seen, a V notch is formed in the clamping limb to provide a space in which the drill can operate. The work should be supported on a piece of ebonite, hardwood, or metal in order to protect the table from

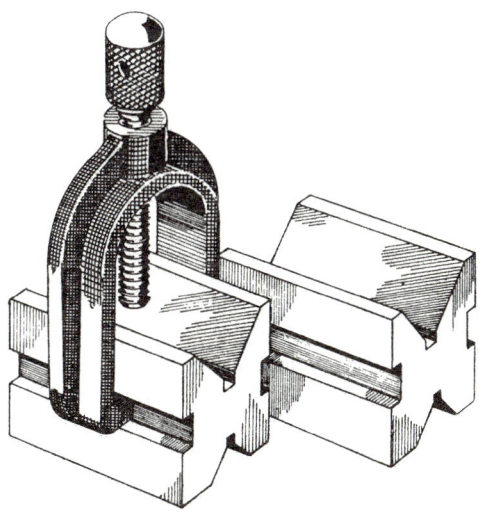

Fig. 12

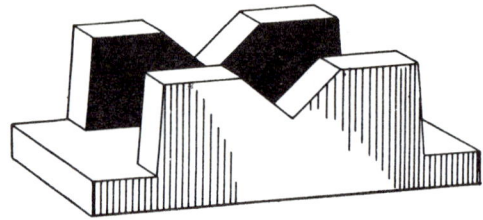

Fig. 13

possible damage and also to prevent a burr being formed on the under-side of the work.

Drill Chuck. It is always advisable to fit a best-quality chuck to the drilling machine, for this will ensure that the drill is always held truly and securely, provided that the chuck is treated in a reasonable manner.

Table Stop. During some drilling operations it is necessary to swing the drill table to the side and, at the same time, to maintain exactly the height to which it is set. This can be ensured if an adjustable stop collar, of the form shown in Fig. 14, is fitted to the column of the machine. When the height of the table has been set, the stop is brought into contact with the under surface of the table bracket and then clamped in place.

Full directions for making this attachment are given in Chapter Six.

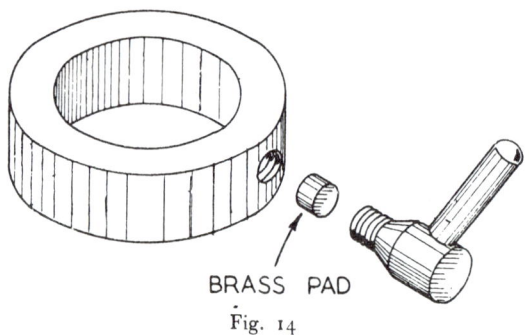

BRASS PAD

Fig. 14

Depth Drilling Stop and Gauge. When it is required to drill a number of holes to an equal depth, it saves much time and uncertainty if the drilling machine can be set to drill to a definite limited depth. In the case of a machine such as the Champion, illustrated in Figs. 4 and 5, this is readily ensured by using the adjustable clamp collar fitted to the spindle.

The collar is set by means of a rule, as shown in Fig. 15,

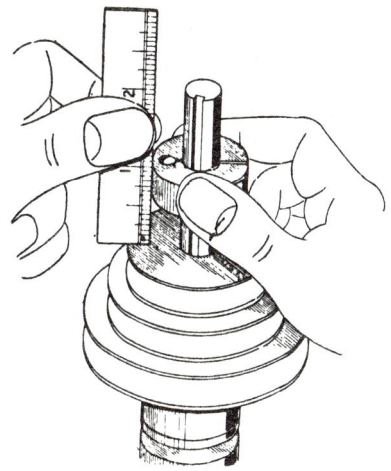

Fig. 15

and, when the adjustment has been made, the collar is secured in place on the spindle by tightening the clamping screw ; the downward travel of the spindle is then limited by the collar coming into contact with the face of the driving pulley.

To measure the downward feed of the drill when using a quill-type of machine, the quill itself is sometimes graduated, or as an alternative method, a portion of a rule is fitted into the split quill-housing, as shown in Fig. 16. Here, a small leaf spring is fitted behind the rule to provide frictional contact, and thus enable the rule to be set to the zero position at an inch mark at the start of the drilling operation.

The simple lever-feed drilling machine can also be fitted with a depth stop and gauge, but the actual construction must depend on the design of the individual machine.

Drilling Operations. The general principles involved in drilling with a drilling machine are similar to those employed when using a hand drill, as described in Part One which of course should be read before the present volume. In the former case the machine has its own motive power and ensures accuracy of drilling alignment, leaving only the feeding of the drill and, perhaps, the steadying of the work to the operator.

As before, the location of the drill hole is accurately set by marking-out, and its centre is then marked with a centre punch.

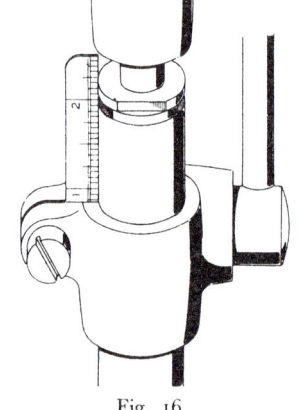

Fig. 16

If a large drill is started in the small punch mark so formed, it is quite possible that it will wander from the true centre owing to lack of guidance. To obviate this, the punch mark is enlarged with a small centre drill of the form illustrated in Fig. 17. When drilling small holes it will be advisable to use the smallest standard size of centre drill with a body of $\frac{1}{8}$ in. diameter and a drilling tip of 3/64 in. diameter.

These fine drills should be run at high speed with plenty of lubrication and the feed should not be forced or the slender drill tip may be broken off.

The centre drill is fed in until a countersunk hole is formed equal to the diameter of the following drill. Should the diameter of the hole to be drilled be appreciably greater than ⅛ in., it is advisable to drill a preliminary pilot hole both to save time and to enable the larger drill to cut more freely and with less feed pressure.

The next step is, therefore, to drill an ⅛ in. pilot hole in the work, and there need be no fear of this being out of centre if the ⅛ in. centre drill has been previously entered to its full diameter.

Fig. 17

Finally, the hole is enlarged to its full diameter in one or more stages, but it should be borne in mind that when larger drills are used the drilling speed should be reduced accordingly by altering the position of the belt on the step pulleys.

When drilling holes in sheet metal, it is advisable to secure the work to the drilling table by means of a clamp as illustrated in Fig. 11, and, in addition, the rate of feed should be reduced when the drill is nearly breaking through or it may grab and dig into the work.

If the drill is carried right through the work, take care that the drill point does not come into contact with the table ; a work table honeycombed as a result of thoughtless drilling is the sign of a careless workman. Damage of this sort can be avoided, either by allowing the drill to pass through one of the table slots, or by supporting the work on a piece of metal, ebonite, or hardwood. Before drilling a second hole, remove any burrs formed by the previous drilling as these will prevent the work from lying flat on the drill table.

When fine drills are used, there is a tendency for the drill to become jammed in a deeply drilled hole ; this

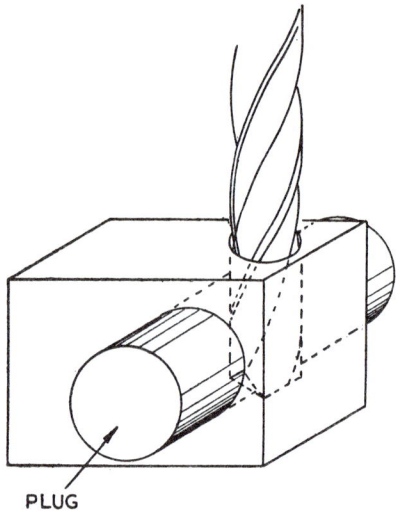

PLUG

Fig. 18

can be avoided by withdrawing the drill at frequent intervals and freeing it from cuttings with an oily brush while the machine is still running.

Drilling into a Hole. Where a hole has to be drilled to meet the side of a previously drilled hole, as shown in Fig. 18, there is the danger of the unsupported drill point being broken off as it breaks through. This can be avoided if a plug of material similar to that of the work is fitted to the first hole, so that the drill point is supported throughout its travel.

Drilling on an Inclined Surface. Should an attempt be made to drill a hole on an inclined surface, the drill will naturally tend to travel down the slope, and the side-strain imposed may break a slender drill or, at best, it will cause the hole to be drilled out of position. It is advisable, therefore, to prepare a flat work surface, either by filing, chipping or machining, prior to the marking-out and drilling operations.

Cross-drilling Shafts. An operation often required in the workshop is the drilling of a hole exactly across the centre of a round shaft. When a jig suitable for this purpose is not available, the following method may be adopted : a line is scribed through the centre of the shaft, as described in the section on marking-out in Part I, and this line is

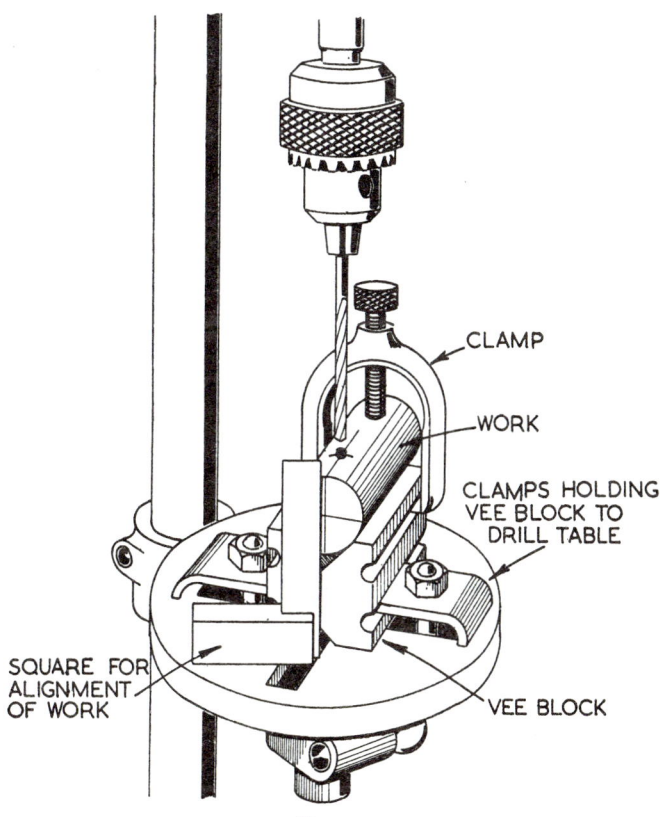

Fig. 19

continued for some distance along the shaft, as represented in Fig. 19. A centre punch mark is then made on this line to locate the hole at the required distance from the end of the shaft.

Next, the shaft is clamped in a V block resting on the drill table, with the scribed diameter line set vertically by means of a square.

A small centre drill is then used to enlarge the punch mark and to form a bearing for the point of the drill which follows to form the cross-hole.

Drilling Holes for Tapping. Although a list of tapping size holes is given in most books of reference, these holes will in many cases be found too small for general use and may be the cause of broken taps and out of line threads.

A method of selecting the correct size of tapping drill for a particular tap was described in Part I ; briefly, this consists in trying the tip of the taper tap in the holes of the drill gauge until a hole is found which admits the tap as far as the line indicating the bottom of the first thread.

If a parallel hole is drilled and tapped, the result will probably resemble the appearance shown in Fig. 20A, where it will be seen that the metal surrounding the hole has been raised in an irregular burr which will prevent the proper seating of a component against this surface. To avoid this, the hole, prior to tapping, should be enlarged to the full clearing size for a depth equal to some one-and-a-half threads, as shown in Fig. 20B.

If an attempt is made to enlarge the hole after the tapping operation has been completed, the mouth of the hole will not be formed concentric with the bore as the inclination of the threads will cause the point of the drill to be pushed to one side of the hole.

Tapping in the Drilling Machine. Although a tap will tend to keep upright in a hole which has ample clearance, and its squareness with the surface can be checked during a hand-tapping operation, machine tapping has the advantage that the tap is entered and guided truly in the work throughout the tapping operation. In commercial practice the tap is mounted in a drilling machine or in a special tapping machine, and a friction-driven tapping attachment is used to drive the tap and to prevent breakage when the bottom of the hole is reached.

This principle can be readily applied to the drilling machine with the tap held moderately tightly in the ordinary drill chuck. The tap is rotated either by pulling on the belt or, preferably, by turning the spindle by means of a handle secured to its upper end. The construction of a handle specially designed for this purpose is fully described in Chapter Six.

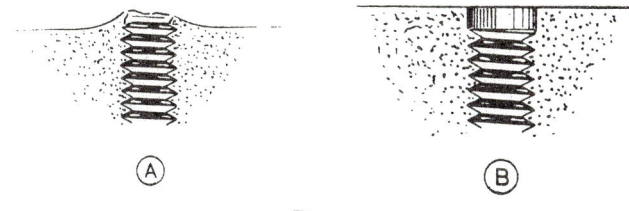

Fig. 20

As, when tapping in this way, both hands are occupied in holding the work and turning the machine, the downward pressure required to start the tap can be applied by means of a length of cord attached to the feed lever, and having at its lower end a loop to form a stirrup for the foot.

Countersinks. In order to allow screws with conical heads to lie flush with the surface of the work, the screw holes are recessed with a countersink having its cutting edges formed to an included angle of 90 deg. The commercial cutters with four or more cutting lips are liable to chatter and form a recess with a rough, waved surface; and although better results are obtained by using a very slow speed, this is not always possible in the case of the small drilling machine.

If, however, a flat-faced countersink having a single-cutting edge and a guide edge is used, this tendency to chatter will be prevented.

Full directions for making a cutter of the type suitable for use in the small drilling machine are given in Chapter Six.

Counterbores and Pin Drills. It is a rule in good engineering practice that where a nut or screw seats on a component it must do so on a flat surface truly square with the line of the screw hole.

When, therefore, a rough casting is drilled for the passage of a bolt, it is essential that, at the same time, the surface against which the nut bears must be correctly machined.

Again, where the work is recessed to receive the head of a cheese-headed screw, the bottom of the recess must be formed with a flat surface to afford a proper seating for the screw head.

These machining operations are usually carried out by means of a tool known as a counterbore, pin drill, or spot-face cutter.

Directions for making two types of this cutter are given in Chapter Six, and reference to the illustrations in that section will show their usual form.

When using these cutters a pilot hole is first drilled to fit the central guide peg, and after the machining with the cutter has been completed, the pilot hole is enlarged to its finished size.

It is advisable to run these tools at a slow or moderate speed in order to avoid chatter and to enable the depth of machining to be more readily controlled.

CHAPTER TWO

The Grinding Head—Driving the Machine Electric Grinding Machine—Angular Grinding Rest—Grinding Operations—Grinding Twist Drills.

As it is impossible to do good work with blunt or incorrectly sharpened tools, the importance of installing proper grinding equipment and adopting a sound method of sharpening the workshop tools can hardly be overstressed.

THE GRINDING MACHINE

Apart from the minor sharpening operations carried out with the aid of carborundum or oil bench stones, as described in Part I, the bulk of this work is done on a carborundum wheel mounted on the spindle of a grinding head.

A simple and inexpensive form of grinding head is illustrated in Fig. 21, where it will be seen that the spindle carries a grinding wheel at either end; usually, a coarse wheel for roughing and a fine wheel for finish grinding are fitted.

The spindle runs in bearings machined in the iron casting, and a small range of adjustment is provided by splitting the bearings on one side to enable them to be closed on the shaft by means of a clamp screw.

Needless to say, precision fitted bearings can hardly be expected in a machine of this type where the first cost is low, but if the spindle and bearings are later accurately hand-fitted by an experienced worker, the machine will run almost noiselessly even at high speed. A rather more elaborate form of grinding machine is shown in Fig. 22, and although the grinding rests are not designed for angular

Fig. 21

setting when grinding tools on the side of the wheel, this could be made good by fitting angular tool rests of the type described later in this chapter and in Chapter Six.

Driving The Machine Small machines can be driven from an electric motor by means of a sewing machine belt joined with a U fastener, as described in the case of the drilling machine.

The grinding heads illustrated have a pulley fitted to the spindle between the two bearings; this usually entails driving the machine from a motor or lineshaft situated either above or behind the grinder, as shown in Fig. 45, in Chapter Four.

If, on the other hand, the pulley is fitted to one end of the spindle and a single wheel only is mounted on the shaft, then a belt drive can be taken from a motor fixed below the bench.

Where, as shown in Fig. 46, Chapter Four, the driving

pulley projects beyond the edge of the bench, there is no need to cut a gap in the bench top for the passage of the belt.

A motor mounted below the bench has the advantage of being well protected from the abrasive dust formed during grinding and, further, it does not then occupy valuable space on the bench top.

It is true that with this arrangement a single wheel only is available, but this may be found sufficient for most purposes in the small workshop.

Should it be decided, however, to install both a rough and a finish-grinding wheel, then this method of driving can still be employed if two grinding heads are used and are driven from a single motor; but in this case the grinding head nearer the operator should be mounted on a wooden base so that it can be readily detached from the bench top to give full access to the second machine.

When this form of installation is adopted, the grinding rest can be made to serve either machine if each is furnished with a base bracket to which the rest can be transferred when required for use.

Where the grinding machine is installed near the other machine tools, it is essential that they should be protected

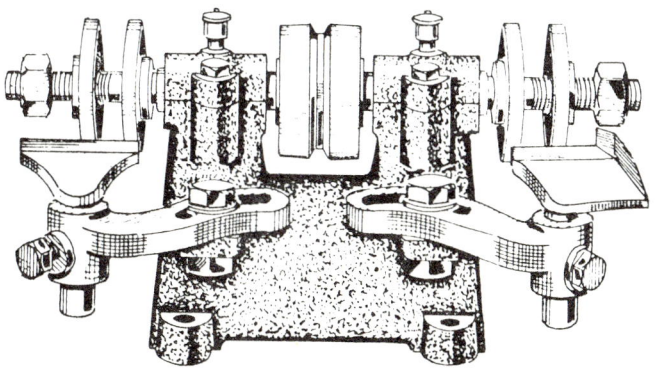

Fig. 22

from abrasive dust either by means of a light wooden screen or by the temporary use of a large sheet of cardboard.

If the best results are to be obtained when grinding tools, it is important that the wheel should be driven at a surface speed of approximately 5,000 ft. a min. in accordance with the following table :

Wheel diameter	Rev. per min.
1 in.	19,000
2 ,,	9,500
3 ,,	6,400
4 ,,	4,800
5 ,,	3,800
6 ,,	3,200

The tool merchant will supply grinding wheels suitable for ordinary tool grinding in the small workshop, but if further information on this subject, or about tool grinding in general, is sought, reference may be made to *Sharpening Small Tools*, published by Argus Books Ltd.

The Electric Grinding Machine. The "Black and Decker" self-contained grinding machine, illustrated in Fig. 23, has the advantage that it can be placed in any required position on the bench, or on a side bench where the danger from abrasive dust is well removed from the machine tools; in addition, its position can be fixed without reference to the requirements of a belt drive.

Two 5 in. diameter grinding wheels are attached to the spindle to provide for rough and finish grinding respectively.

Although the grinding rests fitted are intended for use in connection with the periphery of the wheel, it should not be a difficult matter to make and fit adjustable angular rests for grinding tools on the side faces of the wheels. As already mentioned these rests are described here and also in Chapter Six.

Fig. 23

Angular Grinding Rest. Some form of adjustable rest is required to support the tool and to enable it to be presented to the grinding wheel so that the correct angle is automatically ground at the cutting edge.

In factories the periphery of the wheel is generally used for tool grinding, but in the small workshop this work will be facilitated if, instead, the flat sides of the wheel are used ; for it is much easier to set the grinding angle from the flat side surface than from the curved periphery of the wheel.

It is recommended, therefore, that a simple, adjustable, angular rest of the pattern illustrated in Fig. 24, should be used when fixed to the bench adjacent to the grinding head, or to the machine itself.

A convenient way of making an adjustable rest is to use the hand rest belonging to the lathe, as shown in Fig. 25. The base portion is fitted with a pillar which at its upper end carries a work table that is readily adjustable to any required angle by means of the engraved graduated scale. In addition, the table can be raised or lowered to enable angular grinding to be carried out on the periphery of the wheel. The base is secured to the bench by a stud fitted with a wing nut to allow the rest to be set in position as required.

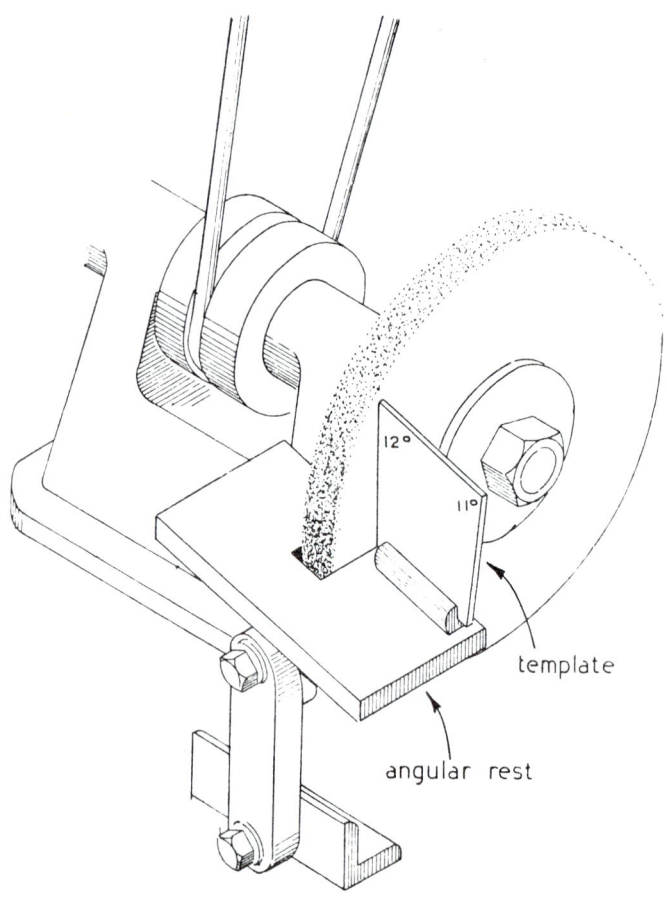

Fig. 24

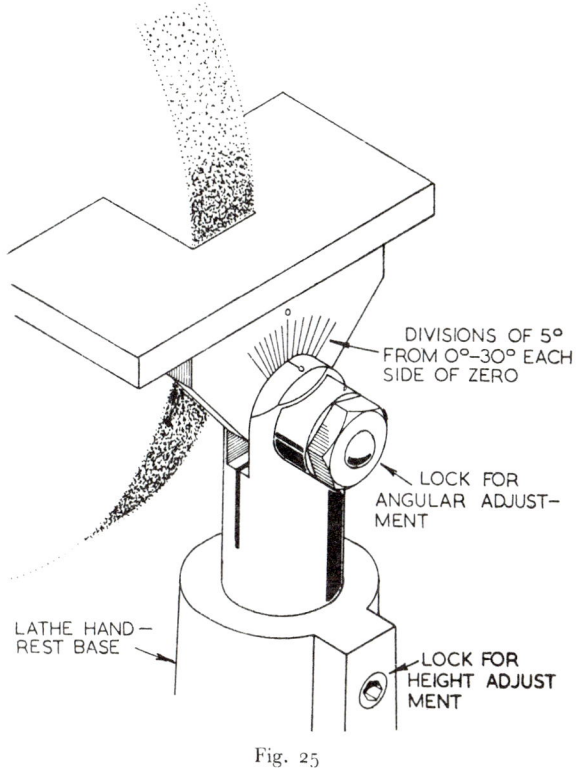

Fig. 25

Although grinding heads are obtainable with grinding rests incorporated, these rests, except in the more expensive machines, are generally designed for grinding tools on the periphery of the wheel as in the case of the grinding machine illustrated in Fig. 22 ; but just as an angular rest can be made for attachment to the bench, as described in Chapter Six, so also can this type of rest usually be fitted to the machine itself without great difficulty, if the method of grinding the tools on the side-face of the wheel is preferred.

Grinding Operations. Apart from grinding twist drills, the chief use made of the grinding machine in the small workshop is for sharpening the lathe tools. Now, this operation must be carried out with considerable accuracy, otherwise the free-cutting properties of the tool may be impaired or the strength of its cutting edge reduced.

If a new lathe tool or one that has been ground in a factory is examined, it will be found that the areas ground to form the cutting edges are flat, uniform surfaces, but on the other hand, a tool ground by an inexperienced workman without proper equipment will, in all probability, show a series of small ground surfaces crossed by uneven ridges. The even, flat surfaces in the former case give the true tool form, and the ridges and hollows in the latter largely detract from the cutting efficiency.

This difference of surface finish probably results from an angular grinding rest being used in the factory, and a method of free-hand grinding being adopted by the casual worker.

The advantages gained when using a proper rest are so outstanding that they should not, if possible, be neglected ; moreover, when attempting to grind free-hand and using the eye and the hand to guide the tool, any small slip may result in much time and labour being wasted in making good the grinding error.

As has already been mentioned, the use of the side faces of the wheel is to be preferred for ordinary tool grinding in the workshop. When the periphery of a small wheel is used to grind a tool, the surfaces so formed will be markedly concave, and where two such surfaces meet at the tool's cutting edge, this edge will be undercut and weakened ; further, not only is it a difficult matter to adjust the height of the rest to grind an exact angle, but the setting of the rest will necessarily vary according to the thickness of the tool.

If, on the other hand, the side of the wheel is used, the rest can be readily set to grind an exact angle on the tool irrespective of the tool's thickness.

A convenient method of setting the rest is illustrated in Fig. 24, where it will be seen that a sheet-metal template, cut to the required angle, rests on the work table and the upright edge is brought into contact with the wheel. In the drawing the template is shown mounted in a rule holder, but a rectangular block may be used to maintain the template in a vertical position.

Fig. 26

To set the work table, the upper hexagon-headed screw is slackened, and it may be necessary, at the same time, to slacken the lower screw to enable the gap in the table to be adjusted to clear the sides of the wheel. When these adjustments have been made, both these screws should be firmly secured to prevent the table from shifting during the subsequent grinding operations.

It will be noticed that the template is cut to an angle of 12 deg. at one end and to 11 deg. at the other. The reason for this is that when grinding the tool on the coarse wheel to form the clearance angle the 12 deg. setting is used, and this is followed by finish-grinding to 11 deg. on the fine wheel.

In this way little metal will have to be removed at the final grinding operation, and not only will the whole grinding process be quickened, but there will be less danger of overheating the tip of the tool.

Although the question of the form and the angles at the cutting edges of lathe tools is dealt with in Chapter

Five, it will be advisable here to consider briefly how angular grinding is employed to form a typical lathe tool. Other tools vary in form, but the methods used for grinding their cutting angles are the same.

The stages in the finish grinding of a knife tool are illustrated in Fig. 26. First, the side clearance is ground with the grinding rest set to 11 deg.; next, the front clearance angle is formed with the rest in the same position; then, with the rest reset to 20 deg. in the opposite direction, follows the operation of grinding the slope on the upper surface, or the side-rake angle as it is termed and which will be explained in Chapter Five.

When applying the tool to the grinding wheel, the tool must be kept moving in a direction parallel with the side-face of the wheel; it must not be allowed to dwell and only light pressure should be used, otherwise it may be overheated and its cutting properties spoilt.

In spite of advice that is sometimes given, on no account should the tool be dipped in water to cool it during the course of the grinding operation, for this will almost certainly result in the formation of surface cracks in the cutting edge, and, when the tool is put to work, particles of metal will break away leaving the cutting edge blunt or jagged.

Nevertheless, where much metal has to be removed, the tool must be allowed to cool during the grinding operation, and this can be hastened by letting the tool lie on a metal block. Should several tools have to be ground, it is better to deal with each in turn for a short time so that cooling can take place meanwhile.

The final sharpening operation consists in honing the tip of the tool to an angle of 10 deg. on an oil stone; this is carried out with the aid of a stoning jig, and the process will be described in the appropriate place in Chapter Five.

Grinding Twist Drills. Although an experienced workman can, with the aid of a gauge, grind a large drill with some degree of accuracy, this is far from being the case where a novice is concerned and the drill is of small diameter.

If the drill is ground so that the cutting lips are of unequal length or do not lie at the same angle with the long axis of the drill, then the drill will neither cut a hole true to size nor will it pursue a straight path.

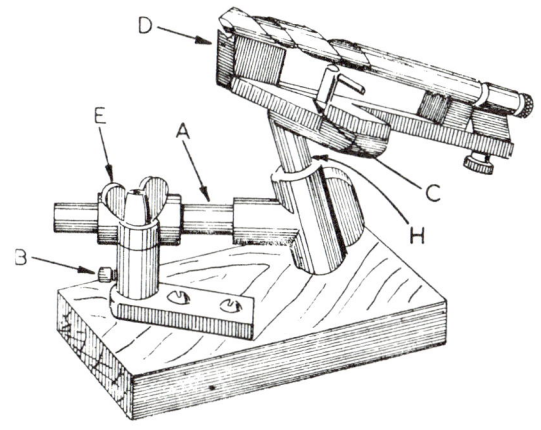

Fig. 27

If, from lack of proper equipment, free-hand grinding has to be used, some idea of the hand movements required when grinding can be gathered by rolling the conical face of a large drill against the side of the stationary grinding wheel. These movements should be practised until the tip of the drill can at all times be kept in level contact with the wheel ; and after making a trial passage of the drill on the revolving wheel, the tip should be measured with the rule and protractor to see if the grinding has been carried out correctly.

On the other hand, a quick and reliable method of grinding twist drills is to use a grinding jig in accordance with ordinary workshop practice.

A small, accurately made jig suitable for use in the small

workshop is the Potts drill grinding jig, illustrated in Fig. 27 ; this appliance will sharpen drills up to ½ in. in diameter.

The jig itself is attached to the bench by means of the base bracket shown in the drawing, and after the spindle (A) has been set parallel with the axis of the wheel spindle, the clamping screw is tightened. To give the correct back-off or clearance angle, the calliper jaws (C) are set to the diameter of the drill shank.

Next, the spindle (A) is moved towards the wheel until the drill carrier (D) is just clear of the side of the wheel ; the wing nut (E) is then tightened.

The drill is then placed in the jig, as shown in the drawing, with one lip in contact with the lip gauge attached to the carrier (D).

When the grinding wheel has been started, the drill is fed towards the wheel by means of the feed screw shown at the extreme right of the drawing. The grinding operation is then carried out by swinging the jig about its pivot (H).

Both lips of the drill are ground in this way, with the same setting of the feed screw, until they are evenly ground over the whole of their surfaces.

Some makers of both belt-driven and self-contained electric grinders supply twist-drill grinding jigs for attachment to their machines, but when purchasing these appliances it is advisable to make sure that they will deal with the smallest drills that are likely to be used.

CHAPTER THREE

General Description—Types of Small Lathes
—Methods of Driving—Lathe Accessories
—Lathe Maintenance.

As will be seen in the drawing in Fig. 28, which represents a small lathe of the type generally used in the small workshop, the modern lathe is a highly developed machine capable of a wide range of work in addition to ordinary turning operations.

THE LATHE

The smaller components shown in the drawing are named so that they can be readily identified when referred to both here and in later chapters.

The Bed. This is the main casting on which the other components are assembled, and on its proper design and construction the accuracy of the lathe as a whole will largely depend.

When the bed is supported on two widely-spaced feet it may be distorted if bolted down to an uneven surface such as the top of a wooden bench. This can be readily demonstrated by applying a test indicator to the free end of a long bar held in the lathe chuck and then tightening the holding-down bolts ; if the surface of the bench is untrue, the test indicator will record the deformity imparted to the bed.

Should the bed be distorted in this way, the lathe will not machine truly, and packing strips must be placed under the bed feet to level the surface on which the lathe stands.

The bed of the lathe illustrated has what amounts to a single foot-piece, and, here, distortion is much less likely to arise, when bolting down, as this part represents the most rigid portion of the bed.

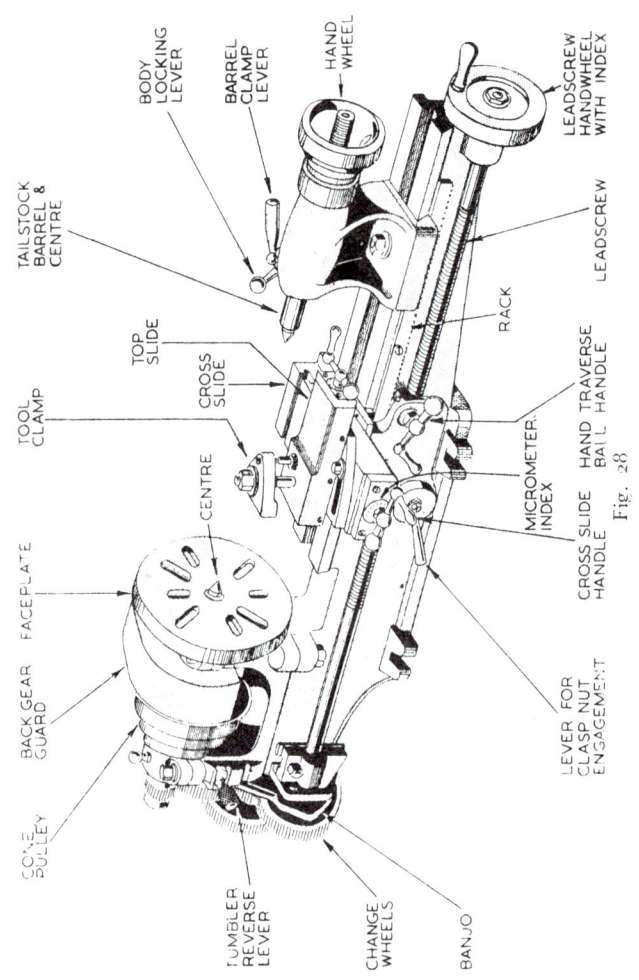

Fig. 28

On the upper part of the bed an accurate slide-way is machined, composed of two shears, as they are termed; this carries the headstock and the tailstock in true axial alignment and, at the same time, the saddle and the tailstock are guided on a straight path as they are moved along the bed. The bed shears fall short of the headstock, leaving a gap to allow for turning work of large diameter.

The Headstock. This is a rigid casting fitted with bearings in which the lathe mandrel rotates. Different types of bearings are used for this purpose, but plain parallel bearings are, in general, to be preferred.

In order to provide the low mandrel speeds required for some classes of work, a back gear, not unlike a motor car gearbox, is fitted, consisting of a gear wheel reduction drive between the belt pulley and the mandrel.

The lathe has, therefore, six speeds : three direct, and three indirect through the back gear; these are arranged in even steps from the lowest to the highest mandrel speed.

The Saddle. As shown in the drawing, the base or sole plate of the saddle, which is guided by the shears of the lathe bed, carries a cross-slide on its upper surface. This slide has a travel of several inches and is controlled by means of a feed-screw fitted with an operating handle and an index. The index is divided into thousandths of an inch and is adjustable so that it can be set to the zero position when turning work to an exact diameter.

Bolted to the cross-slide is the top or tool-slide which also has an index fitted to its feed screw. The slide can be set to any required angle by means of its graduated scale, and in this way it is used for forming bevels or turning short tapers.

A vertical plate, called the apron, is attached to the front of the saddle sole plate; this carries the quick or hand-traverse gear which engages the toothed rack bar attached to the front of the bed. The apron has also attached to it the divided clasp-nut with its operating gear which closes the nut on the leadscrew and thus provides the normal feed for the saddle.

The Tailstock. The body of this component is usually formed in two parts : a sole plate to engage the slides of the lathe bed, and an upper portion capable of being set over across the line of the bed to enable tapers to be turned on work mounted between the lathe centres. When the tailstock has been set either centrally or to one side, the two portions are secured with a clamp bolt. The sole plate is secured to the bed by means of a quick-acting clamp and locking lever.

Fig. 29

The tailstock barrel, which receives support from the whole length of the upper part of the tailstock casting, is secured in place by the action of a clamp and locking lever whenever work is mounted between the lathe centres.

To facilitate drilling holes to an exact depth, the tailstock barrel should be graduated.

The Feed Gear. Where a separate feed shaft is not fitted, the saddle is traversed along the lathe bed by means of the leadscrew when engaged with the clasp-nut attached to the saddle apron.

A handle is attached to the right-hand end of the leadscrew to enable the saddle to be fed by hand when turning short lengths ; in addition, the hand wheel carrying this handle is fitted with an index graduated in thousandths of an inch to permit of an exact length being machined on the work.

When an automatic feed for the saddle is required, the leadscrew is turned by the mandrel through a train of gear wheels mounted on the lathe quadrant, or banjo as it is sometimes called.

The relative speeds of the mandrel and leadscrew depend, of course, on the size of the wheels used, but reference to the makers' chart will show the wheel trains required for either screwcutting or for ordinary turning.

To enable the saddle to be traversed either towards or away from the headstock, a tumbler gear, consisting of a secondary gear train, is sometimes fitted to the mandrel ; this has the further advantage of providing a neutral or no-drive position in addition to the forward and reverse movements.

Lathe Types. There is no need to give, here, a detailed description of the lathes briefly referred to below, for full information in each case, together with illustrations showing the constructional details, can be found in the respective manufacturers' catalogues.

The Perfecto Lathe. illustrated in Fig. 29, is of robust design having an anvil bed that enables the purchaser to mount the Lathe on the bench without fear of distorting the machine and impairing its accuracy.

The Perfecto Lathe is available in three models. The basic machine is not provided with a driving motor or self-contained countershaft whilst the other two models have motor driving units supplied as standard. The more expensive model, seen in the illustration, has adequate protection by guards fitted over the change wheels and final drive belt, whilst the intermediate model has a guard over the mandrel belt only.

The centre height of the Perfecto lathe is $3\frac{1}{2}$ inches (85.7 mm) and its capacity between centres 16 inches (406.7 mm). The mandrel is bored 5/8 in. diam. (15.9 mm) allowing the user rather more scope than is sometimes obtainable in a small lathe.

Fig. 30

The Myford ML10 Screwsetting Lathe, illustrated in Fig. 30 has been designed to provide the user with a simple machine tool at a competitive price. The standard equipment included is comprehensive and there is a range of additional fitments obtainable that will greatly extend the versatility of this very useful machine.

The illustration shows the lathe mounted on its stand and equipped with self-contained motor drive through V-belts.

The Myford ML7 Lathe. This machine has been more recently designed and embodies many up-to-date features which will be found particularly useful by the model engineer, and also by those undertaking other forms of mechanical work where a wide range of adaptability is essential. The design includes the provision of a robust and rigid mandrel which enables heavy cuts to be taken when required. A very extensive range of accessories and fittings is available, including gear cutting and taper turning attachments.

As shown in Fig. 31 a very effective form of self-contained motor-drive is fitted.

The Lathe Drive. Formerly, the alternative to foot

power was a belt-drive taken from a power-driven countershaft, but nowadays, manufacturers usually supply their lathes with a self-contained electric motor driving-unit, fitted either as a standard part of the equipment or at an extra cost.

The ML7 lathe illustrated in Fig. 31 is fitted with a driving unit of this type attached to the rear of the bed; the constructional details of the device are shown in Fig. 32.

Fig. 31

The electric motor is mounted on a swinging platform to allow the tension of the motor-driving belt to be correctly adjusted. This belt drives the countershaft seen at the top of the figure, and the swinging bracket carrying this shaft is controlled by a ball-ended lever for releasing the belt tension when changing speed.

In addition, the position of this bracket can be adjusted to set the belt tension correctly for the final drive to the lathe pulley.

As will be seen, a neat, well-fitting, sliding cover is provided to guard the belts.

Other methods of driving the lathe when installed in the workshop will be described in the next chapter.

Lathe Accessories. Although the makers furnish their lathes with certain accessories, the purchase of others is essential before the lathe can be put to work on the more usual turning operations ; some accessories, however, such as a tool turret, whilst not indispensable, certainly do add to the pleasure and convenience of using the lathe.

Fig. 32

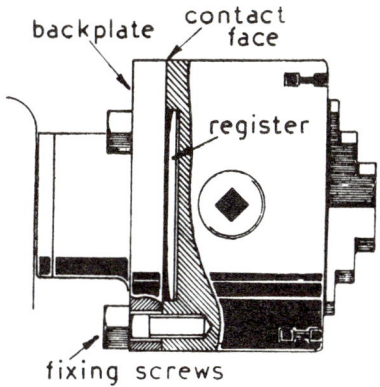

Fig. 33

Chucks. These are attached to the mandrel either directly by having a thread cut at the back of the chuck itself, or more commonly by being bolted to a back plate which is in turn screwed on to the threaded nose of the mandrel.

The method of fitting a chuck to its back plate is illustrated in Fig. 33, where it will be seen that a raised bolting face is formed on the back of the chuck, and, as shown, it is to this face that the back plate is bolted.

The Self-centring Chuck, illustrated in Fig. 34, usually has three jaws, and it will hold the work firmly and with but little error of centring.

Two sets of jaws are provided for holding either on the outside or on the inside of the work.

When changing the numbered jaws, they must not only be inserted in their right slots, but the end of the thread on the scroll which operates the jaws must be engaged with the jaws in the correct order, starting with No. 1 and finishing with No. 3 jaw.

The Four-Jaw Independent Chuck is shown in Fig. 35. Here, the individual jaws are moved one at a time either

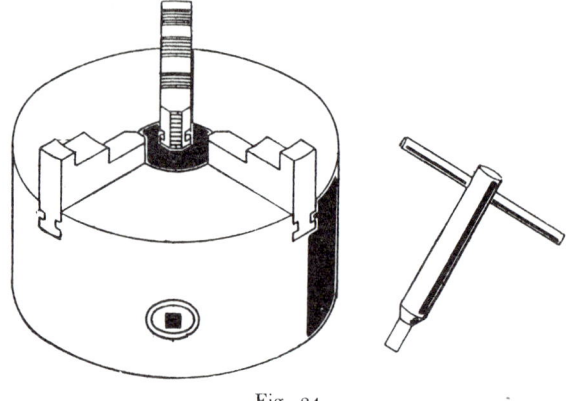

Fig. 34

to centre the work accurately or to set it in any other position required.

Directions for setting work in this type of chuck are given in Chapter Five. As the chuck has four jaws it will hold very securely even when the work is of irregular shape.

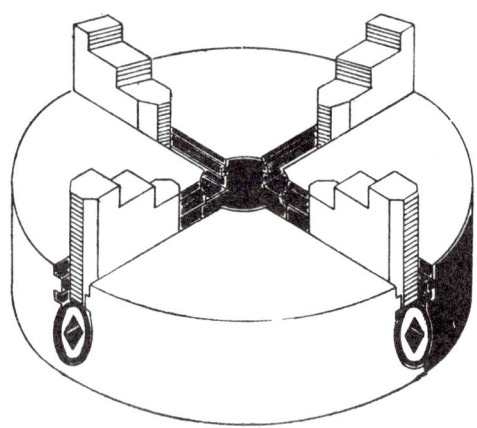

Fig. 35

When changing the jaws to give inside or outside gripping, they are merely reversed in their slots, for each is actuated by its own feedscrew.

Either of the two mandrel chucks described can be fitted to the tailstock, if required, by means of the adapter shown in Fig. 36, which has one end formed to engage the taper in the tailstock barrel, and the other end is a replica of the screwed nose of the mandrel.

The Drill Chuck. When drilling work, held in the mandrel chuck, by means of a drill mounted in the tailstock, as described in Chapter Five, the drill is preferably secured in a true-holding key chuck of the type illustrated in Fig. 37A ; in this case, the chuck is mounted on a double-taper arbor of the form shown in Fig. 37B.

The Drill Pad. If, however, the drill is held in the mandrel chuck and the work is supported and fed forward

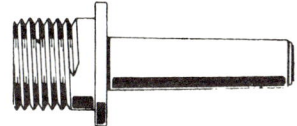

Fig. 36

by the tailstock, then a drilling pad, as illustrated in Fig. 38, is used both to protect the tailstock barrel from possible damage, and also to afford a greater area of support for the work.

As will be seen, two heads are supplied to fit on to the arbor when secured by its taper in the tailstock barrel ; the plain, flat head is used for ordinary work, and the V-grooved fitting will locate a round bar to enable a hole to be drilled through its centre.

Four-tool Turret. This device, which is illustrated in Fig. 39, replaces the usual single-tool clamp fitted to the lathe top slide.

As four tools of different forms can, at the same time, be mounted in it, tool changing for each turning operation

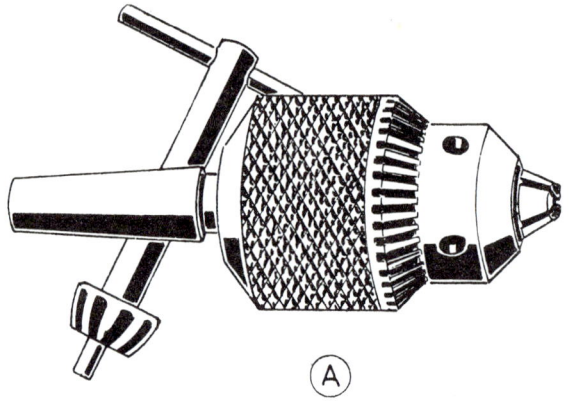

Fig. 37A

is avoided, for the turret has merely to be rotated to bring any tool required into the correct position.

To facilitate accurate repetition turning of parts, a ratchet gear locates the turret at any one of eight stations, thus enabling the tools to be accurately reset to the work as they are successively brought into use.

The clamping lever shown in the photograph secures the turret firmly in place after its position has been set.

The Fixed Steady. When clamped to the lathe bed, as illustrated in Fig. 40, this appliance is employed to support

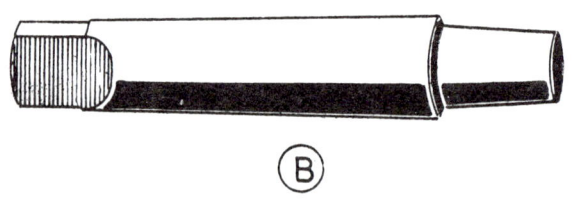

Fig. 37B

the overhanging end of the work, such as a long shaft, held in the mandrel chuck. This becomes necessary when the work has to be faced and axially drilled as described in Chapter Five. The steady is fitted with three adjustable, bronze jaws which are set to make contact with the work and thus afford it a supporting bearing.

Fig. 38

Fig. 39

The Travelling Steady. As its name implies, this form of steady, which is illustrated in Fig. 41, travels in the wake of the tool and gives support to the work in both a vertical and a horizontal direction against the tool's cutting thrust.

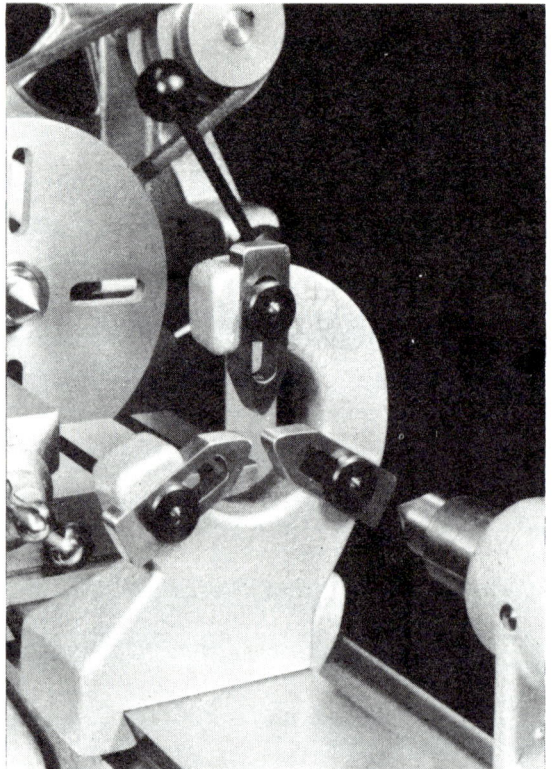

Fig. 40

Either hardened steel or bronze jaws are used, but the latter may be preferred as they do not damage the finished surface of the work. It is essential that the construction should provide for fixing the pressure pads securely, otherwise they may become displaced during the course of the turning operation.

Hand Rest. The rest illustrated in Fig. 42 is employed when turning work with hand tools, as described in Chapter Five,

Fig. 41

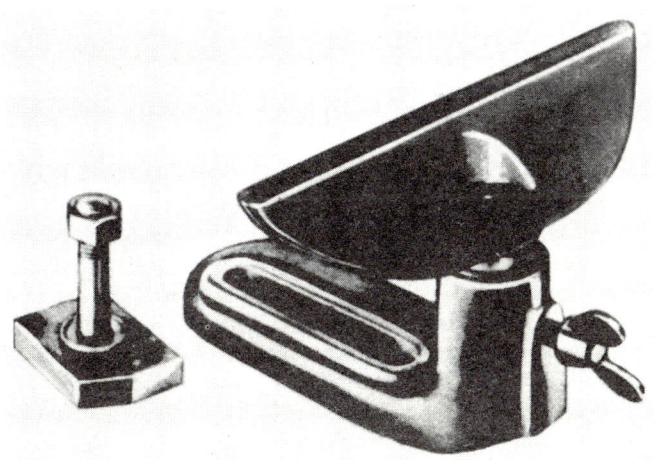

Fig. 42

For this purpose, it is bolted to the lathe cross slide, and after the rest itself has been adjusted to the correct height to suit the tool used, it is secured in place by tightening the wing nut shown in the figure.

Lathe Maintenance. The first essential in looking after a lathe is to keep the working parts clean and well oiled.

Not only should the slides and other parts be kept free from metal chips, but when not in use, the lathe should be covered with a cloth or sheet to exclude the dust that is so harmful to the working parts.

A small brush can be used for clearing the chips from the slides, after which they should be wiped with a clean rag and then lubricated. Medicinal paraffin is a useful lubricant for the lathe bed and slides as it does not become sticky and form a varnish-like film on the lathe parts. Where oil is used, any dried deposit can be readily removed from the metal parts or paintwork with the aid of methylated or surgical spirit.

A good quality thin oil should be used for lubricating the mandrel and other bearings.

The leadscrew and the feed screws of the slides should also receive periodic cleaning and lubrication.

As the mandrel bearings of a new lathe become bedded-in, they may require adjustment to remove any play both in the journals and in the thrust bearing ; this should be carried out in accordance with the instructions issued by the manufacturers.

The gibs fitted to the saddle and slides must also be kept in proper adjustment to eliminate play, but over-tightening of the slides should be avoided as this causes needless wear in the feed mechanism ; moreover, a well-fitted slide should move quite freely and without play if given only a very small working clearance when the gib is adjusted.

The thrust nuts fitted to the feed screws of the slides should be kept in adjustment so that excessive backlash, which would interfere with the proper working of the feed mechanism, is not allowed to develop.

CHAPTER FOUR

Setting out the Machine Tool Bench—Line-Shafts and Countershafts—Direct Drive from Electric Motors — Installation of Motors.

In previous chapters the driving of the individual machine tools has been considered, but where the tools are grouped, as often happens in the small workshop, and more particularly perhaps in the indoor workshop, then it is advisable to adopt a definite plan in arranging the machines and their drives so that they can be used to the best advantage.

DRIVING MACHINE TOOLS IN THE WORKSHOP

As the question of economy as well as convenience may arise, in some instances a single electric motor may be made to drive more than one machine. Where a room within the house is fitted out as a workshop, compactness may be desirable both to save space and to maintain a idy appearance.

In these circumstances, it is not unusual to find the machine tools grouped on a single bench with sufficient space left for installing the vice and carrying out hand work.

A convenient form of layout is illustrated in Fig. 43. It shows the lathe and drilling machine mounted on the bench and coupled to a common lineshaft driven by a single motor.

When the operator works alone and only one machine at a time is used, a $\frac{1}{4}$ h.p. motor will generally be found sufficient for driving a $3\frac{1}{2}$ in. lathe, unless high speeds are required and the lathe makers recommend the fitting of a larger motor.

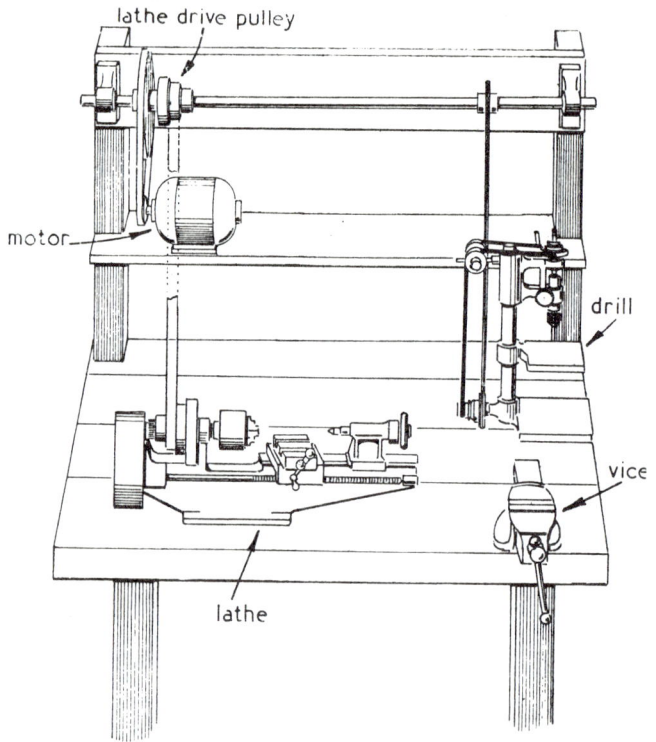

Fig. 43

Although the lineshaft can be mounted to run in plain bearings, ball-bearing shaft brackets are strongly recommended for this purpose, as frictional losses are greatly reduced and lubrication and other attention are then required only at long intervals.

Shaft brackets of the plain or ball-bearing type, as well as the necessary pulleys and shafting, are standard commodities and can normally be obtained from the tool merchant.

Lathe makers usually recommend that the countershaft speed should be some 400 r.p.m. ; this figure must, therefore, be taken into account, when fitting the belt pulleys, to ensure that the reduction ratio obtained will provide the correct countershaft speed.

If the motor installed runs at, say, 1,200 r.p.m., the ratio of the diameters of the pulleys used should, therefore, be 1 : 3, which means that if a 2 in. pulley is fitted to the motor, a 6 in. diameter pulley is needed on the countershaft or lineshaft.

When V pulleys are used in conjunction with a V belt,

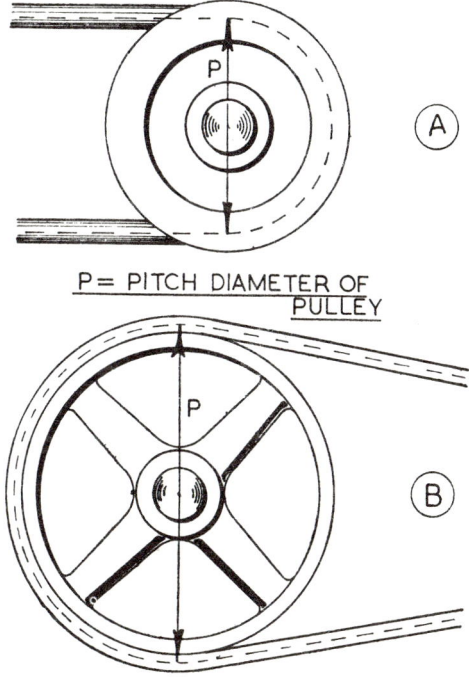

Fig. 44

these pulley sizes refer to the pitch diameter which is measured from the middle line of the belt's thickness as it lies in the groove of the pulley.

This is illustrated diagrammatically in Fig. 44A, where the belt is shown bedding deeply into the pulley.

The pitch diameter or effective diameter of the pulley is then represented by the arrow-headed dimension line which indicates the diameter taken up by the centre line of the belt when lying in the pulley groove.

Where the belt runs on a large plain-faced pulley, as shown in Fig. 44B, the pitch diameter of the pulley is again measured between two diametrically opposite points lying on the belt centre line.

In the arrangement illustrated in Fig. 43 the lineshaft takes the place of a separate countershaft to save complication and expense, and the machines are started and stopped by using the switch controlling the electric motor. Either machine can be temporarily put out of action by removing its belt from the driving pulley and then suspending the belt from a hook to keep it clear of the driving shaft.

It will be seen in the drawing that the position of the motor necessitates a very short belt drive; this is best catered for by using a V belt in conjunction with a V pulley fitted to the motor shaft, but the large driven pulley should have a plain, flat face as the frictional contact obtained will be ample for an efficient drive. The shelf on which the motor is mounted will also provide space for storing the lathe chucks and other accessories.

The vice is fitted directly over one of the bench legs in order to afford a rigid mounting, and although some space has been allowed for hand work, this might well be increased by lengthening the bench for large work.

It is intended that the complete bench assembly should be placed in a good light near a window and, when artificial lighting is needed, an adjustable lamp bracket can be attached to the motor shelf to allow the light to be swung into a position to illuminate either of the machine tools or the bench vice.

It will be noticed that a grinding machine has not been fitted to the bench, for in a compact assembly of this form it is usually preferable to mount the grinder on a separate shelf or small bench in order to keep abrasive dust well away from the machine tools.

A rather more ambitious arrangement is illustrated in Fig. 45, where it will be seen that a larger bench is used which not only provides more space for hand work, but at the same time allows the grinding machine to be mounted in a safe place on the bench top.

More floor space will, of course, be needed, and it is intended that the far end of the bench, as seen in the drawing, should be placed towards the window so that the operator has room to work and use the tools installed on either side of the bench.

The grinding machine is mounted at one end of the bench and a plywood baffle or screen is fitted to protect the lathe from abrasive dust.

Although, for the sake of clarity, it is not shown in the drawing, a metal dust shield should be fitted to the grinder itself to limit, as far as possible, the dispersion of emery dust and afford greater protection for the machine tools.

The grinder is directly driven from the motor shaft by a pulley of the correct diameter to drive the grinding wheel at the proper speed. As in the previous example, the lathe and the drilling machine are driven from either end of the lineshaft which may, in addition, carry a pulley for driving attachments, such as a milling device, fitted to the lathe saddle ; but it should be made clear that the amount of power that can be transmitted in this way is limited by the whip of the shaft when under load and the distance of the pulley from a supporting bearing.

In order not to confuse the drawing, a stretcher or tie-bar has been omitted, but if this is fitted across the tops of the upright bench members, the rigidity of the assembly will be increased and, in addition, the tie-bar will form a convenient point of attachment for the bracket of the adjustable lamp used to light the bench.

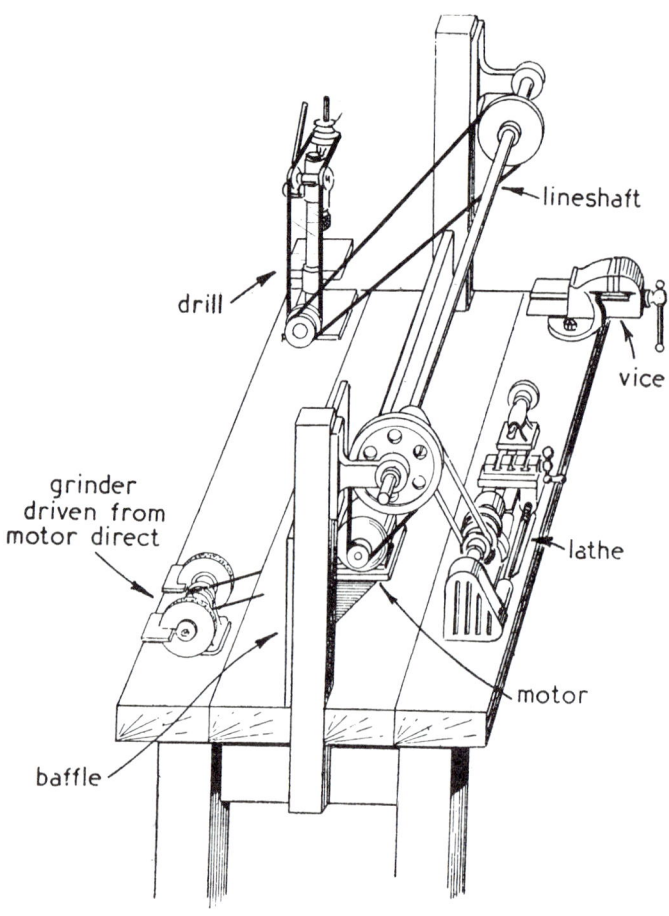

Fig. 45

There is much to be said for providing the extra space shown in the drawing, for it will be apparent that on the left side of the bench ample room is left for installing a hand-shaping machine, or a larger drilling machine with self-contained drive.

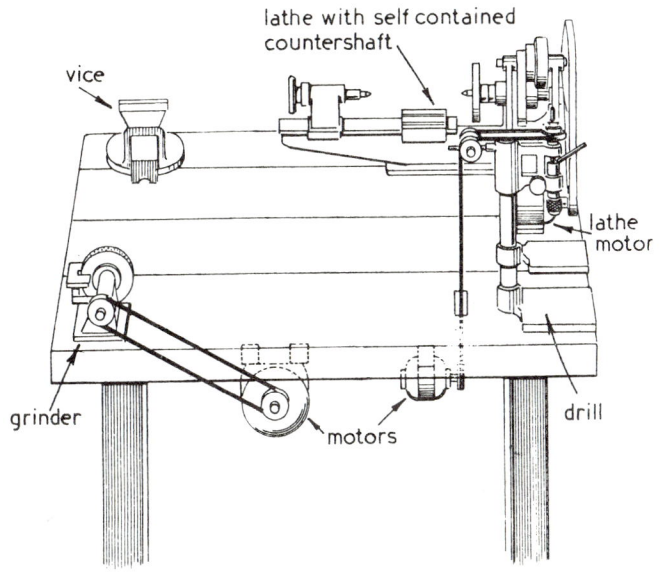

Fig. 46

The arrangement illustrated in Fig. 46 is designed to afford the maximum of free space on the top of a small bench by making the drives of the machine tools as compact as possible.

The lathe is driven by a self-contained motor driving-unit of the type now supplied by the makers of many well-known lathes.

This unit has the advantage of taking up but little bench space as it requires no separate countershaft or supporting uprights. The lathe with its drive-unit can thus be mounted on the bench exactly where required and without reference to any outside source of drive.

The motor driving the drilling machine is mounted, as described in Chapter I, below the bench where it does not encroach on the bench surface and, moreover, it is there well-protected from chips although readily removable when required. The belt passes through a hole cut in the bench top and leads directly to the guide pulleys fitted to the head of the drilling machine.

The grinding machine is also driven by a motor fixed to the under-side of the bench top. These motors can be easily removed for cleaning and lubrication if they are attached to a wooden base which slides in runners fixed to the under surface of the bench top.

Although, to simplify the arrangement of the drive, a grinding machine with a single wheel is used ; as mentioned in Chapter II, a second grinder can be installed in order to provide both a coarse and a fine wheel for tool sharpening. In this case, either the bases of the grinders are secured to the bench by means of bolts fitted with wing nuts, or the bases are made to travel in slides to enable either machine to be moved into place when needed.

The motor is, here, in a convenient position for driving any other machine that may be brought into temporary use, such as rotary cutters and polishing wheels attached to a flexible shaft carrying a driving pulley.

Although a bench of comparatively small size is shown in the drawing, it will be seen that space is available for hand work or for mounting additional tools.

It sometimes happens that, owing to lack of space, a machine has to be installed in the workshop in a position where a drive from the lineshaft or from an adjacent motor cannot be easily arranged.

The best solution of this difficulty is to drive the machine from a motor specially installed for the purpose ; but, on the other hand, the expense may seem hardly warranted when the machine in question is but rarely used, and there

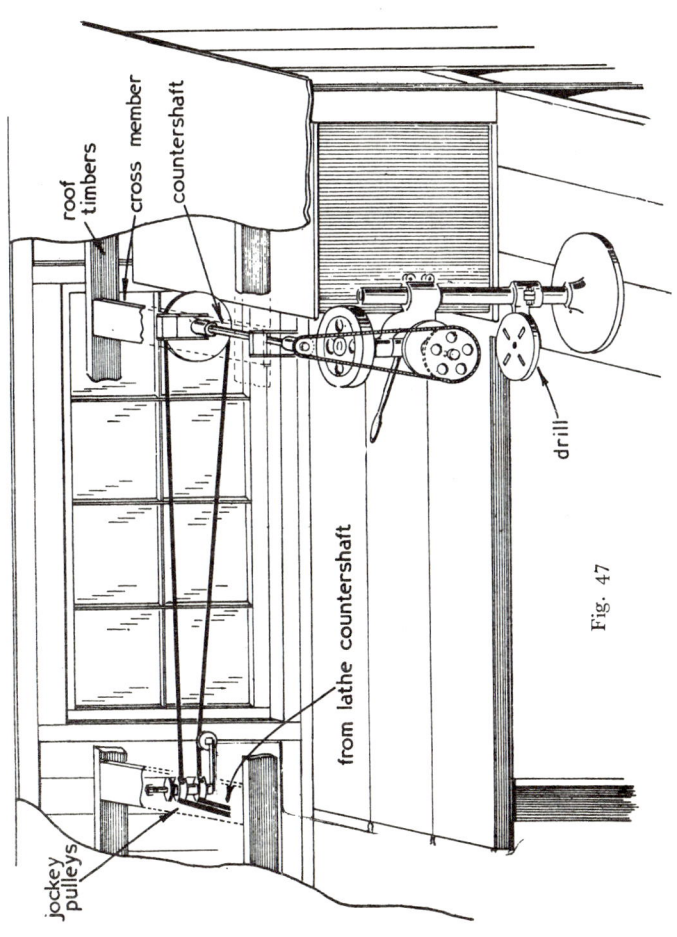

Fig. 47

is also the possibility that at some future date the tool may be replaced by a machine with a self-contained motor drive.

Nevertheless, a drive from some distant point can usually be arranged with the exercise of a little ingenuity, and the manner in which this difficulty has been overcome in a shed workshop is shown in Fig. 47.

A long belt-drive is taken from the lathe countershaft, installed near the roof of the building, to a second countershaft attached to a beam at the other end of the workshop. The belt is guided on its course by means of suitably placed jockey pulleys.

The final drive to the $\frac{1}{2}$ in. capacity drilling machine shown in the drawing is by a chain and sprockets ; this form of drive is used to give the necessary speed reduction and to avoid the slip which would inevitably occur if a short belt-drive were employed in this situation.

Two long cords, attached to the belt shifting gear of the lathe countershaft, are brought to the drilling machine by passing over guide pulleys ; these are used for starting and stopping the drill.

Moreover, as an ordinary measure of safety, a switch that can be operated by either hand should be fitted near every electrically-driven machine to enable it to be stopped instantly in an emergency.

CHAPTER FIVE

> Lathe Tools — Measuring Instruments — Chuck Work—Sliding—Surfacing—Boring —Use of the Faceplate—Turning Work between Centres—Mounting the Work— Use of Steadies—Boring Work on the Saddle—Drilling from the Tailstock—Depth-drilling—The D-bit—Tapping and Dieing —Screwcutting—Turning with Hand Tools.

Lathe Tools. Before any turning operations are described, it will be advisable to consider the formation and sharpening of the lathe tools in greater detail, for on these factors will depend almost entirely the success of the machining processes described later in this chapter. Moreover, even if a set of tools is purchased sharpened and ready for use, these will inevitably become blunted and will need to be resharpened in the same methodical manner as that employed in the first instance by the toolmaker.

OPERATING THE LATHE

When grinding methods were described in Chapter Two it will be remembered that the use of an adjustable, angular grinding rest was strongly advocated and the resort to free-hand grinding was deplored.

In this chapter is was also shown how the commonly used angles could be readily ground at the end of the tool to form the cutting edges.

It will now be advisable to consider in greater detail the purpose of these angles and to indicate the names by which they are generally known.

The Knife Tool. The most generally useful and therefore the lathe tool most used in the small workshop is the right-handed knife tool, shown in Fig. 48, where the form angles are named and their values for ordinary work specified.

These angles, which fall naturally into three classes according to the purpose they serve, can be described as clearance angles, rake angles, and relief angles. Clearance angles are those which keep the tool clear of the work *after* it has passed the cutting edge, so that only the line of the cutting edge makes contact with the work. The rake angle represents the obliquity of the cutting surface presented to the work and on which the cuttings impinge. Relief angles are formed to reduce the extent of the cutting edge in contact with the work to allow the tool to cut freely.

Clearance Angles. These are given to allow the tool to cut and not merely rub against the work. As shown in Fig. 48A and B, it is necessary to provide clearance both at the front and at the side of the tool, for the cutting edges come into contact with the work in both these situations. Clearance angles of 10 deg. can be used for all ordinary purposes, but in any tool of slender form this should be reduced to maintain the strength of the tool's tip.

The principle underlying the provision of clearance is common to all tools, and its application should be clearly understood to enable tools of various forms to be sharpened correctly.

Lathe tools should be examined frequently to make sure that the cutting edges are in good order, because when the clearance angles become reduced or obliterated by wear, the tool's cutting efficiency will be impaired and the finish of the turned work will suffer.

Rake Angles. The rake angles provided in a knife tool are shown in Fig. 48A and C, and it will be apparent that, in this case, the side-rake is the more important as it ensures that the steeply sloping surface behind the cutting edge allows the metal to be easily sliced off in the direction of the tool's travel.

The front rake, that is to say the slope from the front edge of the tool towards its shank, is of less importance in a knife tool, which normally cuts but little on its front edge, and it is therefore often omitted as in Figs. 48A and B.

One advantage of dispensing with the front rake is that the height of the cutting edge does not decrease when the front of the tool is reground.

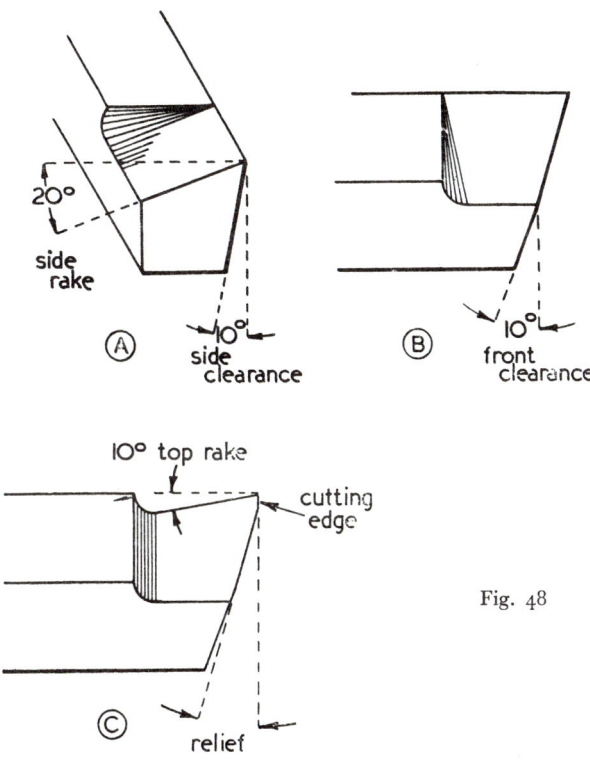

Fig. 48

A side-rake of 20 deg. in a knife tool will ensure free-cutting in mild steel, but both this and front-rake are either much reduced or omitted for machining brass in order to prevent the tool from digging into the work.

When a tool such as a parting tool is used to cut on its front face, front-rake is given where the tool is made for

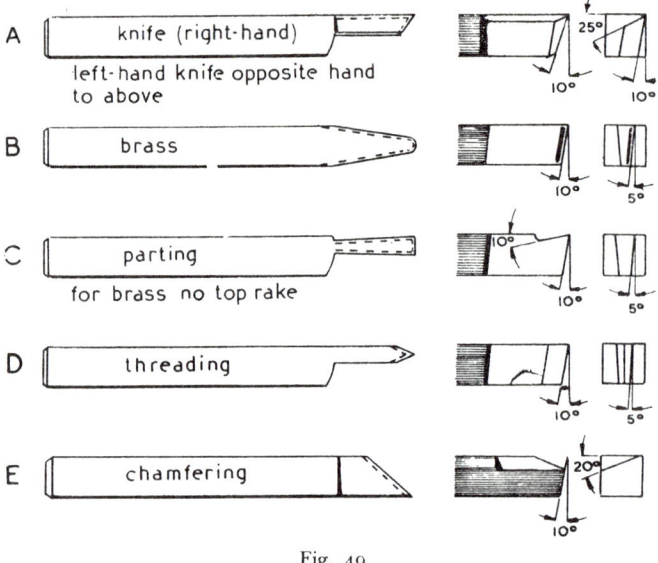

Fig. 49

machining steel, as shown in the drawing in Fig. 49c, but, as before, top-rake must be omitted in a tool formed for cutting brass.

Relief Angles. In the drawing of the knife tool in Fig. 49c, it will be seen that the front cutting edge slopes sharply away from its point of contact with the work; this ensures that only a short length of the front edge comes into contact with the work surface, and any tendency to chatter is thereby reduced.

In practice, it will be found that the less rigid the work being turned, the narrower must be the front cutting edge if chatter is to be avoided. If the extreme tip of the tool is slightly rounded, a better finish on the work will result both when the tool is traversing along the work or taking a facing cut across it.

From what has been said regarding tool forms, the

purpose of the various angles and tool shapes represented in the drawings should now be clear, and no difficulty should be experienced when sharpening these tools or others intended for special purposes. Finally, the importance of keeping the tools really sharp must be stressed, for on this will depend very largely the quality of the work turned out.

An oilstone slip can be employed to give the final finish after grinding, or to restore the tool's edge after it has had a little use. It is, however, difficult to avoid rounding the cutting edges when using the oilstone free-hand, and it is preferable to employ a jig or guide block for this purpose.

An easily made stoning jig with a wooden base and steel side pieces is illustrated in Fig. 50. The base should be clamped to the bench top, and the stone is guided by

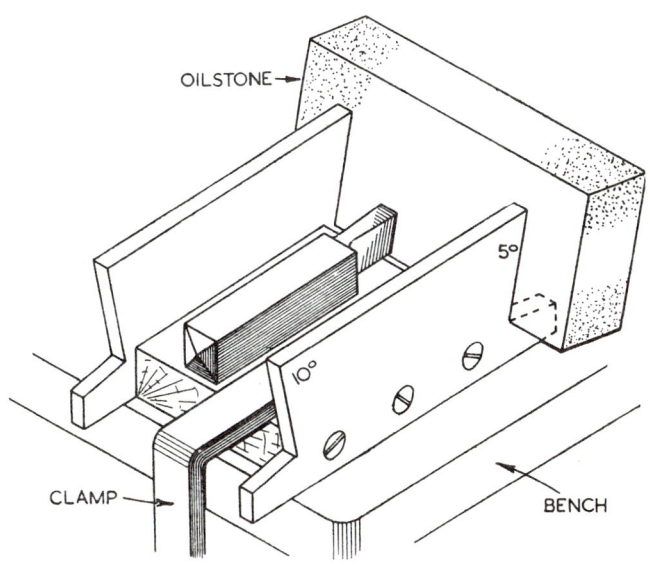

Fig. 50

the side-members as it is moved to and fro across the end of the tool held in place with the fingers. The double-ended guide members allow an angle of either 5 or 10 deg. to be stoned on the tool's tip.

The drawing shows the front clearance of a parting tool being stoned to 5 deg., and if the tool is held in contact with the side-member, this will ensure that the front edge is formed at right angles across the tool.

Those who desire further information on the subject of grinding and stoning lathe tools may refer to *Sharpening Small Tools*, published by Argus Books Ltd.

Material for Lathe Tools. Formerly, lathe tools were hand-forged from tool-steel to the rather elaborate shapes then in common use even in large workshops. In some patterns the ends were bent over to form a swan-necked tool which was difficult to grind accurately as it would not lie flat on the grinding rest.

Nowadays, it is more usual to use tools of simple form to enable accurate grinding of the cutting edges to be readily carried out ; in addition, tough alloy steels with enhanced cutting qualities are now generally used even in the most modest workshops.

The Eclipse brand of super high-speed steel is available in short lengths and in sizes suitable for use in either the tool-post or the four-tool turret of the small lathe.

This material is supplied with the ends obliquely ground to save heavy grinding when shaping the tool tip, and as the steel is ground flat on all its sides, it will lie evenly on the grinding rest and accurate forming of the cutting edges is facilitated.

Measuring Instruments. Two instruments are commonly employed in lathe work to ensure accuracy of machining as well as to save time ; these are the screw micrometer for making exact measurements of the length and diameter of components, and the test indicator used for setting and aligning work in the lathe.

The Micrometer. This instrument is shown in Fig. 51, and its component parts are lettered to make clear the construction and method of using. It will be seen that a thimble *A*, attached to the screwed spindle *B*, can be turned with the fingers to advance *B* towards the anvil *C*. When these two surfaces are brought into contact with the work lying between them, their distance apart, and so the diameter of the work, can be read on the scales engraved on the thimble and on the sleeve, as shown in the drawing.

The spindle, where it lies within the sleeve, has a fine thread of 40 t.p.i., so that for each turn of the thimble the

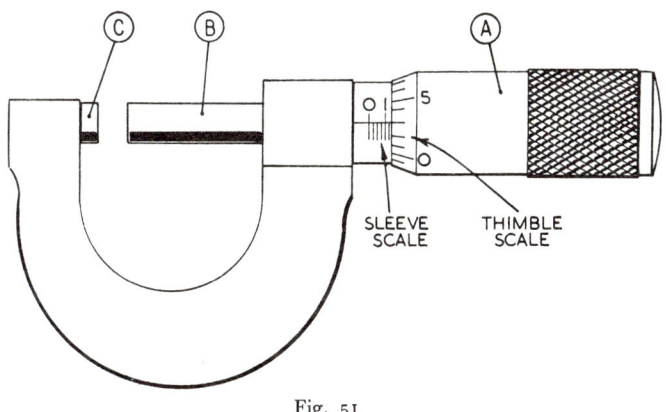

Fig. 51

spindle advances 1/40 in. (0.025 in.), as denoted on the scale on the sleeve. The bevelled edge of the thimble is divided into 25 equal parts, and one division of this scale is, therefore, equal to 1/25 of a turn of the spindle or 1/40 × 1/25 in., which is one thousandth of an inch. As an example of how to read the micrometer, reference to the drawing will show that the reading on the sleeve scale is one large division, which equals four small divisions of 25 thousandths, or 0.1 in., and in addition, a further small division, making a total of 0.125 in. The thimble scale reading of three thousandths must be added to this, so that the micrometer reads 0.128 in.

The micrometer is a finely-made but delicate instrument, and if its accuracy is to be preserved it must be carefully treated.

On no account should it be forced on to or off the work being measured, and when not actually in use it should be placed on a clean surface and where it cannot be damaged by other tools or exposed to metal cuttings.

Although internal micrometers are available for measuring the diameter of holes or bores, the external micrometer described can be made to serve this purpose in the small workshop by setting the internal callipers to the bore, and then using the micrometer to measure across the points.

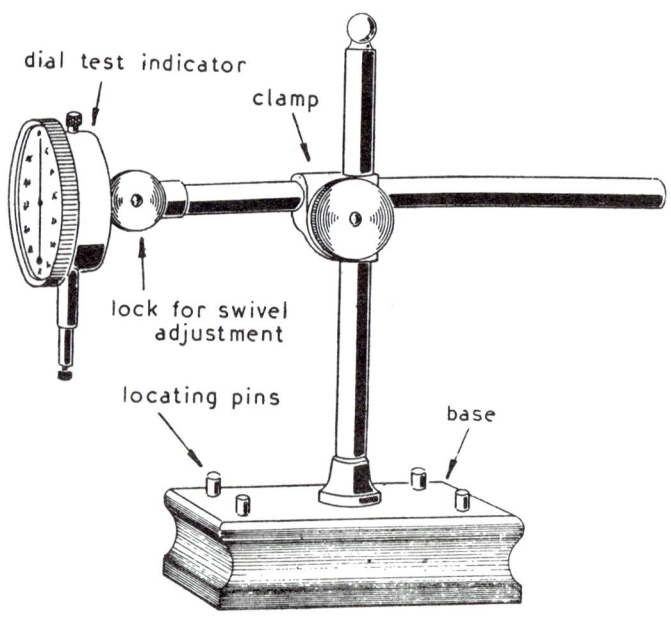

Fig. 52

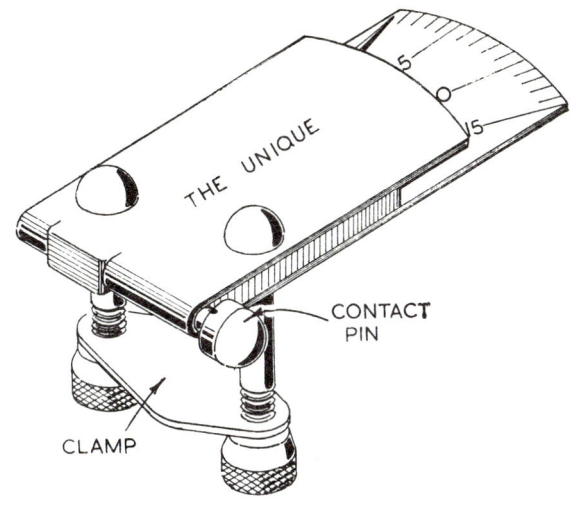

Fig. 53

The Test Indicator. The more expensive form of this instrument, the dial-test indicator, is illustrated in Fig. 52, and here it is shown attached to the pillar of a base mounting, but it can, if required, be secured either in the chuck or in the tool post of the lathe. When the contact point, which usually has a range of movement of $\frac{1}{4}$ in., is pressed against the work, the indicator hand records this movement in thousands of an inch.

Where the instrument is clamped in the tool-post with its point in contact with a component mounted in the lathe, any eccentricity of the work will be indicated when the part is revolved by hand.

An attachment with a pivoted lever can be used with the instrument for setting the work from the internal surface of a bored hole.

A much less expensive pattern of test indicator, named the "Unique" and illustrated in Figs. 53 and 54, was once available.

This well-made and serviceable instrument, in spite of its smaller range of movement, proved adequate for carrying out all the work-setting operations generally encountered in the small workshop. As will be seen in the drawing, it can readily be clamped to a lathe tool or to a piece of material secured in the lathe-tool post. A window is provided in the base portion carrying the scale, to allow the position of the pointer to be read from either side of the instrument. As in the previous example, a lever attachment, shown in Fig. 54, can be fitted to enable the work to be set from an internal surface.

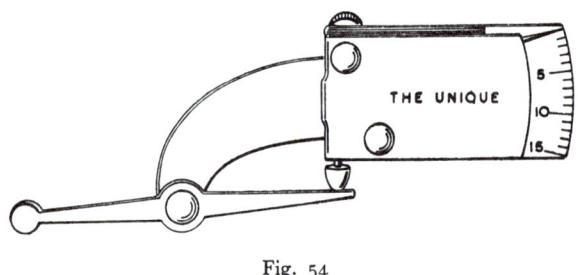

Fig. 54

Turning Operations. When the lathe is used to machine a component, three questions arise which have to be settled at the outset, namely : the lathe speed ; the rate of feed ; and the depth of cut.

Cutting Speeds. In commercial undertakings output is maintained by running the machines at the highest economic speed and by providing, where necessary, a system of forced lubrication for the cutting tools. In the small workshop, however, both this urgency and the special equipment are usually lacking.

High speeds, used with a normal depth of cut, also have the disadvantage that they cause heating and distortion of the work, as well as more rapid blunting of the lathe tools.

Although a surface speed of the work as high as 120 ft. per min. can be used when turning mild-steel, the ordinary lathe user will generally find it better to restrict the work speed to between 50 and 80 ft. per min. When machining cast-iron, these speeds should be halved, but doubled for turning brass and aluminium.

As the circumference of a 1 in. diameter round-bar is approximately $\frac{1}{4}$ ft. in length, it follows that to attain a surface speed of 50 ft. per min. the work must revolve at 200 r.p.m., or 320 r.p.m. for a surface speed of 80 ft. per min. The slow direct gear should, therefore, be used in this instance, but if the diameter of the work is reduced to a half, the lathe speed can then, of course, be doubled.

Rate of Feed. If the feed is too coarse, or the cutting edge of the tool in contact with the work is too narrow, a spiral groove similar to a fine screw-thread will be formed on the surface of the work ; but as chatter and other forms of inaccurate turning must be avoided by keeping the edge of the tool narrow, it follows that it is the rate of feed that must be adjusted to give a good finish to the work.

A feed of between 200 and 300 turns of the mandrel for a feed of 1 in. will generally be found most suitable for light accurate turning.

Depth of Cut. When a deep cut is taken with a normal rate of feed, not only will both the work and the machine be heavily stressed, but the heat engendered will cause further distortion of the work.

Roughing cuts for the quick removal of metal are, of course, permissible, but, except to save time, it is as a rule preferable to take two cuts of medium depth rather than a single heavy one.

The depth of cut to apply in any particular case will be learnt by experience and will depend, in part, on the rigidity of both the machine and the work. The finishing cut to bring the component to size should be limited to a few thousandths of an inch, in order to leave a smooth surface and ensure accuracy.

When surfacing, that is to say taking a facing cut across

the work, even finer feeds can be employed, and the use of an automatic surfacing feed is here an advantage.

Use of Chucks. It will be found that most of the work carried out in the small workshop consists in turning parts held in the chuck but unsupported by the tailstock centre.

The self-centring chuck may, as a rule, be expected to hold material within some two thousandths of an inch of the true centre, but if the chuck is worn or has been strained this error may be much greater.

Where a piece of work, without being removed from the chuck, is turned, drilled, bored, and then parted off, it matters little if the material is mounted somewhat off-centre, for the accuracy of the machining of the various surfaces in relation to one another will be unaffected. If, however, the work is removed from the self-centring chuck and then rechucked by one of its turned surfaces, any subsequent machining will be out of line with the previously turned parts ; also, the amount of this error will depend on the chuck's lack of truth.

Although it is sometimes possible to make the chuck hold truly by using a packing on one of the jaws, it will often be found that the correction is required at some point lying at an unequal distance from two of the jaws ; moreover, the problem is further complicated when the chuck's error of holding varies with the position in which the jaws are set.

Setting Work in the Four-jaw Chuck. These difficulties of untrue centring can be overcome by using the four-jaw independent chuck, which ensures that parts can be chucked or rechucked to run truly.

Although an experienced worker will set the work remarkably quickly, it is advisable for the novice to adopt a methodical way of working from the start, in order to save time and effort and to ensure that each adjustment of the chuck brings the work nearer to the centre. In the first place, the guide circles turned on the face of the chuck should be used to set the jaws holding the work nearly central. If a tool mounted in the tool-post is then brought close to the part while the lathe is turned by hand, the position of any eccentricity will readily be seen. When the gap between the tool and the work is at its narrowest point, the jaw farthest from the operator is slackened and the opposing jaw is tightened. This procedure is continued until the work appears to run truly. A piece of chalk held to the work while the lathe is revolving will then mark any high spot, and the chuck is reset accordingly.

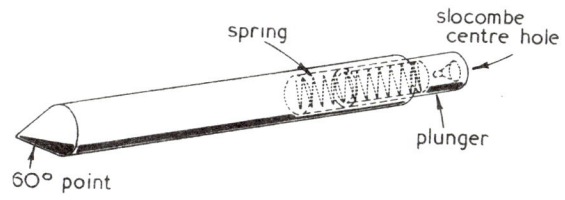

Fig. 55

To obtain real accuracy of centring, the test indicator is mounted in the lathe-tool post, and its button is brought into contact with the work while the lathe is slowly turned by hand; this will enable the smallest error of centring to be detected and easily corrected.

If, for example, the variation shown by the test indicator is 10 thousandths, then the work should be set-over half this amount, or 5 thousandths; this procedure is repeated when making any subsequent correction needed.

A component mounted in the chuck can be centred with reference to an internal surface in a similar manner, if the lever attachment is fitted to the indicator as previously described.

When the work has to be centred in the chuck with reference to a previously drilled centre hole, the tailstock centre can be pressed into the work to act as a guide at the outset; the centring is then completed by using a device known as a centre finder or wobbler and illustrated in Fig. 55.

The conical point of the wobbler is engaged with the

drilled centre in the work, and the centre formed in the plunger at the other end of the device is applied to the tailstock centre ; the tailstock feed is then used to press the plunger inwards against its spring. The point of the test indicator is next brought into contact with the centre finder close to the work ; and when the chuck is turned by hand, the eccentricity of the wobbler is indicated and then corrected as in the previous example.

When centring a part with reference to its bore or to a drilled hole, a plug can be fitted to the bore and then centred with the test indicator ; if the plug has a truly formed centre hole, this hole can be centred by means of the wobbler.

Turning Work in the Chuck. Here, the work is held in either the four-jaw or the self-centring chuck and the turning and other operations are carried out without support being given by the tailstock. To illustrate the methods employed, the machining of the small part shown in Fig. 56A will be followed step by step.

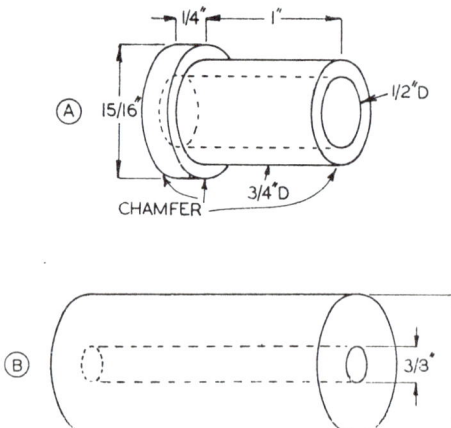

Fig. 56

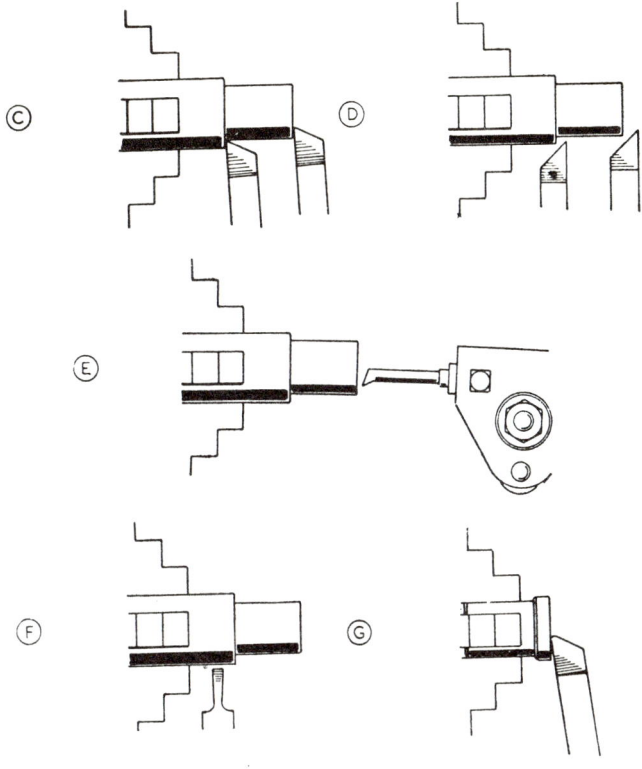

Fig. 56

The component in question is a mild-steel, shouldered bushing with chamfered edges and having a through bore of ½ in. diameter; the dimensions to which the part has to be machined are shown in the drawing.

A length of 1 in. diameter mild-steel rod, as shown in Fig. 56B, is used, and, to suit our present purpose, we will take it that a bore of some ⅜ in. has already been drilled through it as will be described later in this chapter.

The rod can be mounted in the self-centring chuck as it does not matter if it runs slightly out of truth, for there is plenty of metal to spare; but if the four-jaw chuck is used, the work can, of course, be adjusted to run truly, and, in addition, it will overhang less and so will receive more rigid support from the mandrel bearings.

Before describing the actual turning operations, it should be emphasised that, as mistakes resulting in spoilt work are easily made when machining, it is advisable to guard against this by adopting a methodical way of working which keeps a continuous check on the progress of the work. To save the machine drawings from damage

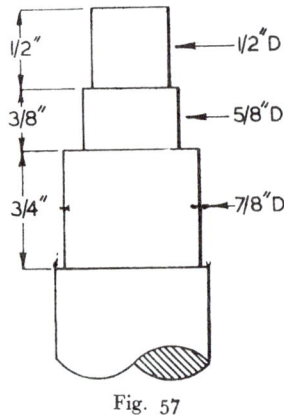

Fig. 57

and to make clear exactly what is required, make a simplified dimensioned sketch of the actual part to be machined.

As illustrated in Fig. 57, mark on the left of the sketch the length of any turned portions, and on the right note the diameters to be turned. To avoid errors when feeding in the tool, start with the cross-slide index set to its zero position with the tool touching the work. If the diameter of the material is 1 in. and it has to be reduced to ⅞ in., then the final reading of the index will be approximately 60.

Measure the diameter of the work with the micrometer after taking a cut, and note on a piece of paper both the work diameter and the index setting. A further measurement should be made before taking the finishing cut to ascertain the exact setting of the cross-slide required. If the diameter of the work and the cross-slide settings correspond throughout the turning operation, there should be little chance of making a machining error.

To begin the machining operation, add a few drops of machine oil to the mandrel lubricators, and then clamp a right-hand knife tool in the tool post with its cutting edge set to the exact centre height of the lathe ; this is best done with the aid of a specially made height gauge standing on either the saddle or the bed of the lathe, or the ordinary surface gauge may be used for this purpose.

As the material to be machined is 1 in. in diameter, the low direct-speed of the lathe should be used to give between 200 and 300 r.p.m., in accordance with the calculations previously cited.

The next step is to face the end of the work with the knife tool as shown in Fig. 56c ; the tool is fed to the work by means of the top slide after the leadscrew index has been set to the zero position. If the tool is set correctly to the centre height, no unsightly central pip will be formed when a solid bar is faced.

To reduce the diameter of the bar from 1 in. to $\frac{3}{4}$ in., the lathe is stopped and the cutting point of the knife tool is brought gently into contact with the work on its outer diameter ; the cross-slide index is then set to zero, and when the tool has been moved clear of the work to the right by means of the leadscrew feed, a cut of some 30 thousandths, or so, is put on with the cross-slide feed. When turning short lengths of material, hand-feed for the saddle can quite well be used, but the automatic feed will, as has been pointed out, give better results and should be used in this instance.

It will be clear that, where the pitch of the leadscrew is $\frac{1}{8}$ in., to cover the 1 in. length to be turned, the leadscrew index will have to revolve exactly eight times, starting from its zero position as previously set when facing the end of the work.

In addition, the tool will have to be fed inwards by the cross-slide for approximately 125 thousandths to reduce the diameter of the bar to the finished size.

Start the lathe, and when the leadscrew index has turned a few thousandths of an inch short of eight full turns, throw out the leadscrew feed. The full number of turns made by the leadscrew can be determined with the aid of a rule or from a chalk mark made on the work.

This operation is repeated until the work has been turned to the correct diameter as determined with either the micrometer or the outside callipers ; but for the finishing cut a feed of a few thousandths only should be allowed in order to produce a good finish on the work. To turn the reduced portion to an exact length of 1 in., the final few thousandths of an inch of traverse are made by turning the leadscrew by hand until its index reaches the zero position.

Next, the diameter of the head of the bushing is reduced in the same way to 15/16 in. in accordance with the dimensions given in Fig. 56A, and the edges are chamfered as shown in Fig. 56D, but the lathe may have to be run at a slower speed for this latter operation if there is any tendency to chatter. The form of chamfering tool used is illustrated in Fig. 49E.

Boring. This completes the turning of the outside diameters, and the forming of the bore to size is now undertaken with a small boring tool, as represented in Fig. 56E. The form of boring tool used for this purpose is illustrated in Fig. 58, and the position of the cutting edge when at work is also shown in Fig. 58c.

As the diameter of the work being turned is now less than half of what it was when the machining was begun, the speed of the lathe can safely be doubled, but only light cuts should be taken to avoid overstressing the rather slender boring tool. The automatic feed for the saddle is used, and the depth of entry of the boring tool must be controlled by reference to the leadscrew index, in order

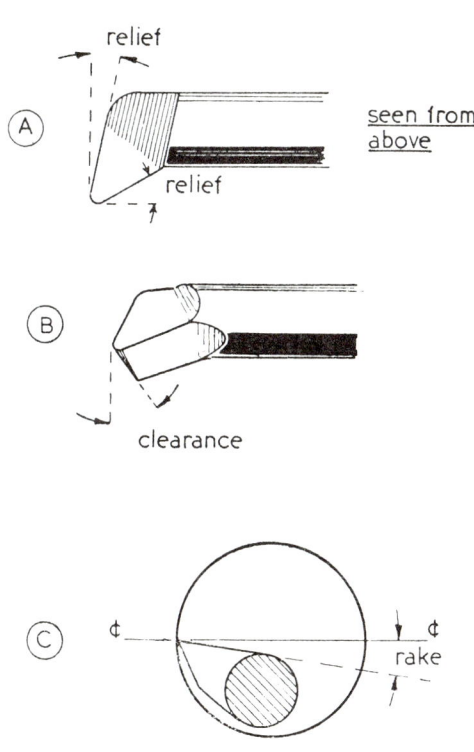

Fig. 58

to prevent the tip of the tool from being forced against the shoulder formed at the end of the bored hole. Should the bore pass right through the work, a packing of rag or cotton wool should be inserted to prevent the cuttings from reaching the working parts in the interior of the chuck.

The next operation is to part-off the component. This is done, as illustrated in Fig. 56F, with a narrow parting tool of the form shown in Fig. 49C. Until some experience has been gained, it is advisable to use the back gear of the lathe for this operation, and great care should be taken to maintain an even rate of feed so that a coiled shaving is produced which readily clears itself from the groove cut in the work. Oil should be applied continuously with a brush to promote free cutting, but should the tool dig in and become jammed in the work, it is advisable to slacken the clamping screws and remove it carefully, otherwise its tip will almost certainly be damaged. When using the parting tool it is essential that the cross-slide should be properly adjusted to remove slackness and undue backlash in the feed mechanism.

The final operation, after reversing the work in the chuck, is to face its end as shown in Fig. 56G, and then to chamfer the rim in accordance with Fig. 56D.

Use of the Faceplate. Where the work is too irregular in shape or too bulky to be held in the chuck, it can usually be clamped to the faceplate for machining, but if the turning is to be accurately carried out, the faceplate must, of course, run quite truly. The true running of the faceplate can be checked with the test indicator, mounted in the lathe toolpost and with its contact point brought to bear on the surface of the plate while slowly turned by hand.

Untrue running may result from the presence of dirt or chips on the mating surfaces of the mandrel nose or faceplate, and may not be due to inaccurate machining.

Fig. 59 shows an engine casting attached to the faceplate by means of clamping pieces and bolts. The rear face of the casting has been previously turned so that it beds evenly on the faceplate and thus ensures that, when the crankshaft bearing is bored, as illustrated in the drawing, it will lie truly at right angles to the surface in contact with the faceplate.

Should the form of the work not permit it to be mounted

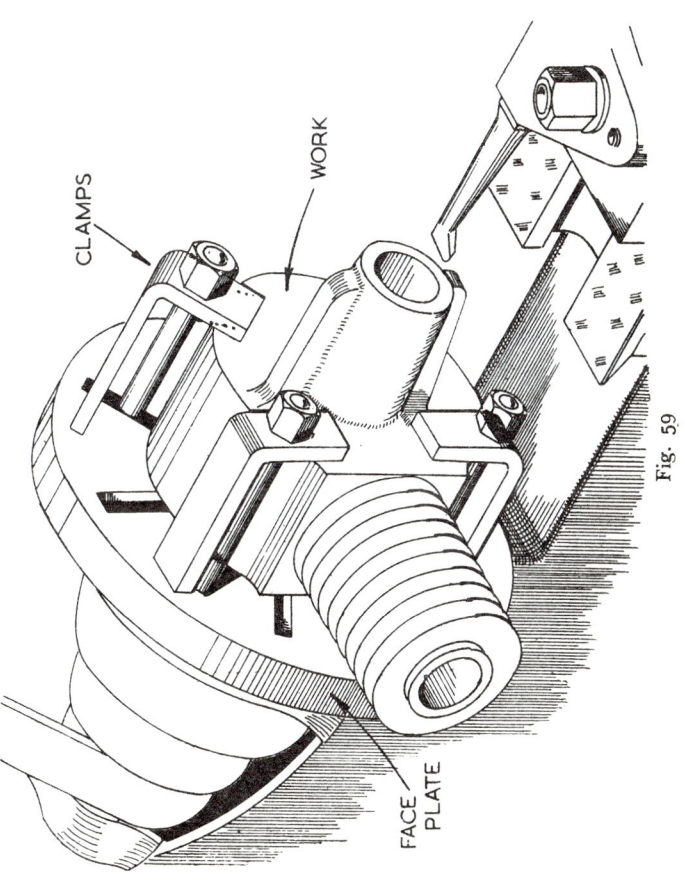

Fig. 59

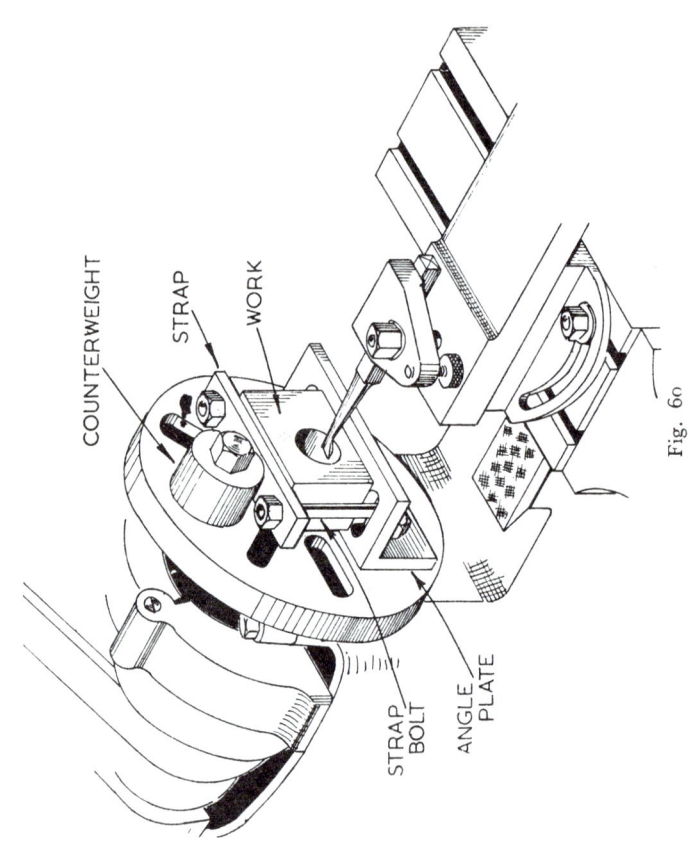

Fig. 60

in this way, or if, as shown in Fig. 60, the bore has to be machined truly parallel with the base surface, then the work can be clamped to an angle-plate which is in turn secured to the faceplate.

This method of mounting allows the position of the work to be readily adjusted when centring the bore.

It will be observed that a counterweight has been attached to the faceplate. This should always be done if the work is out of balance, otherwise inaccurate machining may result. The position and size of the weight are adjusted until the lathe mandrel, when running free and turned by hand, has no tendency to stop in any one position.

When mounting work on the faceplate in the ways described, a firmer hold will be obtained if a single sheet of paper is placed between the opposed flat clamping surfaces.

Turning Work Between Centres. Components that project for some distance from the chuck in which they are mounted often require additional support from the tailstock centre to provide the rigidity necessary for machining.

To allow of this, the faced end of the work is drilled with a centre drill of the type illustrated in Fig. 17, in Chapter One.

The form of the hole so made is shown in section in Fig. 61A, and Fig. 61B represents the appearance when the tailstock centre is engaged. It will be seen that the centre itself remains clear of the bottom of the hole, and a space is left which forms an oil reservoir for lubricating the working surfaces. Should, however, a defective centre drill be employed, the centre may bottom in the hole, as shown in Fig. 61C, and no proper guidance will be provided.

Shafts, such as crankshafts and machine spindles, are turned between the two lathe centres, and this method of mounting the work has the advantages that no bending strain is imposed on the shaft, and should remachining be required at any time, the shaft can be mounted to run truly on the original centre holes.

When centre-drilling the ends of a long shaft which

will not pass through the bore in the lathe mandrel, one end is set to run truly in the four-jaw chuck and the other is supported in a fixed steady secured to the lathe bed, as illustrated in Fig. 62.

The end of the shaft so mounted is faced and afterwards drilled with a centre drill ; the shaft is then reversed in the chuck and the other end is machined in a similar

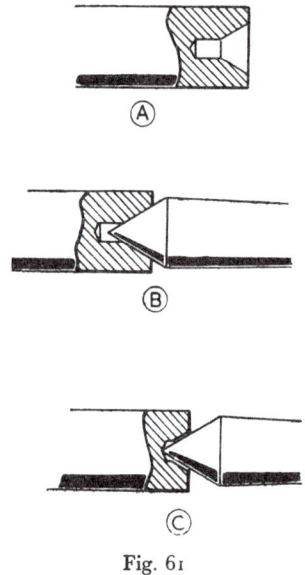

Fig. 61

manner. This method of mounting and driving the work can also be employed when turning the taper bore in the end of a machine spindle or mandrel.

To provide for driving the shaft when it is mounted between the lathe centres, as illustrated in Fig. 65, a lathe carrier is attached to its end, as shown in Fig. 63 ; in addition, to ensure that the carrier does not slip, particularly when cutting a screw thread on the shaft, a small flat may be filed on unfinished work to give a bearing for

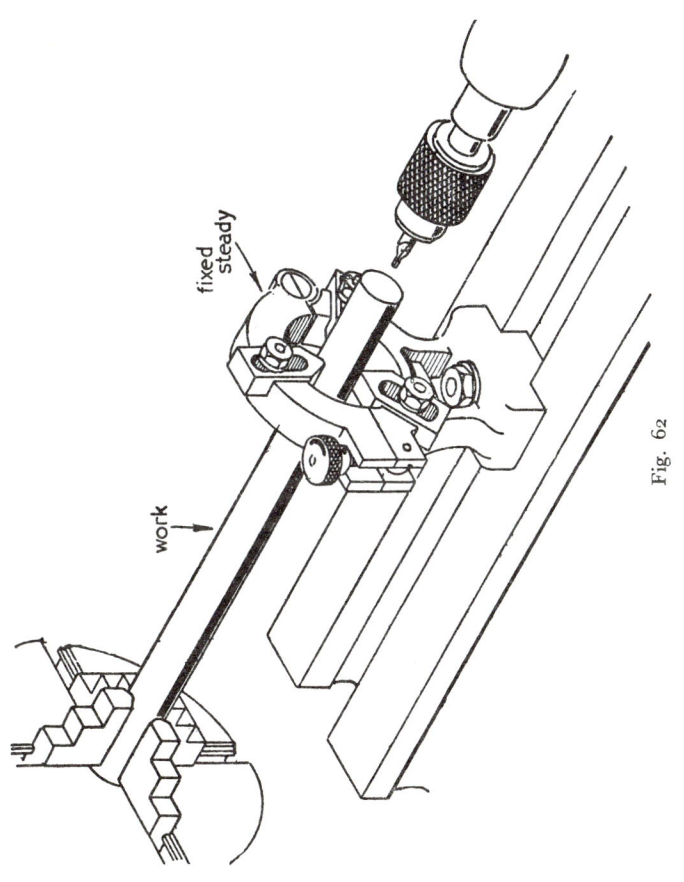

Fig. 62

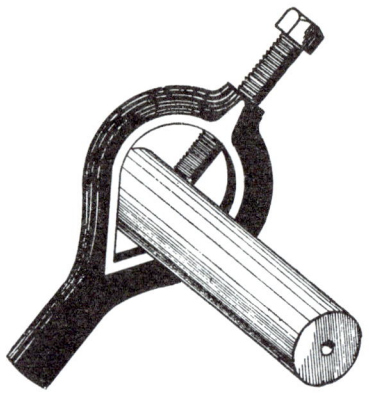

Fig. 63

the point of the clamp screw. Where finished work is held in this way, a piece of sheet-copper should be wrapped round the shaft to prevent it being damaged.

When the work has been mounted between the lathe centres, the tail of the carrier is driven by a dog or bolt attached to the driver-plate screwed on to the mandrel nose of the lathe.

To prevent the dog from knocking against the carrier during the turning operation, the parts should be lightly bound together with a piece of wire.

If the end of a shaft where it is engaged with the tail-stock centre has to be turned to a small diameter, it may be found that the ordinary form of back centre will not allow the point of the tool to be fed far enough inwards;

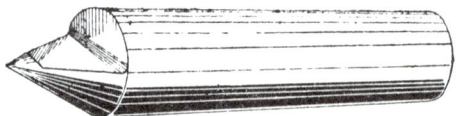

Fig. 64

to overcome this difficulty a special cut-away or half-centre is used with the flat surface at the tip turned towards the operator. A centre of this type is shown in Fig. 64.

The back centre should be kept clean and well-lubricated, and it is engaged with the work just sufficiently firmly to ensure that all side-play is taken up; during the subsequent turning operations the tailstock centre should be reset in the work from time to time, as the heat

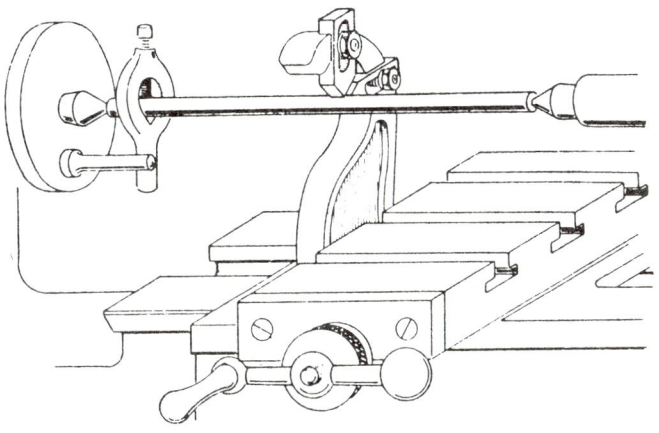

Fig. 65

engendered by the machining causes the work to expand in length and tighten on the centre.

The actual machining of the shaft is carried out as in the previous example, but when a long or slender shaft is being turned, it may be found necessary to give it support against the thrust of the tool by using a travelling steady, as illustrated in Fig. 65.

This device is attached to the lathe saddle, and its two contact pads support the work as they follow in the wake of the tool.

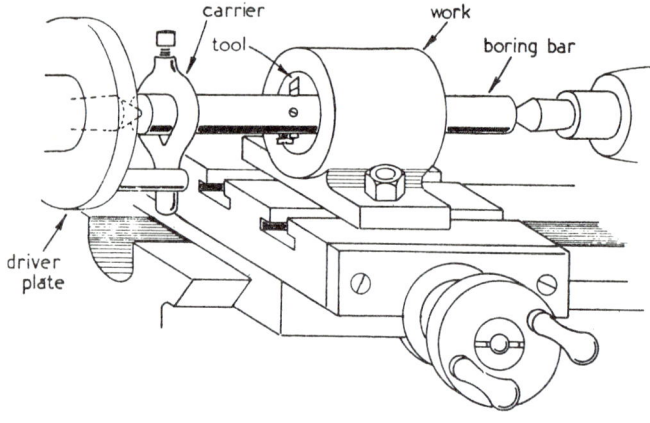

Fig. 66

It is necessary, of course, to readjust the pads after each passage of the tool along the work.

Boring Work on the Saddle. When a casting is too large to be held in a chuck or mounted on the faceplate, it can sometimes be bored and machined if clamped to the lathe saddle, as illustrated in Fig. 66. The boring operation is then carried out by means of a boring bar mounted between the lathe centres.

This bar is fitted with a cutter which can be adjusted, as shown in Fig. 67, to the radius required to machine the bore to size.

An alternative method of driving the bar is to grip it close to its end in the four-jaw chuck and to support the other end with the tailstock centre. This allows the radius of the cutter point to be accurately set by adjusting the chuck with the aid of the test indicator. This fine adjustment is made, when the bore is nearing its finished size, by mounting the indicator on the lathe and resetting the bar in the chuck with the point of the cutter in contact with the button of the indicator. If the lathe is turned slowly backwards by hand, a reading of the indicator can be taken both before and during the setting operation to enable an exact amount of feed to be given.

Drilling from the Tailstock. When a drilling machine is not available, the lathe may be used as a substitute by mounting a drill in the mandrel chuck and supporting the work against a drilling pad fitted to the tailstock. A drilling fitment of this type is illustrated in Fig. 38 in Chapter Three, which shows a tapered adapter fitting into the tailstock taper and having a parallel portion at its front end to carry either a plain or a V-slotted pad to accommodate round work.

On the whole, this is not a very satisfactory method of drilling, for it is difficult in this case to keep the work in position and to locate holes accurately.

If, however, the work is mounted in the mandrel chuck and the drill is fed from the tailstock, very accurate work can be done if reasonable care is taken.

For this operation the drill is held in a drill chuck mounted in the tailstock taper by means of a tapered arbor. As so many less experienced workers complain that they are unable to drill a true axial hole in this manner, it may be worth while to describe the operation in detail.

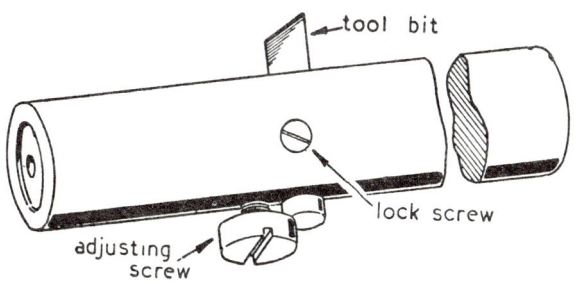

Fig. 67

In the first place, the tailstock must be truly aligned with the headstock, and properly sharpened drills are essential for accurate work. Let us take as an example the drilling of an axial hole $\frac{3}{16}$ in. in diameter in a piece of round material mounted in the lathe chuck. The end surface of the work must first be turned flat and without a central pip. A small standard centre drill with a body $\frac{1}{8}$ in. in diameter and with a 3/64 in. drilling point is secured in the drill chuck fitted to the tailstock taper. With the lathe set to run at high speed, the drill is fed into the work until the parallel body portion has entered for at least $\frac{1}{8}$ in. An $\frac{1}{8}$ in. twist drill is then secured in the drill chuck and is entered for the full depth of the hole required. The guidance afforded by the drilled centre will ensure that the $\frac{1}{8}$ in. drill starts truly, and if it is fed in carefully a true hole should result.

The mouth of the hole is now enlarged with a larger centre drill to form a guide centre for the $\frac{3}{16}$ in. drill which follows and enlarges the hole to its finished size.

Should a hole smaller than $\frac{1}{8}$ in. have to be drilled, the parallel, drilling portion of a centre drill can be used to form the guide hole for the pilot drill, and the hole formed by this drill is then enlarged to the full size to complete the operation.

Depth Drilling. Where the tailstock barrel is graduated as illustrated in Fig. 68A, the depth of entry of the drill

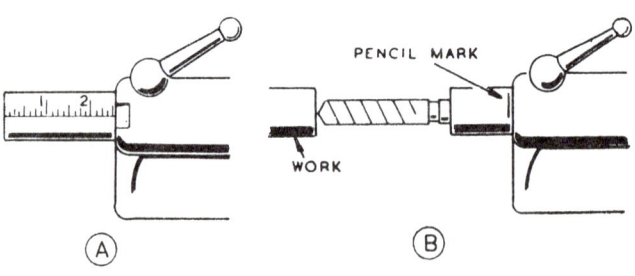

Fig. 68

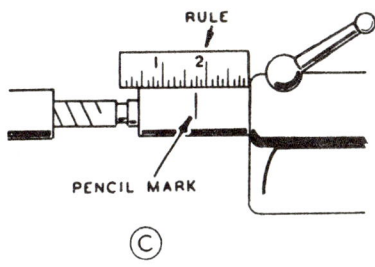

Fig 68

can, of course, be read directly, but when the barrel is left plain, a pencil mark is made, as in Fig. 68B, to denote the start of the drill in the work, and its progress is determined by measuring with a rule the distance between this mark and the edge of the tailstock casting, as represented in Fig. 68c.

The 'D' Bit. A ready and accurate method of drilling deep holes from the tailstock is to use a D bit of the form shown in Fig. 69.

This tool is easily made from a length of silver-steel, filed to the shape shown in the drawings, and then hardened and tempered in the manner described in the instructions for making a countersink in Chapter Six. It will be seen that both clearance and relief angles are formed at the cutting point of the tool, and the flat surface behind the cutting edge lies a little above the diameter in order to maintain guidance.

It is essential when using these cutters to start them in a truly centred hole of a diameter exactly equal to that of the tool ; to give adequate guidance at the start, this hole must be formed to a depth equal to the diameter of the cutter.

Dieing and Tapping in the Lathe. If reasonable care is taken, parts, held in the lathe chuck and turned or bored to size, can be threaded sufficiently accurately for most purposes by means of a die or tap guided by the tailstock.

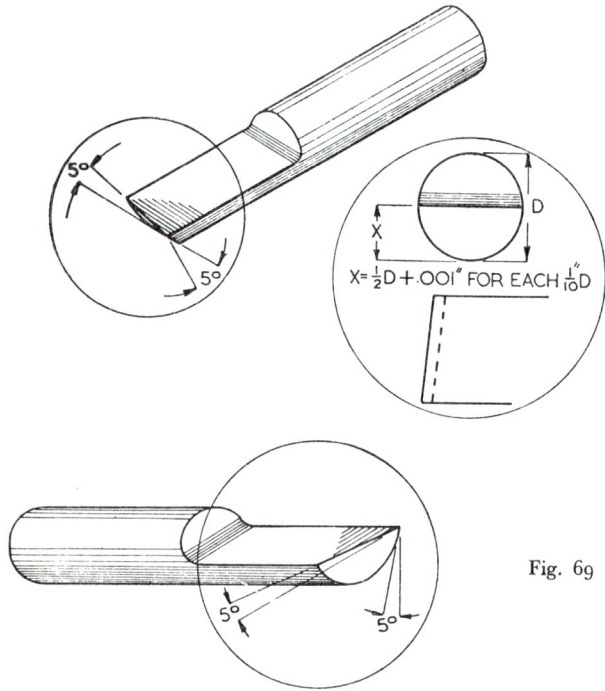

Fig. 69

$X = \frac{1}{2}D + .001''$ FOR EACH $\frac{1''}{10}D$

For cutting external threads, a dieholder, such as that made by Messrs. Myford, and illustrated in Fig. 70, is mounted by its tapered shank in the tailstock barrel.

The die, which is secured in the head of the die holder by the adjusting screws, is then fed forward by means of the tailstock screw-feed to engage the work as it is slowly rotated.

The lathe mandrel is rotated either by pulling on the belt or, preferably, by means of a special handle secured to the rear end of the mandrel itself. While the first few threads are being cut, some pressure should be exerted by the tailstock to overcome the cutting pressure and so prevent these threads being thinned; but as soon as the die has obtained a fair hold it will continue to cut as it feeds itself along the work.

During the threading operation, the handle attached to the die-head can either be controlled by the hand, or allowed to engage some part of the lathe, in order to prevent the die turning with the work.

When a large thread is being cut in this way, once the die has obtained a good hold the work can be removed from the lathe and the threading operation completed at the bench ; this safeguards the chuck, which might otherwise be strained in an attempt to prevent the work from slipping in its jaws.

Tapping a hole centrally drilled in the work mounted in the chuck is carried out by supporting the shank of the tap in the tailstock drill chuck. The jaws are closed sufficiently to provide guidance for the tap without preventing it from turning freely.

A small lathe carrier is secured to the tap to afford the necessary turning leverage, and, with the lathe mandrel locked, the tap is worked to and fro until the threading is completed.

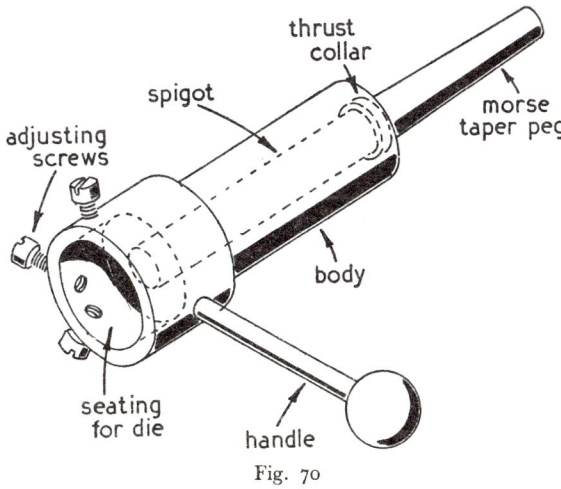

Fig. 70

Here, again, if much resistance is encountered when cutting the thread, the work should be removed from the lathe and the operation completed at the bench.

Screw Cutting. Clearly, if a tool with a V-shaped point is mounted in the lathe tool post, and a cut is taken along a piece of work with a rather coarse automatic feed, a spiral groove will be formed which is essentially a screw thread. Reference to the makers' screw-cutting chart will show the arrangement of the change-wheels necessary for cutting any particular thread; but the operation will be simplified if the beginner is content, for a time at least, to cut only thread pitches that are a multiple of the leadscrew thread of 8 t.p.i., that is to say 16, 24 and 32 threads per in. for example.

The corresponding wheel trains are simple, too, and merely call for a reduction of 2 to 1, 3 to 1, and 4 to 1 respectively.

There is also no difficulty in engaging the leadscrew nut at the right moment, as any position relative to the work will be correct; but when odd pitches are cut, if the leadscrew nut is not engaged correctly a second thread will be cut on top of the previous thread.

It is now usual, however, for manufacturers to fit a thread indicator to enable the operator to engage the leadscrew nut at the proper time.

To put the matter briefly, if a V-pointed tool, formed to the correct angle, is mounted at centre height in the lathe-tool post, and is used to make a series of cuts with a feed equal to a multiple of the leadscrew pitch, then a satisfactory thread can be readily formed on either the external or the internal surface of the work.

The commonly used Whitworth form of thread has an included angle of 55 deg., and thread cutting tools should have their points ground to this angle, as shown in Fig. 49D, but when sharpening these tools additional clearance must be given to allow for the spiral course of the thread.

It is important to secure the tool exactly at centre height, otherwise it will not cut the thread to the correct form.

An initial cut of 5 thousandths of an inch may be taken, but this must be reduced as the work proceeds or the slender tip of the tool may be damaged.

Until experience is gained, the slow speed of the back gear should be used to allow time for the tool to be withdrawn at the end of the cut ; if possible, a groove should be turned in the work at this point to safeguard the tool.

Fig. 71

When the end of the thread is reached, the tool is withdrawn, the leadscrew nut is disengaged, and the saddle is returned to the starting point. As the thread being cut is a multiple of the leadscrew thread, the clasp nut can be engaged at any point when taking the next cut. This procedure is continued until the thread has been formed to the full standard depth.

Internal threads are cut in the same way, but additional care is required to ensure that the tool is not damaged when it reaches the end of the thread, for in this case it will be out of sight and its depth of entry must be controlled by reference to the leadscrew index. The usual form of tool for cutting internal threads is illustrated in Fig. 71. Only a brief outline of screw-cutting procedure has been given, and the question of cutting threads of odd pitch, and the method of screw-cutting with the tool-slide set at an angle have necessarily been omitted, but this subject is fully dealt with in any practical text-book on lathe work.

Hand Turning Tools. In the days when the small lathe was not often fitted with a slide rest, hand-turning tools were largely used by the amateur and also by the professional instrument maker.

In the hands of the skilled craftsman the graver, shown in Fig. 72A, is capable of doing accurate turning over a wide range of work, such as both parallel and taper turning, and also forming parts with curved surfaces.

The amateur, however, uses the graver mostly for rounding the edges of work where he finds the slide-rest of little help.

A graver can be made from a discarded square file by grinding the tip to the lozenge shape shown in the drawings; the teeth on the blade of the file should be ground smooth to save the hands from damage. To form a fine cutting edge, the sharpening must be completed by stoning the diamond-shaped area at the tip with the aid of a stoning jig which maintains the tool in correct alignment with the surface of the oilstone; this is fully described in *Sharpening Small Tools*, published by Argus Books Ltd.

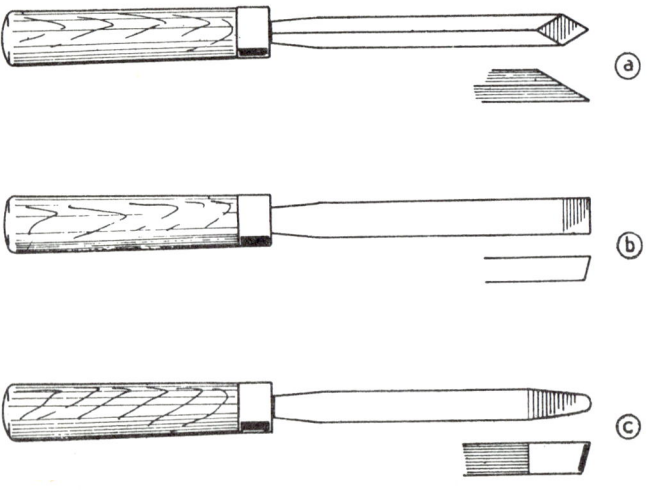

Fig. 72

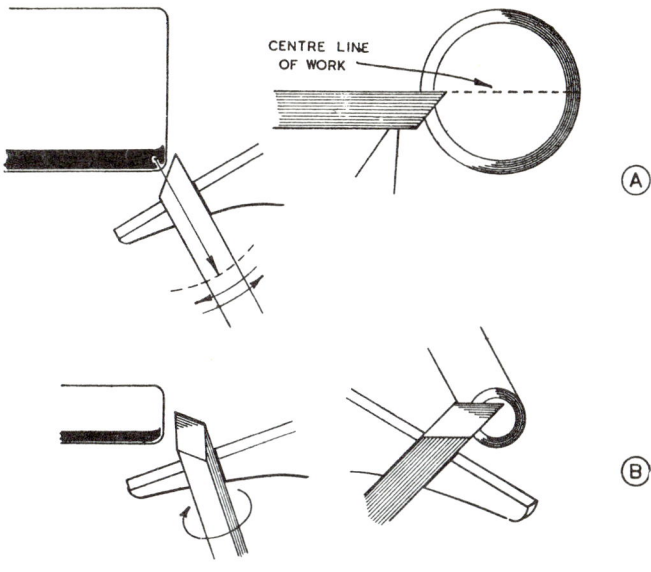

Fig. 73

The blade of the tool should not be less than 4 in. in length to provide a grip for the left hand, and a wooden handle is fitted to afford the right hand a secure grip when steadying the tool at its further end.

The method of using the graver is illustrated in Fig. 73, and it is important that the tool-rest should be set as closely as possible to the work to prevent the point of the tool from being drawn downwards and caught in the gap between the work and the rest.

When the tool is presented to the work as shown in Fig. 73A, it has no top or side rake and will then turn brass to a good finish, but an even better finish can usually be obtained by rotating the tool until it has a negative rake in relation to the work surface.

The arrows in the figure indicate the direction in which

the handle is moved when forming a radius on the edge of the work.

When turning steel, the graver is applied to the work, as shown in Fig. 73B, and the rake angles then cause a slicing cut to be taken as the tool is turned on its long axis to form a radius on the work.

As only light cuts are, as a rule, taken with the graver, the turning speed can be high, but if there is any tendency to chatter, the speed should be reduced.

With practice, small parts can be turned parallel by hand-turning with the graver ; the handle of the tool is steadied with the right hand, and the left is used to pull the graver along the tool-rest for a short distance towards the left ; the grip of the left hand is then shifted and a further cut is taken. Finally, the turned sections are merged to form a continuous parallel surface.

If preferred, hand tools of the ordinary lathe tool form can be used instead of the graver for finishing curved surfaces ; these tools are particularly useful for turning brass and aluminium.

The square-ended tool, shown in Fig. 72B, can be used to form an external radius by swinging the handle horizontally while the end of the tool is allowed to pivot on the hand rest ; and, as in the previous case, if the handle is raised to give a negative rake to the tool, a very fine finish can be imparted to the work.

The round-ended tool, depicted in Fig. 72C, is used in the same way for forming hollow-curved surfaces.

CHAPTER SIX

Colleted Die-holders — Drilling Machine Tapping Handle—A Countersink—Pin Drills—Drilling Machine Table Stop—Centre Finder—Angular Grinding Rest.

As mentioned in earlier chapters it is now proposed to describe the making of some useful articles of workshop equipment. This will serve a twofold purpose in enabling

TOOLS AND EQUIPMENT TO MAKE

the worker to put his reading to practical account and, at the same time, to provide himself with tools which may not be readily procurable.

It should, however, be borne in mind that the designs suggested are intended rather as a guide, and modifications can be introduced where needed, either to suit individual requirements, or to adapt them for use with other equipment.

Fitting a Collet Adapter to the Die Holder. As was previously explained, it is a difficult matter to cut a thread truly with a die holder that has no guide for aligning the die with the work, but when a guide collet is fitted, as in the American type of holder, accurate threading is a simple and certain procedure.

The easiest way to make a holder of this pattern is to fit an adapter for carrying the collet to a standard die holder of the type illustrated in Fig. 74, which also shows the adapter and its collet fitted in place and secured by two countersunk screws.

The first step is to form a true seating for the adapter in line with the die housing, for it is quite possible, as represented in Fig. 75, that the existing surfaces will require remachining to bring them into correct alignment.

To do this, a short length of round-steel of a diameter greater than 13/16 in. is mounted in the self-centring chuck, and its end is turned down to form a firm press-fit in the die housing of the holder.

The die holder is pressed into place on the spigot and, to give additional security, the grub screws used to hold the die are screwed firmly home.

Reference to the working drawing in Fig. 76 will show that the register on the adapter where it fits into the holder is 11/16 in. in diameter; the corresponding bore in the

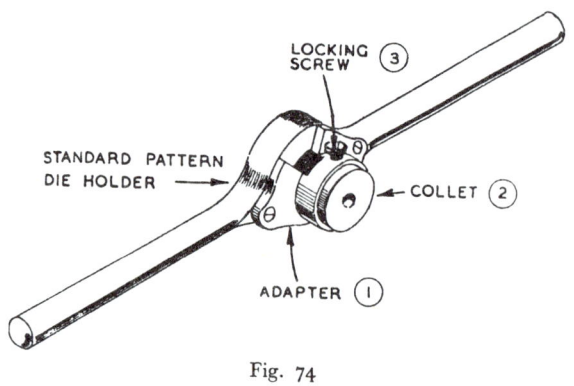

Fig. 74

holder is, therefore, turned to this dimension and the face of the holder is machined flat with a knife tool.

The adapter itself is now taken in hand, and for its construction a piece 1½ in. in length is cut off from a steel bar 1 in. wide and ½ in. thick.

Prior to machining, the work is marked-out in accordance with the working drawing and as shown in Fig. 77A. The cross-centre lines are scribed with the jenny callipers, and from the point of intersection the screw hole centres are marked-out with the dividers set to 7/16 in. These centres are then drilled with a No. 34 drill to provide clearance holes for the 6 B.A. fixing screws. The centre

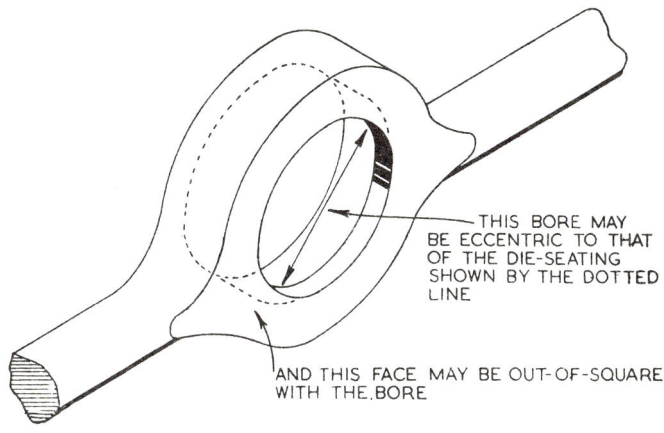

Fig. 75

of the work is drilled with a centre drill to form a bearing for the centrefinder when setting the part in the chuck.

The appearance of the work when mounted in the lathe is then as illustrated in Fig. 77A.

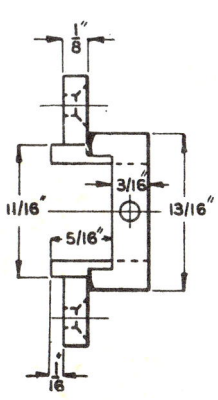

Fig. 76

It should be noted that packing pieces must be placed behind the work to bring it forward in the chuck jaws so as to allow $\frac{5}{16}$ in. to project for forming the collet boss shown in Fig. 77c. The next step is to drill and bore the part to 15/32 in., as in Fig. 77B. The collet boss is then turned to $\frac{13}{16}$ in. diameter for a length of $\frac{5}{16}$ in., as shown in Fig. 77c.

The work is now reversed in the chuck and held by the collet boss. The machining in the lathe is completed by turning the register to a depth of $\frac{1}{16}$ in. and

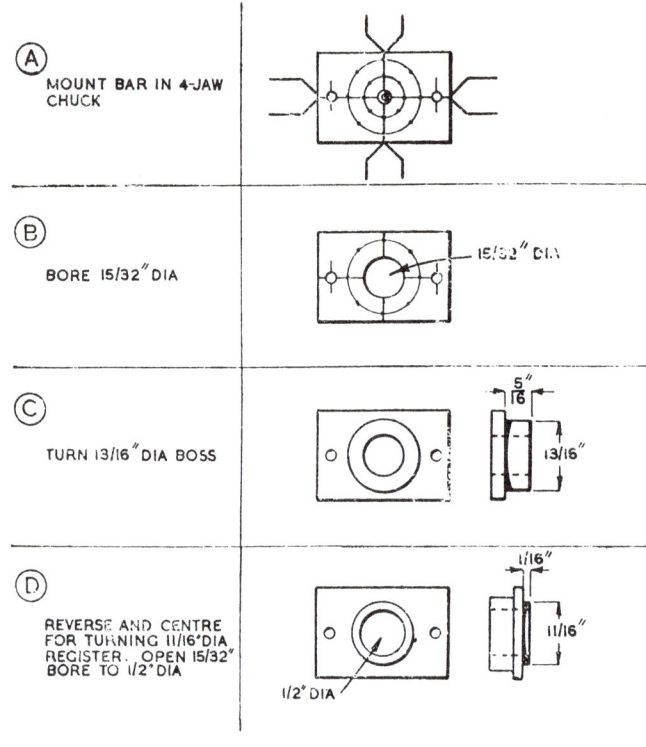

Fig. 77

then finishing the bore to exactly $\frac{1}{2}$ in., as depicted in Fig. 77D.

The next operation is shown in Figs. 77E and F and consists in cutting the chip clearance slots with the hacksaw and file.

After this, as seen in Fig. 77G, the screw holes are countersunk, and the adapter is filed to its finished shape. Finally, the hole for the 6 B.A. collet clamp screw is drilled and tapped, and, with the adapter clamped in place in the

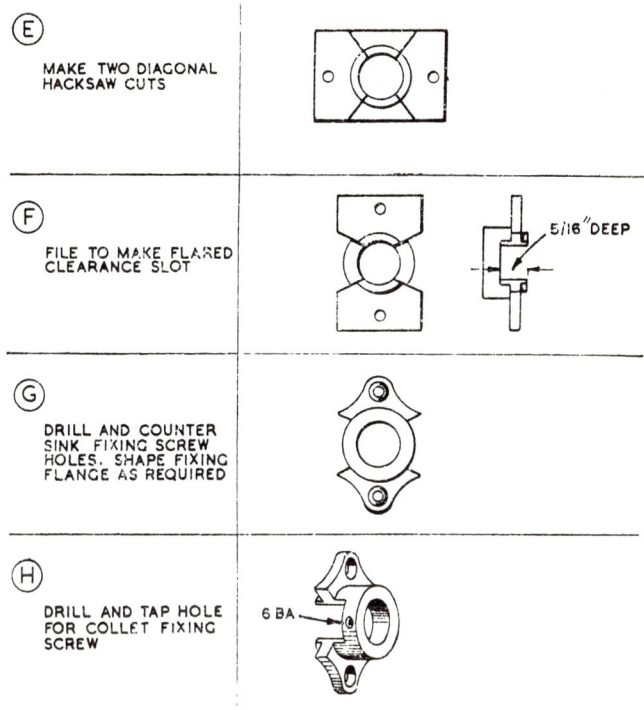

E MAKE TWO DIAGONAL HACKSAW CUTS

F FILE TO MAKE FLARED CLEARANCE SLOT — 5/16" DEEP

G DRILL AND COUNTER SINK FIXING SCREW HOLES. SHAPE FIXING FLANGE AS REQUIRED

H DRILL AND TAP HOLE FOR COLLET FIXING SCREW — 6 BA

Fig 77

die holder, the holes for the 6 B.A. fixing screws are drilled and tapped.

Collets. The standard form of collet shown in Fig. 78, can be machined from a length of $\frac{5}{8}$ in. diameter mild- or silver-steel mounted in the lathe chuck. The spigot is turned to $\frac{1}{2}$ in. diameter to fit the adapter, and a groove should be cut with a V-pointed tool to receive the point of the fixing screw.

The guide hole is drilled centrally in accordance with

the method described for drilling from the lathe tailstock and, finally, the collet is parted off. If the collet is to have much use it should be case-hardened or hardened in the manner already described, but, as a rule, this will be found unnecessary in the small workshop especially if silver-steel is used for the construction.

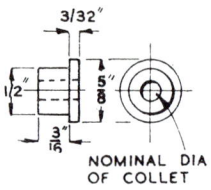

Fig. 78

A Colleted Die Holder. This die holder, which is illustrated in Fig. 79, has a central body piece machined from the solid and carrying two handles.

Although the holder is primarily intended for hand threading, it can be used as a tailstock die holder when one handle is unscrewed. For the latter purpose, an arbor is used with a tapered shank to fit the tailstock taper, and a parallel portion on which the die-holder collet slides to guide the die.

The holder is machined to take the standard form of collet used in the previous example.

Three screws are fitted for holding the die when resting against the shoulder of the die housing shown in the drawing, and the flared slot provided for chip clearance will be seen towards the lower part of the front face of the device.

The working drawings given in Fig. 80 will make clear the actual construction of the holder, and it will be apparent that it can be made from a $\frac{3}{4}$ in. length of 1 in. sq. mild-steel bar.

One end of the bar is filed flat and the centre is marked-out and drilled with a centre drill. The work is then secured in the four-jaw chuck, and after it has been centred with the aid of the centre finder, it is faced and then drilled and bored right through to ½ in. diameter to fit a standard collet.

This bore is enlarged to 13/16 in. for a depth of 5/16 in. to form the housing for the die, but before finishing the bore to size, the diameter of the circular dies used should be measured as these vary in size in different makes, and it is essential that the die should fit closely in its housing if it is to be truly centred.

When the machining has been completed, the work is removed from the chuck and the positions of the screwed holes to receive the handles and the collet fixing screw are marked-out, in accordance with the dimensions given in the drawings.

These holes are then drilled and tapped ¼ in. 40 or 26 threads per inch for the handles, and 6 B.A. for the fixing screw.

The chip clearance slot is marked-out as shown, and the bulk of the metal is removed by drilling a series of 5/32 in. holes right through the work from side to side.

The slot is then filed to shape and its mouth on either side is flared as depicted in the drawing.

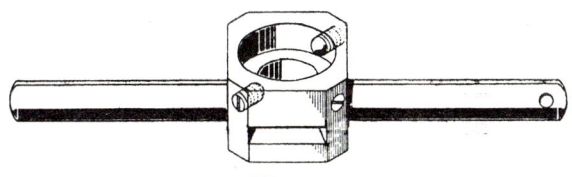

Fig. 79

The four corners of the body are filed to form flat surfaces for the reception of the die-fixing screws. The position of these screws must be determined by reference to the particular dies used, as these vary both in construction and in the position of the recesses provided for the points

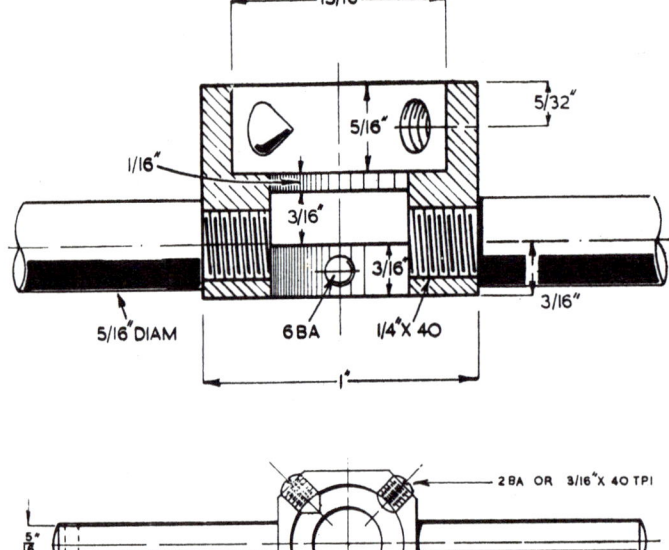

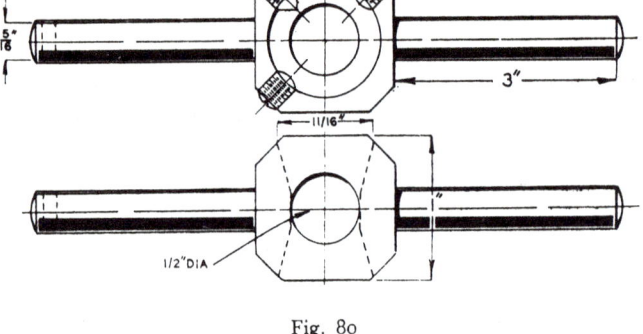

Fig. 80

of the fixing screws; but if three screws are fitted, as shown in the drawings, these should be suitable for holding most dies.

The handles are made from lengths of 5/16 in. steel rod, reduced at the ends to 1/4 in. for threading and screwing into the body.

If the die holder is to be used for threading from the

lathe tailstock, it is advisable to drill a cross-hole near the outer end of one handle to take a tommy bar, so that the arm can be readily removed when required.

A Tapping Handle for the Drilling Machine. As described in Chapter One, the drilling machine can be used for tapping holes when a tap is mounted in the chuck and the spindle is turned by a handle secured to its upper end.

An easily made handle for this purpose is shown in Fig. 81, and the full working drawings are reproduced in Fig. 82.

The collar (1) that carries the handle bar (3) is clamped to the drilling machine spindle by the screw (6) whose point engages in the spindle keyway. To alter the leverage obtained, the screws (5) holding the clamp plate (2) are slackened, and the handle bar can then be moved to any position required.

The Handle Bar (3) is made from a length of $\frac{1}{2}$ in. by $\frac{1}{8}$ in. mild-steel. A $\frac{1}{4}$ in. diameter hole to receive the shank of the handle is drilled $\frac{1}{4}$ in. from one end, and both this and the opposite end of the bar are rounded off by filing as shown in the drawing. The sides and edges of the bar are then draw-filed with a fine file to complete the work on this part.

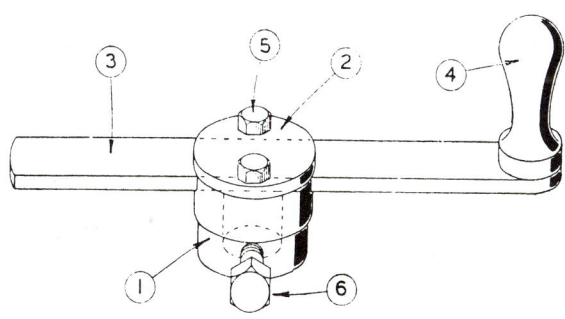

Fig. 81

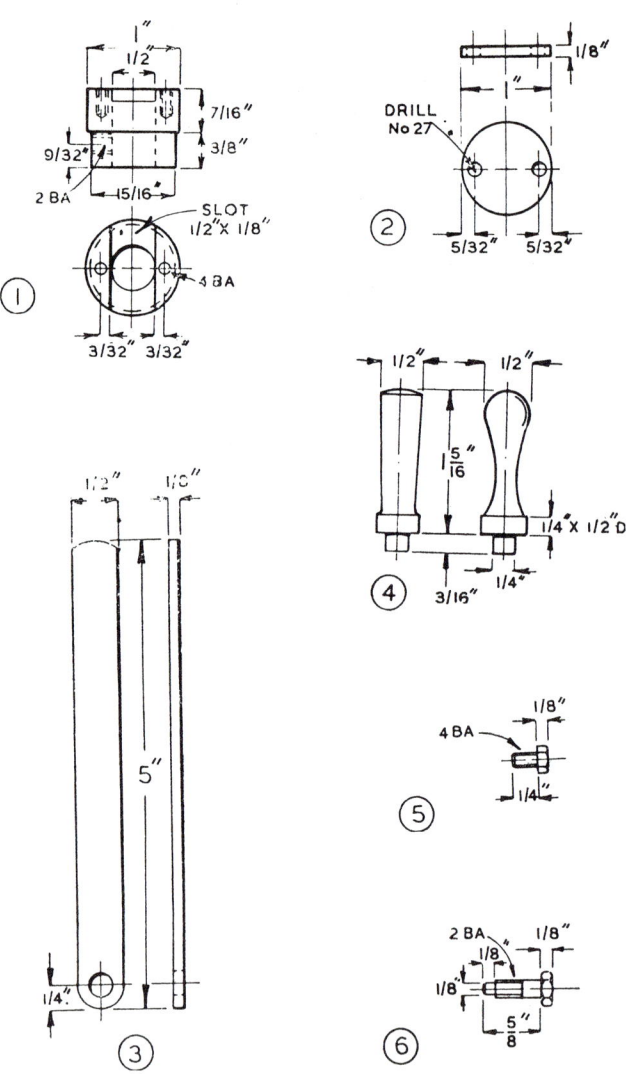

Fig. 82

The Handle (4) of the rounded form shown in the drawing is turned to shape with hand tools from a piece of ½ in. diameter round bar ; this is followed by using a fine file and emery cloth on the rotating work until a good, smooth finish has been obtained.

To avoid using hand tools, the handle can, if preferred, be made in the form of a straight taper as in the drawing.

This taper is machined by setting the lathe top-slide to an angle of some 2 deg., and the top of the handle is then rounded or chamfered to give a good appearance.

After the handle has been turned to shape it is parted off, but care must be taken to ensure that both the upper end of the handle and the collar at its base are of equal diameter, to enable it to be held securely in the chuck for turning the spigot.

The handle is gripped in the self-centring chuck over its two ½ in. diameters, but a piece of thin card or sheet-copper should be interposed to prevent damage to the work surface.

The spigot is turned to a good press-nt in the handle bar, that is to say it should be made about a thousandth of an inch larger in diameter than the hole.

The polishing operation is best carried out with the spigot of the handle secured in the chuck of the drilling machine, for a high speed is then available, and, in addition, there is no danger of the abrasive dust formed causing damage to the machine, as may happen when the lathe is used for this purpose and the slides are not well-protected by temporary coverings.

After it has been polished, the handle is pressed into the bar with the aid of the vice, and the part projecting is lightly riveted over with a hammer to make the joint secure.

The Collar (1) is turned from a short length of 1 in. diameter round mild-steel bar held in the self-centring chuck. The central hole is drilled and finally bored to fit the drill spindle, and after the lower part has been reduced to 15/16 in. in diameter, the collar is parted off ⅞ in. in length.

The work is then reversed in the chuck to face the upper surface of the collar. The dimensions of the slot to receive the bar are marked-out by clamping the work in a V block standing on the surface plate, and scribing parallel lines with the surface gauge from the upper and lower edges of the bore.

The depth of the slot is marked-out with the surface gauge while the collar is standing on end on the surface plate.

Cuts are then made with a hacksaw inside the scribed lines and to a depth just short of the dimension lines scribed on the outer diameter. The slot is filed to shape to fit the bar, but the latter must stand slightly proud so that it receives the pressure of the clamping plate.

The Clamping Plate (2) is best made by facing the end of a short length of 1 in. diameter round-bar held in the self-centring chuck and then parting off a disc $\frac{1}{8}$ in. in thickness. The central pip left on the work can be removed with the aid of a scraper.

The position of the screw holes is determined by scribing a line through the centre of the plate and marking-out the two drilling centres with the jenny callipers set to 5/32 in. ; the two screw holes are drilled with a No. 27 drill.

The collar with the clamping plate in position is clamped in the upright position in the machine vice, and the No. 27 drill is entered in the previously drilled holes and fed into the collar for $\frac{1}{16}$ in. This drill is followed by a No. 32 drill, and the holes so formed are tapped No. 4 B.A. in the drilling machine without disturbing the setting of the parts in the vice.

It now remains to fit the two 4 B.A. hexagon-headed screws for the clamping plate and the 2 B.A. clamp screw to the collar.

After the position of the clamp screw has been marked-out, the collar is secured in the machine vice and a No. 2 B.A. tapping size hole is drilled on the diameter with a No. 22 drill and then tapped.

The three screws required are best made from hexagon rod, but if this is not available, round steel-rod may be used. The shanks of the screws are turned to size in the lathe and then threaded with the aid of the tailstock die holder. The hexagon heads are formed, when necessary, by filing the round rod to shape, using a standard nut screwed on the screw blank to act as a filing guide. It is advisable to form the same size of hexagon on all the screws so that a single spanner will serve for all adjustments.

When making the 2 B.A. clamp screw, its tip should be reduced in diameter to allow it to enter the spindle keyway, and a brass disc should be used to take the clamping pressure to save the keyway from damage.

As an alternative, the screws can be turned from square rod held in the four-jaw chuck; this will save the filing work necessary in the previous case to form the heads to shape.

To add to the appearance of the work, the screws can be blued by heating them in the flame of a spirit lamp and plunging them into oil as soon as the desired colour is reached.

Making a Countersink. As has been pointed out commercial countersinks with several cutting lips are liable to chatter when used in small drilling machines, and, to overcome this, the single-lip form of cutter should be adopted.

A cutter of this pattern is illustrated in Fig. 83, where it will be seen that the point is formed to include an angle of 90 deg., and the flat cutting face lies a little above the diameter. This construction gives a single cutting edge whilst the other lip acts as a guide or steady to prevent chatter.

To make the cutter, a short length of $\frac{1}{2}$ in. diameter round silver-steel is set to run truly in the four-jaw chuck, and the shank is turned to a diameter of $\frac{1}{4}$ in. to enable it to be held in the chuck of the small drilling machine.

The work is then reversed in the chuck and, after it has been set truly, the tip is turned to an angle of 90 deg.

by setting the lathe top slide to 45 deg. The knife tool used for this operation should be set to the exact centre height; this can be checked, when facing the end of the work, by adjusting the tool so that no central pip is formed.

The cutter is then removed from the lathe and secured in the vice for filing the flat face on the tip as shown in the

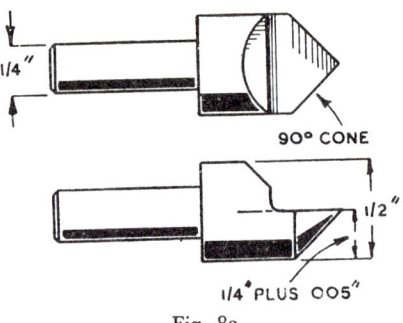

Fig. 83

drawing; this face must be formed slightly above the diameter, and a measurement taken with the micrometer will help to determine this exactly.

The next step is to harden and temper the tool; it is, therefore, heated to a bright cherry-red and plunged into cold water; test the steel with a file, and, if the file slides over the surface without cutting the metal, the cutter is fully hardened.

Clean the work with a piece of fine, worn emery cloth, and heat the shank carefully in a small flame until the tip assumes a straw colour, then plunge the cutter into cold water and the tempering is completed, leaving the tool tough and not brittle as in the fully hardened state.

Finally, the flat face of the cutter should be honed on an oilstone to finish the sharpening of the cutting edge, but in both this and in any subsequent sharpening operations care must be taken to maintain the cutting edge above the diameter, otherwise the non-chattering properties of the tool will be lost.

Counterbores and Pin Drills. The purpose for which these tools are used has been described in Chapter One, and there are two forms in common use; the two-lipped flat cutter with a solid central guide pin, as shown in Fig. 84, and the cutter with two or more cutting lips and a detachable guide-pin as illustrated in Fig. 85. The latter is usually referred to as a pin drill, and it has the advantage that guide pins of various sizes can be used in a single cutter.

To make the flat form of cutter, a length of silver-steel is centred in the four-jaw chuck and the shank is turned to the required diameter and length. The work is then reversed in the chuck and, after it has been faced and a light cut taken over the body, the central pin is formed with a knife tool leaving a square shoulder.

The cutter is next gripped in the vice and the flat faces are formed by filing, but care must be taken not to damage the central pin. The two lips are then shaped with a fine file to form the cutting edges as shown in the drawing.

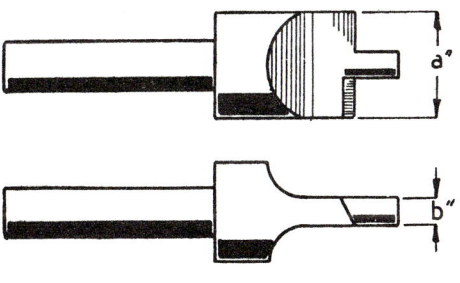

Fig. 84

After the cutter has been hardened and tempered, as described in the case of the countersink, the cutting edges are carefully honed with an oilstone slip to impart the final sharpness.

The pin drill shown in Fig. 85 is also made of silver-steel, and it will be an advantage to make a set of these useful tools to cover the range of work normally undertaken.

In the smaller sizes 3/32 in. diameter guide pins can be used, but for sizes above and including $\frac{5}{16}$ in. a $\frac{1}{8}$ in. diameter pin will be found more serviceable.

When making large cutters, a shank of reduced diameter, as in the previous examples, may be required to fit the chuck of the drilling machine, but smaller cutters can be made parallel throughout, as shown in the drawing in Fig. 85A.

A length of silver-steel is centred in the four-jaw chuck and its end is faced with a knife tool ; then, as described in Chapter Five, the central hole for the guide pin is drilled to the required depth. The two cutting lips are formed by making a cut on the diameter with a fine hacksaw, as shown in Fig. 85B, and at the same time the saw

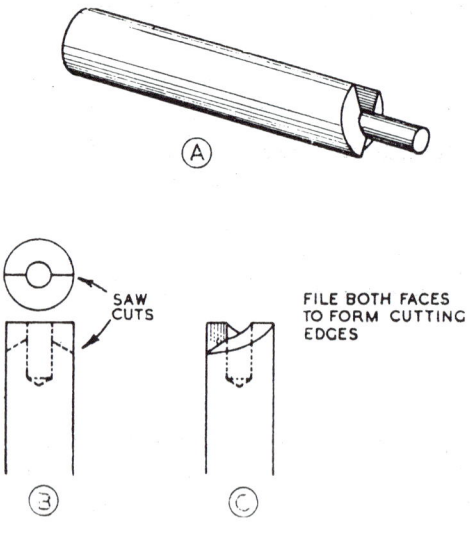

Fig. 85

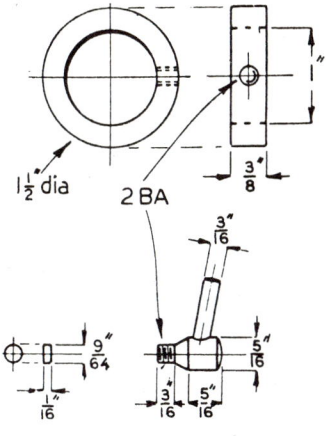

Fig. 86

is inclined to make the cuts slope in accordance with the drawing.

If preferred, two further saw cuts can be made to remove the surplus metal prior to filing the cutting lips to the shape depicted in Fig. 85c.

Should an error be made when filing the lips to shape, this can be retrieved by again mounting the cutter in the chuck and taking a facing cut across its end.

When filing the lips, the edge of the file should make contact with the vertical face of the cutting edge in order to give it a smooth finish. If a fine file is used for this purpose, the edges will be quite sharp and oil stoning after the cutter has been hardened and tempered may not be needed.

The guide pins are made of silver-steel and there should be no need to harden them as they are readily renewed when worn; in addition, there is no danger of an unhardened pin breaking when in use.

Drilling Machine Table Stop. This device, which will be found a useful addition to the drilling machine, is illustrated in Fig. 14 in Chapter One, and the working drawings from which it can be made are given here in Fig. 86.

The collar, made of mild-steel or cast-iron to be in keeping with the rest of the drilling machine, can usually be machined from a piece of scrap material, but if this is not available the part should be turned from a short length of steel bar.

The turning operations involved are quite straightforward and consist in turning the outer diameter, drilling and boring the part to make it a good sliding fit on the machine column, and then parting off to the required length.

The collar is finally drilled with a No. 22 drill, and tapped to take the 2 B.A. clamping screw.

After the body of the clamping screw has been turned and threaded as previously described, it is secured in an inclined position in the machine vice. The hole for the handle is formed by first entering the point of a fine centre drill in a deep depression made with a centre punch; a small drill is then put right through the work, and this is followed by a larger centre drill to make a bearing for the No. 13 drill which enlarges the hole to the finished size.

The next step is to grip the rod in the self-centring chuck and part off the screw to the correct length; the screw is then reversed in the chuck and its end is faced and finally rounded or chamfered.

The handle is made from a short length of $\frac{3}{16}$ in. diameter steel-rod which is held in the chuck of the lathe or drilling machine, to enable one end to be slightly tapered with the aid of a fine file. The vice is then used to press the handle into place in the screw head.

A small pad, as shown in the drawing, is turned and parted off from a length of brass rod; this pad piece is used to protect the drilling machine column from being marked by the end of the clamping screw.

The Centrefinder or Wobbler. A description of this

appliance was given in Chapter Five, where it was also illustrated ; the working drawings reproduced in Fig. 87 show the details of its construction.

It will be clear that the body piece (A) must be straight, otherwise the indications given by the device when in use will be misleading.

A piece of silver-steel rod should be used to make the body, and its straightness can be checked by mounting it either in the four-jaw chuck of the lathe or in a trueholding chuck in the drilling machine. Although the trained eye can readily detect any material wobble, it is best to use the test indicator to take readings at various points, and to repeat these tests with the rod reversed in the chuck. Moreover, if the rod is turned in the chuck through an angle of 180 deg., and a second set of readings is taken, errors arising from lack of truth in the chuck can be eliminated.

Should there be any difficulty in finding a straight piece of material, a rod should be turned to size in the lathe using the travelling steady as described in Chapter Five.

The rod is centred in the four-jaw chuck and its end is faced with a knife tool, set at centre height to avoid forming a central pip ; the top slide is then set to 30 deg. and the conical 60 deg. tip is turned to a sharp point.

Next, when the rod has been reversed and centred in the chuck, a $\frac{1}{8}$ in. centre drill is fed in to form a parallel bore for a depth of at least $\frac{1}{8}$ in. ; a $\frac{1}{8}$ in. drill is then entered for the full length of the bore. The mouth of this hole is opened out with a centre drill to form a guide bearing for the drill used to enlarge the bore to its full diameter.

If the drilling is carefully carried out it should be possible to drill this hole accurately with a $\frac{3}{16}$ in. drill, but if there is any doubt about this, a smaller drill should be used and the bore is then finished with a small boring tool.

To make the plunger (B), a length of silver-steel rod is gripped in the chuck and turned down to make it an accur-

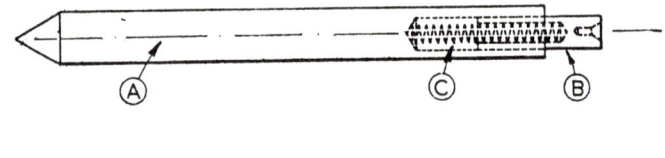

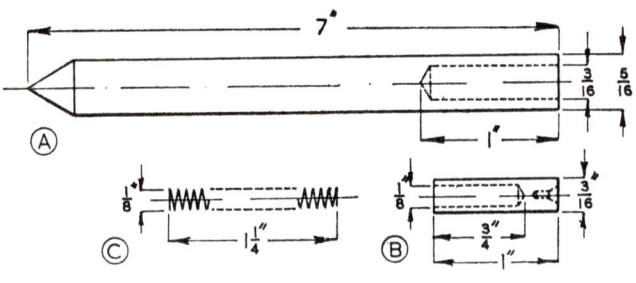

Fig. 87

ate sliding fit in the machined bore; a centre drill hole is then formed in the faced end, as shown in the drawing, and the piece is parted off to the correct length. The plunger is next reversed in the chuck and the hole to receive the spring (C) is drilled as previously described.

The length of the spring fitted should allow the plunger to project as shown. To secure the parts in position, so that the plunger does not fall out, the ends of the spring should be opened out with the pliers to give a firm frictional grip in both the plunger and the body piece. Fit the plunger to the spring by turning the former in a direction to close the coils of the spring, then insert the spring in the body and continue turning the plunger until the parts are correctly assembled.

An Angular Grinding Rest. The method of using the angular grinding rest was described and illustrated in Chapter Two, and the complete rest is shown in Fig. 88.

The rest is attached to the bench by means of the angle bracket (C), to which the swing arm (B) is secured by the lower screw (D).

At the upper end of the arm (B) the tilting work table (A) is attached by the stud and nut (E) to the angle bracket (F), which can rotate on the upper clamping screw (D).

It will be clear that, when the two screws (D) are slackened, the table can be tilted to any angle required and, at the same time, the slot in the table can be set to clear the sides of the wheel.

Reference to the working drawings reproduced in Fig. 89 will show that both the angle brackets (C) and (F) have been made of $\frac{1}{8}$ in. angle-steel as this was the only material available at the time, but stouter material of $\frac{3}{16}$ in. section might have been used with advantage.

The drawings of the bracket (C) show the position of the screw holes for attachment to the bench, and also the location of the tapped hole to receive the screw (D).

The length shown for the arm (B) may need to be altered to bring the surface of the rest some distance below the

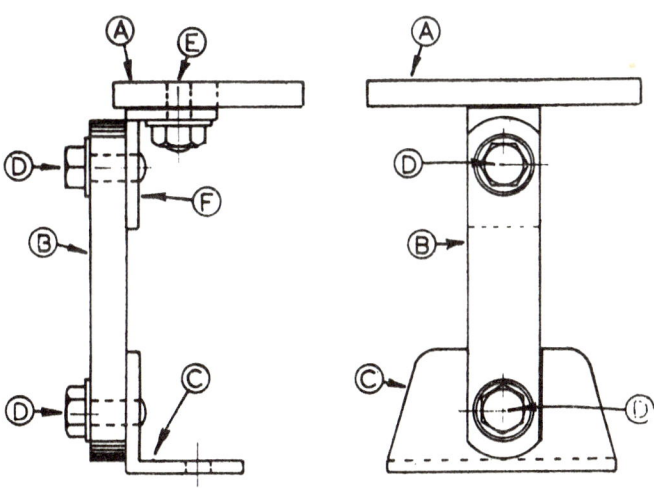

Fig. 88

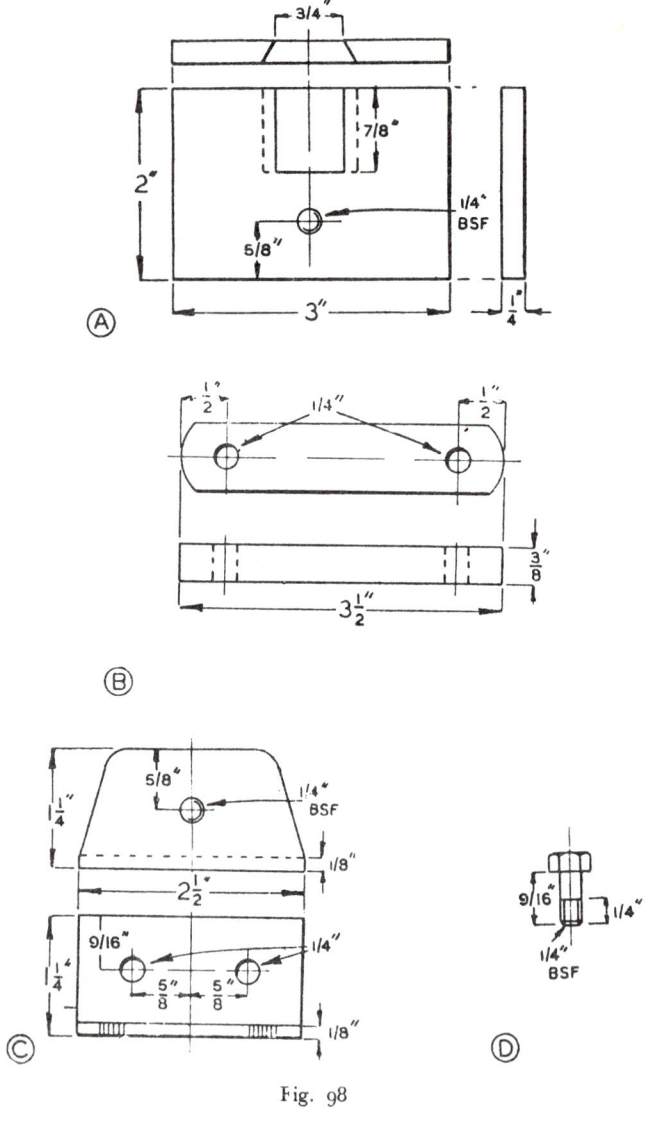

Fig. 98

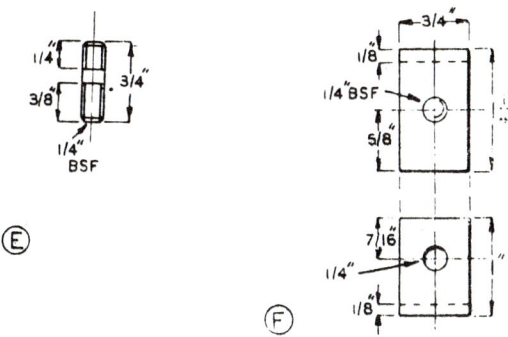

Fig. 89

centre line of the wheel to allow for the thickness of the tool being ground.

Both ends of the arm are drilled to give a working clearance for the screws (*D*).

The mild-steel table (*A*) should be made fully large to give adequate support for the tools; the dimensions of the slot will depend on the size and thickness of the grinding wheel fitted.

The upper surface of the table should be filed to a flat finish so that the tools will lie evenly and without rock.

The table is attached to the angle bracket (*F*) by means of a flush-fitting stud (*E*) fitted with a nut and washer.

For the fixing screws (*D*) either hexagon-headed screws can be used in accordance with the drawing, or, if preferred, studs and nuts can be employed similar to (*E*) only rather longer.

In the latter case, to give additional security, the inward ends of the studs should be lightly riveted over.

TWIST DRILLS

Inch or gauge	mm	Decimal Inch	Inch or gauge	mm	Decimal Inch	Inch or gauge	mm	Decimal Inch	Inch or gauge	mm	Decimal Inch
80		0.0135	72		0.0250	64		0.0360	55		0.0520
	0.35	0.0138		0.65	0.0256		0.925	0.0364		1.35	0.0531
79		0.0145	71		0.0260	63		0.0370	54		0.0550
	0.375	0.0148		0.675	0.0266		0.95	0.0374		1.4	0.0551
1/64		0.0156		0.7	0.0276	62		0.0380		1.45	0.0571
	0.4	0.0157	70		0.0280		0.975	0.0384		1.5	0.0590
78		0.0160		0.725	0.0285	61		0.0390	53		0.0595
	0.425	0.0167	69		0.0292		1.00	0.0394		1.55	0.0610
	0.45	0.0177		0.75	0.0295	60		0.0400	1/16		0.0625
77		0.0180		0.775	0.0305	59		0.0410		1.6	0.0630
	0.475	0.0187	68		0.0310		1.05	0.0413	52		0.0635
	0.5	0.0197	1/32		0.0312	58		0.0420		1.65	0.0650
76		0.0200		0.8	0.0315	57		0.0430		1.7	0.0669
	0.525	0.0207	67		0.0320		1.1	0.0433	51		0.0670
75		0.0210		0.825	0.0325		1.15	0.0453		1.75	0.0689
	0.55	0.0216	66		0.0330	56		0.0465	50		0.0700
74		0.0225		0.85	0.0335	3/64		0.0469		1.8	0.0709
	0.575	0.0226		0.875	0.0344		1.2	0.0472		1.85	0.0728
	0.6	0.0236	65		0.0350		1.25	0.0492	49		0.0738
73		0.0240		0.9	0.0354		1.3	0.0512		1.9	0.0748
	0.625	0.0246									

Contd.

Inch or Gauge	mm	Decimal Inch	Inch or Gauge	mm	Decimal Inch	Inch or Gauge	mm	Decimal Inch
48		0.0760	40		0.0980	31		0.1200
	1.95	0.0768		2.5	0.0984		3.05	0.1201
5/64		0.0781		2.55	0.0995		3.1	0.1220
47		0.0785	39		0.1004		3.15	0.1240
	2.00	0.0787	38		0.1015	1/8		0.1250
	2.05	0.0807		2.6	0.1024		3.2	0.1260
46		0.0810	37		0.1040		3.25	0.1280
45		0.0820		2.65	0.1043	30		0.1285
	2.1	0.0827		2.7	0.1063		3.3	0.1299
	2.15	0.0846	36		0.1065		3.35	0.1319
44		0.0860		2.75	0.1083		3.4	0.1339
	2.2	0.0866	7/64		0.1094		3.45	0.1358
	2.25	0.0886	35		0.1100	29		0.1360
43		0.0890		2.8	0.1102		3.5	0.1378
	2.3	0.0906	34		0.1110		3.55	0.1398
	2.35	0.0925		2.85	0.1122	28		0.1405
42		0.0935	33		0.1130	9/64		0.1406
3/32		0.0938		2.9	0.1142		3.6	0.1417
	2.4	0.0945	32		0.1160		3.65	0.1437
41		0.0960		2.95	0.1161	27		0.1440
	2.45	0.0964		3.00	0.1181		3.7	0.1457
						26		0.1470
							3.75	0.1476

Inch or Gauge	mm	Decimal Inch
25		0.1495
	3.8	0.1496
	3.85	0.1516
24		0.1520
	3.9	0.1535
23		0.1540
	3.95	0.1555
5/32		0.1562
22		0.1570
	4.00	0.1575
21		0.1590
	4.05	0.1594
20		0.1610
	4.1	0.1614
	4.15	0.1634
	4.2	0.1654
19		0.1660
	4.25	0.1673
	4.3	0.1693
18		0.1695
	4.35	0.1713

contd.

Inch or Gauge	mm	Decimal Inch	Inch or Gauge	mm	Decimal Inch	Inch or Gauge	mm	Decimal Inch	Inch or Gauge	mm	Decimal Inch
11/64		0.1719	9		0.1960	1		0.2280	17/64		0.2656
17		0.1730		5.00	0.1968			0.2283			0.2657
	4.4	0.1732	8		0.1990		5.8	0.2323		6.75	0.2660
	4.45	0.1752		5.1	0.2008		5.9	0.2340	H		0.2677
16		0.1770			0.2010	A		0.2344		6.8	0.2716
		0.1772	7		0.2031	15/64		0.2362		6.9	0.2720
	4.5	0.1791	13/64		0.2040		6.00	0.2380			0.2756
	4.55	0.1800	6		0.2047	B		0.2402	I		0.2770
15		0.1811		5.2	0.2055		6.1	0.2420		7.00	0.2795
	4.6	0.1820	5		0.2067	C		0.2441	J		0.2810
	4.65	0.1831		5.25	0.2087		6.2	0.2460		7.1	0.2812
14		0.1850		5.3	0.2090	D		0.2461	K		0.2835
	4.7	0.1870	4		0.2126		6.25	0.2480	9/32		0.2854
	4.75	0.1875		5.4	0.2130		6.3	0.2500		7.2	0.2874
13		0.1890	3		0.2165	E, 1/4		0.2520		7.25	0.2900
	4.8	0.1909		5.5	0.2188		6.4	0.2559		7.3	0.2913
3/16		0.1910	7/32		0.2205		6.5	0.2570	L		0.2950
12		0.1929		5.6	0.2210	F		0.2598		7.4	0.2953
	4.85	0.1935	2		0.2244		6.6	0.2610	M		0.2969
11		0.1949		5.7	0.2264	G		0.2638		7.5	0.2992
	4.9			5.75			6.7		19/64		
10										7.6	
	4.95										

contd.

Inch or Gauge	mm	Decimal Inch	Inch or Gauge	mm	Decimal Inch	Inch or Gauge	mm	Decimal Inch	Inch	mm	Decimal Inch
N	7.7	0.3020	$\frac{11}{32}$	8.75	0.3438	W	9.9	0.3860	$\frac{7}{16}$	11.2	0.4375
	7.75	0.3031		8.8	0.3445			0.3898		11.25	0.4409
	7.8	0.3051	S		0.3465			0.3906		11.3	0.4429
	7.9	0.3071		8.9	0.3480	$\frac{25}{64}$	10.00	0.3937		11.4	0.4449
		0.3110		9.00	0.3504	X		0.3970		11.5	0.4488
	8.00	0.3125			0.3543		10.1	0.3976			0.4528
$\frac{5}{16}$		0.3150	T	9.1	0.3580		10.2	0.4016		11.6	0.4531
		0.3160			0.3583		10.25	0.4035	$\frac{29}{64}$	11.7	0.4567
O	8.1	0.3189	$\frac{23}{64}$		0.3594	Y		0.4040		11.75	0.4606
	8.2	0.3228		9.2	0.3622		10.3	0.4055		11.8	0.4626
P		0.3230		9.25	0.3642			0.4062		11.9	0.4646
	8.25	0.3248		9.3	0.3661	$\frac{13}{32}$	10.4	0.4094			0.4685
	8.3	0.3268	U		0.3680	N		0.4130	$\frac{15}{32}$		0.4688
$\frac{21}{64}$		0.3281		9.4	0.3701		10.5	0.4134		12.00	0.4724
	8.4	0.3307		9.5	0.3740		10.6	0.4173		12.1	0.4764
Q		0.3320	$\frac{3}{8}$		0.3750		10.7	0.4213		12.2	0.4803
	8.5	0.3346	V		0.3770			0.4219		12.25	0.4823
	8.6	0.3386		9.6	0.3780	$\frac{27}{64}$		0.4232		12.3	0.4842
R		0.3390		9.7	0.3819		10.75	0.4252			0.4844
	8.7	0.3425		9.75	0.3839		10.8	0.4291	$\frac{31}{64}$	12.4	0.4882
				9.8	0.3858		10.9	0.4331		12.5	0.4921
							11.00	0.4370		12.6	0.4961
							11.1				

contd.

Inch	m/m	Decimal Inch	Inch	m/m	Decimal Inch	Inch	m/m	Decimal Inch
1/2	12.7	0.5000	39/64		0.6094	47/64		0.7344
	12.75	0.5020		15.5	0.6102		18.75	0.7382
	12.8	0.5039		15.75	0.6201		19.00	0.7480
	12.9	0.5079	5/8		0.6250	3/4		0.7500
	13.00	0.5118		16.00	0.6299		19.25	0.7579
33/64		0.5156		16.25	0.6398	49/64		0.7656
	13.25	0.5216	41/64		0.6406		19.5	0.7677
17/32		0.5312		16.5	0.6496		19.75	0.7776
	13.5	0.5315	21/32		0.6562	25/32		0.7812
	13.75	0.5413		16.75	0.6594		20.00	0.7874
35/64		0.5469		17.00	0.6693	51/64		0.7969
	14.00	0.5512	43/64		0.6719		20.25	0.7972
	14.25	0.5610		17.25	0.6875		20.5	0.8071
9/16		0.5625	11/16		0.6875	13/16		0.8125
	14.5	0.5709		17.5	0.6890		20.75	0.8169
37/64		0.5781		17.75	0.6988		21.00	0.8268
	14.75	0.5807	45/64		0.7031	53/64		0.8281
	15.00	0.5906		18.00	0.7087		21.25	0.8366
19/32		0.5938		18.25	0.7185	27/32		0.8438
	15.25	0.6004	23/32		0.7188		21.5	0.8465
				18.5	0.7284		2.751	0.8563

Inch	m/m	Decimal Inch
55/64		0.8594
	22.00	0.8661
7/8		0.8750
	22.25	0.8760
	22.5	0.8858
57/64		0.8906
	22.75	0.8957
	23.00	0.9055
29/32		0.9062
	23.25	0.9154
59/64		0.9219
	23.5	0.9252
	23.75	0.9350
15/16		0.9375
	24.00	0.9449
61/64		0.9531
	24.25	0.9547
	24.5	0.9646
31/32		0.9688
	24.75	0.9744
	25.00	0.9842
63/64		0.9844
1		1.0000

INDEX.

A

Abrafile, 22, 78.
Angle-Poise Lamp, 9, 10.
Angle Plate, 55.
Angular Grinding Rest, 139-141.
,, ,, ,, templates for, 143.
,, ,, ,, making an 230-233.

B

Bakers' Fluid, 95.
Belt Pulleys, 165-167.
Beltfasteners, Round Belt, 119-120.
Belts, V, 165-166.
Benches, 2, 3.
Blue Marking Compound, 73, 74.
Boring, 190.
,, Bar, 200-201.
,, Work on the Saddle 200-201.

C

Callipers, 41-43.
,, Jenny, 49.
Case-Hardening, 99.
Centre Finder, 185-186.
,, ,, Making a, 228-230.
Centre Lines, 64.
,, Punch, 49, 50.
Centres, Lathe, 198-199.
Chests of Drawers, 6, 8.
Chisels, 30, 31, 82-84.
Chucks, Drill, 126.
,, Four-jaw, 155-156.
,, Self-centring, 155.
,, Setting Work in, 184-186.
,, Turning Work in, 186-190.
,, Use of, 184-192.
Clams, Vice, 13.
Colleted Die-holders, Making, 211-219.
Conventions used in Drawings, 61-65.
Cupboards, 2, 6, 8, 9.
Counterbores, 134.
,, and Pin Drills, Making, 223-224.
Countersinks, 132-133.
,, Making, 223-224.
Countershaft, 165-166.
,, Speeds, 165.
Cross-drilling Shafts, 131-132.
Cut, Depth of, 183-184.
Cutting Speeds, 182-183.

D

D-bit, 203.
Depth Drilling, 202-203.
Depth Gauge, 45.
,, ,, Making a simple, 100-103.
Dies, 25-27
Dieing and Tapping in the Lathe, 203-206.
Die Holders, 27, 28.
Die Holders, Making Colleted, 211-219.

Dimensions, 65.
Dividers, 48, 49.
Draw-Filing, 70-72.
Drawings, Conventions used in, 61-65.
Drawings, Reading Machine, 60-65.
Drill Gauge, 46, 47.
Drill Pad, 157
Drills Grinding, 144-146.
,, ,, Potts Jig, 145-146.
,, Chuck, 126.
,, Chuck Lathe, 157.
Drills, Hand, 22-24.
,, Straight Fluted, 24.
,, Twist, 24.
Drilling with Hand Drill, 85-88.
Drilling Machine, Depth, Stop and Gauge, 127-128.
,, ,, Driving the, 118-120, 163, 170.
,, ,, Electric, 118.
,, ,, Equipment, 123-127.
,, ,, Lever Feed, 109-112.
,, ,, Rack Feed, 112-116.
,, ,, Table Stop, 126.
,, ,, Table Stop, Making, 227.
,, ,, Table V-blocks 124-125.
,, ,, Tapping Handle For, 219, 223-228.
,, ,, Tapping in the, 132-133.
,, ,, Vice, 123-124.
,, ,, Work Clamp, 125-126.
,, Machines, Champion, 115.
,, ,, Model Engineer, 109-112, 119.
,, ,, Wolf, 118.
,, ,, Cowell, 116-118.
Drilling Sheet Metal, 88.
Drilling for Tapping, 132.
,, from the Tailstock, 201-202.
,, into a Cross Hole, 130-131.
,, on an Inclined Surface, 130,131.
,, Operations, 128-134.
,, Speeds, 120-123.
Driving the Drilling Machine, 118-120, 163, 170.
,, ,, Lathe, 152-154.
,, ,, Machine Tools, 163-172.

INDEX

E

Electric Drilling Machine, 118.
,, Grinding ,, 138-139.
,, Motor Drives to Machine Tools, 163-172.
Equipment, Drilling Machine, 123-127.
,, Lathe, 154-162.
Equipment for Marking-out, 41-49.
Equipment for Screw Threading, 24-28.
Equipment for Soldering, 38, 39.
,, Workshop, 12-40.

F

Faceplate, Use of, 192-195.
Feed Gear, Lathe, 150-151.
Feed, Rate of, 183.
Files, 16-19.
File Card, 70.
,, Handles, Fitting, 18.
Filing, 66.
,, Aluminium, 72.
,, Draw-, 70-72.
Fixed Steady, 158-159.
Floor, The Workshop, 10.
Flux, Soldering, 95, 96.
Four-jaw Chuck, 155-156.
Four-tool Turret, 157-158.

G

Gauge, Depth, 45.
,, a Simple Depth, 100-103.
,, Drill, 46, 47.
,, Surface, 55.
Gear, Feed, 150-151.
Graver, 208-210.
Grinding Machine, 135-138, 167.
,, ,, Driving the, 136-137, 167, 170.
,, ,, Electric, 138-139.
,, ,, Black & Decker 138-139.
Grinding Operations, 142-144.
,, Rest, Angular, 139-141.
,, ,, Angular Templates for, 143.
,, ,, Making an Angular, 230-233.
,, Twist Drills, 144-146.
,, Twist Drills, Potts Jig for, 145-146.

H

Hacksaw, 19-21.
,, Blades, 19, 20.
,, Using the, 76, 77.
Hammers, 37.
Hand Drills, 22-24.
Hand Rest, 160-161.
,, Tools, 16-40.
,, ,, Using, 66-99.
,, Turning Tools, 207-210.
Handles, Fitting File, 18.
Hardening and Tempering, 98, 99.
Headstock, Lathe, 149.
Heating the Workshop, 2, 9.

J

Jenny Callipers, 49.

L

Lamps, Angle-Poise, 9, 10.
Lathe, The, 147-152.
,, Accessories, 154-162.
,, Centres, 198-199.
,, Chucks, 155-157.
,, Dogs, 197-198.
,, Drill Chuck, 157
,, Driving the, 152-154.
,, Equipment, 154-162.
,, Feed Gear, 150-151.
,, Half Centres, 198-199.
,, Hand Turning Tools, 207-210.
,, Headstock, 149.
,, Saddle, 149.
,, Tailstock, 150.
,, Tools, 173-178.
Level, Spirit, 16, 86.
Lighting the Workshop, 9, 10.
Lines, Witness, 53.
Lineshafting, 163-164.

M

Machine Drawings, Reading, 60-65.
Machine Tools, Driving the, 163-172.
Marble Slab, 4-6.
Marking-out, 47-59.
,, ,, a Bearing Bracket, 56-59.
,, ,, Centre of a Shaft, 59.
,, ,, Equipment, 41-49.
,, ,, Sheet Metal Work, 50-53.
,, ,, Solid Objects, 54.
,, ,, Fluid, 48.
Measuring Instruments, 178-182.
Metal Cutting, 79-85.
,, ,, with Shears, 82.
,, ,, ,, Cold Chisels, 82-85.
Metal Sawing, 74-76.
Micrometer, 178-180.
Micrometers, 45.

N

Nuts, Bolts and Screws, Storing, 6, 7.

O

Oilstone, Slips, 177.
,, Stoning Jig for, 177-178.
Oilstones, 40.
Operations, Drilling, 128-134.
,, Grinding, 142-144.
,, Turning, 182-200.

P

Pin Drills, Counterbores and, 225-227.
Pinning, 70.
Pliers, 36, 37.
Polishing with Hand Drill, 88, 89.
Protractor, 46.
Pulleys, Belt, 165-167.
Punches, Centre, 49, 50.
,, Pin, 38.

INDEX

R
Racks, Tool, 2, 6-8.
Rawlplugs, 8.
Reamers, 89.
Reaming, 89-90.
Rest, Hand, 160-161.
Rules, 44, 45.
Rule Stand, 55.
,, ,, Making a Simple, 103-107.
Rust, Prevention of, 9.

S
Saddle, Lathe, 149.
Saws, 19-23.
,, Abrafile, 22.
Saws, "Eclipse" Light Pattern, 21.
,, Fret, 22.
,, Hack, 19-21.
,, Piercing, 21-22.
,, Curves, 78, 79.
Sawing Metal, 74-76.
,, ,, Marking-out Work for, 76.
Scrapers, 31,32.
,, Sharpening, 74.
Scraping, 72-74.
Screwdrivers, 34, 36.
Screw Cutting, 206.
,, ,, Tool, External, 176, 206.
,, ,, Tool, Internal, 207.
Screw Threads, 62, 63.
,, ,, Cutting External, 94, 95.
,, ,, Cutting Internal, 90-94.
Screw Threading Equipment, 24-28.
Scriber, 48.
Self-centring Chucks, 155.
Shafts, Cross-drilling, 131-132.
Shears, 28, 29.
,, Tinman's, 82.
Shearing Machine, 29.
Shelving, 8.
Slab, Marble, 4-6.
Snips, Tinman's, 28.
Soldering, 95-98.
,, Equipment, 38, 39.
,, Flux, 95, 96.
,, Irons, 38, 39.
Spanners, 32-34.
Speeds, Cutting, 165.
,, Drilling Machine, 120-123.
,, Countershaft, 165.
Square, 48.
Steadies, Fixed, 158-159.
,, Using Fixed, 196.
,, Travelling, 159-160.
,, Using Travelling, 199-200.
Stones, Oil, 40.
Storing, Screws, Nuts and Bolts, 6-7.
Stoning Tools, 6-8.
Straight Fluted Drills, 24.
Surface Gauge, 55.
,, Plate, 55.

T
Tailstock, Lathe, 150.
,, Die-holder, 205-206.
,, Drilling from the, 201-202.
Tapping, Drilling for, 132-133.
,, Handle for the Drilling Machine, 219, 223-228.
,, in the Drilling Machine, 132-133.
Taps, 26.
Tap Wrenches, 27.
Tempering, 98, 99.
Test Indicator Dial, 181.
,, ,, "Unique", 181-182.
Threads Cutting, 90-95.
,, ,, External, 94, 95.
,, ,, Internal, 90-94.
Tinman's Snips, 28.
Tool Racks, 2, 6-8.
Tools, Hand, 16-40.
Tools, Lathe, 173-178.
,, ,, Hand Turning 207-210.
,, Using Hand, 66-99.
Turning Operations, 182-200.
,, Tools, 173-178.
,, ,, Hand, 207-210.
,, Work between centres, 195-200.
Turrets, Four-tool, 157-158.
Twist Drills, 24.
Twist Drills Tables of, 234.

V
V-Belts, 165-166.
V-Block, 56.
V-Blocks, Drilling Machine Table, 124-125.
Vice, 12.
,, Clams, 13.
,, Correct Height for, 15, 16.
,, Drilling Machine, 123-124.
,, Fixing the, 14, 15.
,, Jaws, 12, 13.
,, Yankee, 16.

W
Witness Lines, 53-58.
Work Clamp, Drilling Machine, 125-126.
Workshop Equipment, 12-40.
,, Floor, 10.
Wrenches, Tap, 27.